Emerging Market Mu
in Europe

CU00796909

This book makes a timely and highly stimulating contribution to the discourse on emerging-market multinationals, (EMNCs), as Foreign Direct Investment (FDI) in Europe from emerging countries (especially from the BRICs – Brazil, Russia, India, China) continues to grow in significance. Unsurprisingly, the emergence of EMNCs from emerging economies raises a wide range of challenges and opportunities for scholars, business professionals, and policymakers alike.

While explaining the sudden rise of these companies has become a major concern among scholars, we have very limited knowledge on drivers, motivations, strategies, and impact of these EMNCs in Europe and their policy implications. This volume provides fresh insights into EMNCs activities and their impact in Europe. The contributors argue that EMNCs combine various country specific advantages, existing firm-specific advantages (exploitation), and/or new FSAs (exploration) in their FDI, and that there is considerable heterogeneity across EMNCs, even those from the same southern economy.

Highlighting the importance of considering this divergent behaviour when implementing future European FDI policies, this book will be of interest to students and scholars of European Politics, International Political Economy, International Business and European Integration.

Louis Brennan is a Fellow of Trinity College and a Professor within the School of Business at Trinity College Dublin where he teaches International Business and Global and Operations Strategy. He was formerly Director of the Institute for International Integration Studies at Trinity College Dublin. Louis is the proposer and Chair of EU COST Action IS0905 which encompassed a 26 nation research network addressing the emergence of non-triad MNEs and their impact on Europe.

Caner Bakir is Associate Professor of Political Science, with a special focus on political economy and public policy at Koc University, Istanbul. Caner is Associate Editor of Policy Sciences and Co-director of Center for Globalisation, Peace and Democratic Governance. His work relates to comparative institutional analysis and policy change. His research interests include varieties of national financial systems, the political economy of central banking, financial regulation and governance, Turkish multinationals and economic bureaucracies.

Routledge Advances in International Political Economy

For a full list of titles in this series, please visit www.routledge.com

Emerging Market Multinationals in Europe

Edited by
Louis Brennan and Caner Bakir

Routledge
Taylor & Francis Group

LONDON AND NEW YORK

First published 2016
by Routledge
2 Park Square, Milton Park, Abingdon, Oxon OX14 4RN

and by Routledge
605 Third Avenue, New York, NY 10017

First issued in paperback 2021

*Routledge is an imprint of the Taylor & Francis Group,
an informa business*

British Library Cataloguing in Publication Data
A catalogue record for this book is available from the British Library

Library of Congress Cataloging-in-Publication Data
Names: Brennan, Louis, editor. | Bakir, Caner, editor.
Title: Emerging market multinationals / edited by Louis Brennan and
    Caner Bakir.
Description: Abingdon, Oxon ; New York, N.Y. : Routledge, 2016. |
    Series: Routledge advances in international political economy ; 28 |
    Includes bibliographical references and index.
Identifiers: LCCN 2016013532 | ISBN 9781138920187 (hardback) |
    ISBN 9781315687285 (ebook)
Subjects: LCSH: International business enterprises—Developing countries. |
    Investments, Foreign—Developing countries. | Investments, Foreign—
    Europe. | Developing countries—Foreign economic relations—Europe. |
    Europe—Foreign economic relations—Developing countries.
Classification: LCC HD2932 .E438 2016 | DDC 338.8/891724—dc23
LC record available at https://lccn.loc.gov/2016013532

ISBN 13: 978-1-03-209781-7 (pbk)
ISBN 13: 978-1-138-92018-7 (hbk)

Typeset in Times New Roman
by Apex CoVantage, LLC

Contents

Figures

Tables

Abbreviations

BRIC	Brazil, Russia, India, China
BRICS	Brazil, Russia, India, China, South Africa
CEE	Central and eastern Europe
CEEs	Central European economies
CIS	Commonwealth of Independent States
COST	Cooperation on Science and Technology
CSAs	Country-specific advantages
EFTA	European Free Trade Association
EMEA	Europe, the Middle East and Africa
EMF	Emerging market firm
EMNC	Emerging market multinational corporation
EMNE	Emerging multinational enterprise
FDI	Foreign direct investment
FSAs	Firm-specific advantages
GNI	Gross national income
IB	International business
ICT	Information and communications technology
IDE-JETRO	Institute of Developing Economies–Japan External Trade Organization
IDP	Investment development path
IPA	Investment Promotion Agency
IT	Information technology
JV	Joint venture
KPI	Key performance indicator
LDCs	Least developed countries
LLL	Linkage, leverage, learning
M&A	Mergers and acquisitions
MNC	Multinational company
MNE	Multinational enterprise
MMT	Malaysia, Mexico, and Turkey
NICs	Newly industrialized countries
OECD	Organisation for Economic Co-operation and Development

OEM	Original equipment manufacturer
OLI	Ownership, localization, internationalization
R&D	Research and development
SDoI	Subjective degree of internationalization
SMEs	Small and medium-sized enterprises
SPEs	Special purpose entities
UNCTAD	United Nations Conference on Trade and Development
VA	Value added

Editors

Louis Brennan is a Professor within the School of Business at Trinity College Dublin, where he teaches International Business and Global and Operations Strategy. He was formerly Director of the Institute for International Integration Studies at Trinity College Dublin. Louis is the proposer and Chair of EU COST Action IS0905, which encompassed a 26-nation research network addressing the emergence of non-triad MNEs and their impact on Europe. He has published extensively in his areas of interest research and recently edited the Palgrave Macmillan volume *Emergence of Southern Multinationals: Their Impact on Europe*. His most recent edited books are *Enacting Globalization: Multidisciplinary Perspectives on International Integration*, published in 2013 by Palgrave Macmillan, and *Drivers of Integration and Regionalism in Europe and Asia: Comparative Perspectives* (co-edited with Philo Murray), published in 2015 by Routledge.

Caner Bakir is Associate Professor of Political Science, with a special focus on International and Comparative Political Economy, and Public Policy and Administration at Koc University, Istanbul. He is Co-director of the Center for Globalisation, Peace and Democratic Governance. He is the Associate Editor of *Policy Sciences*. His work relates to comparative institutional analysis and policy change. His research interests include varieties of national financial systems, the political economy of central banking, financial regulation and governance, Turkish multinationals, and economic bureaucracies. He has published articles in leading journals such as *Governance*, *Public Administration*, *Development and Change*, and *New Political Economy*. His books have been published by Koc University Press (2015), Palgrave Macmillan (2013), and Bilgi University Press (2007). He is the recipient of the 2010 Scientific and Technological Research Council of Turkey (TUBITAK) Incentive Award and the TUBITAK Early Career Award in 2008. He has been the principal investigator of various TUBITAK-funded projects, and his research linked with a Cooperation on Science and Technology (COST) project entitled 'The Emergence of Southern Multinationals and their Impact on Europe' (ISCH COST Action IS0905).

Contributors

Nuran Acur is Associate Professor of Innovation and Technology Strategy, University of Strathclyde, UK and Ozyegin University, Turkey. Her research and consulting projects include designing service/technological innovation processes, facilitating operations strategy development, designing customer experience management and service innovation processes, as well as evaluating the entrepreneurship process. She has received Research Council funding to support several projects related to the fields of technology and service innovation. She has also been serving as a board member of EurOMA (the European Operations Management Association) since 2006. She is in the editorial board of *Journal of Product Innovation Management* and *Creativity in Innovation Management*. Her work has appeared in numerous journals, including *International Journal of Operations & Production Management, the Journal of Product Innovation Management, Creativity and Innovation Management* and *Supply Chain Management: An International Journal.*

Filip De Beule is Assistant Professor of International Business at KU Leuven University, Belgium. He holds a BA and MA in Economics (UFSIA), and an MBA from the University of Antwerp Management School (UAMS). He got his PhD from the University of Antwerp on "Belgian Subsidiary Management in the People's Republic of China: Strategic Evolution, Host Country Impact and Policy". Dr. De Beule has lectured as Visiting Professor at the University of Antwerp and the KU Leuven University, where he teaches a course on the economic development of China. Mr. De Beule is a member of the Academy of International Business (AIB) and the European International Business Academy (EIBA). He serves on the board of EIBA as national representative for Belgium. He focuses his research on multinational companies and emerging economies.

Imola Drigă is Associate Professor at the University of Petroşani, Faculty of Sciences, Department of Economics, Romania. She graduated from Babes-Bolyai University of Cluj-Napoca (Romania) Faculty of Economics and Business Administration in 1999, having majored in Finance and Banking, and joined the University of Petroşani (Romania) as Assistant Professor at the end of the same year. She received her Ph.D. from Lucian Blaga University of Sibiu

(Romania) in 2006, based upon the doctoral thesis "Banking Risk Management in Romania". Her research interests include various issues relating to financial institutions and services, risk management in banking, bank marketing, and international finance. Her research has resulted in the publication of 4 books and over 80 articles and scientific papers published in national and international journals and conference proceedings. Imola Driga is Deputy Editor-in-chief of the journal *Annals of the University of Petrosani – Economics*, an academic publication in Romania, indexed in some of the most popular international databases, such as: RePEc, D.O.A.J., EBSCO Publishing, Cabell's, ICAAP, etc. She is a member of the Multidisciplinary Association for Research in the Western part of Romania (ACM – V). In 2012 Imola Driga became Head of the Department of Economics at the University of Petroşani, Romania.

Codruţa Dura is Associate Professor of Management at the University of Petroşani, Faculty of Sciences, Department of Economics, Romania. She graduated from the University of Petroşani in 1996, receiving a five-year Diploma in Economics, specialization in Management. In 2002, she received her Ph.D. in Management, based upon the doctoral thesis "Management Strategies in Equipment Building Companies in Extractive Industry". She is the Director of the master degree programme in Human Resources Management. She is the author and co-author of 10 books and monographs and more than 100 papers and articles published in various scientific journals and international conference proceedings. She is a member of the Editorial Board of the *Journal of Global Economics*. Her general research interests are Management, Economy of Enterprises, and Marketing. She is a member of the Romanian Management and Economic Engineering Association. She serves as the Vice-Rector of Education of the University of Petroşani, Romania.

Stefano Elia, Ph.D. in Management, Economics, and Industrial Engineering, is Assistant Professor at Politecnico di Milano (Italy). His main research interests deal with global sourcing, emerging multinational firms, international alliances, location choices, and agglomeration effects. In 2013 he was awarded the John H. Dunning Visiting Fellowship by the University of Reading. He is member of the European project ISCH COST Action IS0905, "The Emergence of Southern Multinationals and Their Impact on Europe" and is involved in the "Offshoring Research Network" promoted by Duke University and in the European project "POREEN on Partnering Opportunities between Europe and China in the Renewable Energies and Environmental Industries" coordinated by University of Macerata (Italy). He published in international journals such as *Economic Geography, Journal of International Management, Management International Review, Journal of Economic Geography, International Business Review, Journal of World Business, Global Strategy Journal, International Journal of Production Economics* and the *European Journal of International Management*.

Françoise Hay is Associate Researcher at the Centre of Research in Economy and Management (unity of the Scientific Research National Centre), University of

Rennes 1, France. She is also a member of the Management Committee of the European Program COST IS0905 related to "The Emergence of Southern Multinationals and their Impact on Europe". Her research interests are mainly related to the Chinese economy and FDI: FDI in China and FDI from China. She has recently published two books. One is *The Impact of the Global Financial Crisis on the Presence of Chinese and Indian Firms in Europe* published in 2012 by Sussex Academic (with Milelli C. and Shi Y.). Another, published in French in 2013 by L'Harmattan Editions, is related to an analysis of European investments in China and to the opportunity to invest in China (*"Faut-il encore investir en Chine? opportunités, risques et logique économique"*, cowritten with Milelli C. and Shi Y).

Per Heum is a researcher at the Centre for Applied Research at NHH (SNF), Norwegian School of Economics (NHH). His fields of specialization are: industrial dynamics, industrial policy, and economic growth; multinational corporations and foreign direct investments; industrial activities related to upstream oil and gas; and cost-benefit analysis. He was until December 2013 managing director of the Centre for Applied Research at NHH (SNF), Norwegian School of Economics (NHH).

Andreja Jaklič is an Associate Professor of international economics and international business, research fellow and deputy director of the Centre of International Relations, Faculty of Social Sciences, University of Ljubljana. Her teaching areas include International economics, International Finance, International Business, International Business Environment, the EU in a global economy and research seminars. As a visiting scholar and researcher, Andreja Jaklič cooperated with the Vienna Faculty of Economic and Business Administration, Aalto University (Helsinki), Corvinus University (Budapest) and Polytechnic University (Milan). She has cooperated in several international research projects. Her research focuses on competitiveness, internationalization, international trade, foreign direct investment, multinational enterprises and performance, in particular internationalization and creation of multinational enterprises in the former transition economies. Her publications include the monograph *Enhanced Transition through Outward Internationalization* (Ashgate, 2003), several e-books (CIR-Analysis), book chapters (Edward Elgar, Routledge, Palgrave, Ashgate) and over 25 articles in scientific journals (*Services Industries Journal, Eastern European Economics, Post-Communist Economies, Transnational Corporations, Economics and Business Review*, etc).

Reinhard Meckl studied Economics at the University of Regensburg, where he started his academic career. After several years of business experience in multinational companies he returned to university in 2000 as a full professor of General Management. Prof. Meckl has held the position of Chair for International Management at the University of Bayreuth since 2004. In 2012 Prof. Meckl was awarded the title of honorary professor at the School of Management at the Beijing Institute of Technology. Alongside International Management, his main fields of research are M&A, Renewable Energies and Emerging Markets, with a particular focus on China.

Christian Milelli has a Ph.D. in Economics from the University of Paris. He is a Research Fellow at the National Center for Scientific Research (CNRS). He is member of the Management Committee of the COST Action IS0905 (European Foundation for Science) on 'The Emergence of Southern Multinationals and Their Impact on Europe' (2010–2014); he is also a member of the Chinese Economic Association (UK and Europe), and member of the French academic and expert network on Asia-Pacific-Europe (CNRS-FMSH, Paris). He has a general interest in multinational companies and Asian economies. Some of his recently published contributions are: "The Internationalization Of Chinese Car Manufacturers", in: Marin Marinova & Svetla Marinova (Eds), *Emerging Economies and Firms in the Global Crisis*, Palgrave Macmillan, December 2012 (with Hay F. and Shi Y.); and "The Impact of the Global Financial Crisis on the Presence of Chinese and Indian Firms in Europe", Sussex Academic Press, 2011 (with Hay F. and Shi Y.); and "Chinese and Indian Firms in Europe", *International Journal of Emerging Markets*, Vol. 5, N° 3–4, pp. 377–397, 2010 (with Hay F. and Shi Y.).

Armando J. Garcia Pires (Ph.D.) is a researcher at Centre for Applied Research at NHH (SNF), Norwegian School of Economics (NHH). He has been working in the fields of international trade, industrial organization, and economic development. He has published in journals such as: *Economic Theory; Journal of Urban Economics; Economic Letters; Information Economics and Policy; Journal of Media Economics; Journal of Industry, Competition and Trade; Journal of Regional Science; Economics Bulletin*, and *International Economics*. He has been a visiting scholar at the University of Agder (Kristiansand), University of Antwerp, University College Dublin, Fundacão Getúlio Vargas (Rio de Janeiro), University of Modena and University of Bologna.

Lucia Piscitello is Professor of International Business at Politecnico di Milano. Her research interests cover the economics and management of MNEs and the international aspects of technological change. Her recent studies focus on agglomeration and MNEs' location strategies, globalization of R&D and technology development in the global network of MNEs, offshoring and global sourcing, MNEs from emerging countries. She has published in international journals such as *Economic Geography, Journal of Economic Geography, Journal of International Business Studies, Global Strategy Journal, Strategic Entrepreneurship Journal, Industrial and Corporate Change, International Business Review, Journal of International Management, Cambridge Journal of Economics, Regional Studies, Research Policy*, among others. She serves on the editorial review boards of several journals. She has taught extensively in undergraduate and graduate programs, customized executive education, MBA and Executive MBA programs.

Rasha Rezk is currently a Ph.D. student at the Centre for International Manufacturing, University of Cambridge working on the impact of products' configuration on firms' international dispersion. She holds a B.Sc. in civil engineering from Ain Shams University, Egypt and an MPhil in Industrial Systems, Manufacture and Management, University of Cambridge. Rasha supervises undergraduate engineering students at Wolfson College, Cambridge (Material Science Part I) and assists in supervising graduate MPhil students at the Institute for Manufacturing, Cambridge. Her research interests include supply network design, product configuration, emerging economies and foreign direct investment.

Vittoria G. Scalera is a Ph.D. Candidate in Management, Economics and Industrial Engineering at Politecnico di Milano (Italy). Her main research interests are related to Chinese and Indian multinational enterprises, knowledge intensive cross-border acquisitions, international collaborations and knowledge networks and innovative performance. Since October 2013 she has been a visiting scholar at the Department of Strategic Management, Fox School of Business, Temple University (Philadelphia, PA, USA). She is involved in the project "Europe And Global Challenges – the Challenge Of Globalization: Technology Driven Foreign Direct Investment and its Implication for the Negotiation of International Investment Agreements", financed by Riksbankens Jubileumsfond and coordinated by Prof. Cristina Chaminade (CIRCLE, Lund University) and in the European funded project "POREEN on Partnering Opportunities between Europe and China in the Renewable Energies and Environmental Industries" coordinated by University of Macerata (Italy).

Jagjit Singh Srai is Head of the Centre for International Manufacturing, Institute for Manufacturing, University of Cambridge where he completed his Ph.D. in Engineering, Manufacturing and Management. His research work and that of his group involves working closely with Industry in the area of operational capabilities and their associated network configuration models. He has authored numerous articles in leading academic and practitioner journals. Previous roles have been in Industry working as a Supply Chain Director of a Multinational Regional business, Technical Director of a National Business, and other Senior Management and front-line operations. As part of Institute's dissemination activity Jagjit also has significant consultancy experience involving the application of the latest research with leading multinationals and government organisations. He also holds a first class honours degree in Chemical Process Engineering from Aston University and is a Fellow of the Institute of Chemical Engineers.

Marjan Svetličič is Professor at the Faculty of Social Sciences, University of Ljubljana (was also its Dean) teaching; International Economics, International Business, Negotiations and International management. He was nominated Ambassador of Science of the Republic of Slovenia in 2007 and is Fellow of the European Academy of International Business (EIBA). He is teaching also at the Universities of Trento, Trieste, Sarajevo, Skopje and Rijeka and Faculty of Economics, and GEA College in Ljubljana. He was vice chair of COST project The Emergence of Southern Multinationals and President and vice president of the EIBA, a member of FP7 Advisory Group for International Scientific Cooperation, Trans European policy Studies association (TEPSA) board, a member of the Steering Committee of the Standing Group of the European Consortium for Political Research (ECPR). He is a member of many editorial boards of scientific journals and a consultant to many international organisations. He has authored more than 300 articles and books.

Nükhet Vardar has been pursuing both an academic and a business life since 1983. After receiving her B.Sc. from Dokuz Eylul University, Izmir, Turkey in 1983; she obtained her M.Sc. in International Marketing from University of Manchester Institute of Science and Technology (UMIST), UK in 1985 and her Ph.D. in International Advertising in 1990 also from UMIST. She worked as a lecturer at Yeditepe University, Istanbul, Turkey (2002–2008), where she was appointed as Professor of Marketing in 2004. As a professional, she started her career in 1985, as a brand manager at Henkel. She was the founding Managing Director of Initiative Media in Istanbul (1995–2001). In 2002 she established her own marketing and communications consultancy firm, El Izi, where she is currently working. Her first book *Global Advertising: Rhyme or Reason* published in London in 1992, was translated into Korean in 1998. As of July 2014, she is the author of 13 books in total in marketing and branding; 6 book chapters in edited books published by Prentice, Emerald, Routledge; more than 60 papers and 80 talks and presentations. For a detailed CV: http://elizi.net/cv_eng/

Sebastian Weusthoff studied Business Administration at the University of Bayreuth. Since graduation he has been engaged as a research assistant at the Chair for International Management at the University of Bayreuth. Alongside International Management, Sebastian Weusthoff focuses on research topics in the fields of M&A, Emerging Markets and Cultural Diversity.

Michał Zdziarski is Assistant Professor of Strategic Management and International Business at Management Faculty, Warsaw University and Research Director of Executive MBA at International Management Centre, Warsaw University. He was Principal Researcher at global business association The Conference Board, for which he re-designed it's flagship, leadership research program The CEO Challenge™. His research interests include top management teams and leadership, intra-organizational networks, stakeholder analysis, strategy formation, structured decision making, corporate governance and international business.

Part I

Introduction

1 Introducing emerging market multinationals in Europe

Louis Brennan and Caner Bakir

Introduction

This introductory chapter sets out the evolving context of foreign direct investment flows within which the content of the book is positioned. It describes the collaborative process by which the research reported in the book was undertaken. The reasons as to why the research reported in the book is both timely and essential are outlined. In doing so, the critical conceptual, methodological, and empirical issues to be addressed in the book are derived. The aims of this edited volume are set out and the overall conceptual basis and methodology employed in the volume are presented. The chapter concludes with an explanation around the structure of the book and the topics covered.

The evolving context of foreign direct investment flows

The focus of this edited book is emerging market multinational companies (EMNCs, MNCs) in Europe. Traditionally FDI has flowed from advanced developed economies into developed and developing countries. More recently a new trend has emerged in the pattern of FDI. Outward-bound FDI from emerging economies has begun to increase significantly and has been growing at a faster pace than FDI from the advanced developed world. Unsurprisingly, the emergence of MNCs from emerging economies raises a wide range of challenges and opportunities for scholars, business professionals, and policymakers alike. Although explaining the rather sudden rise of these companies has become a major concern among scholars over the last few years, we have very limited knowledge on drivers, motivations, strategies, and impact of these EMNCs in Europe and their policy implications. This book is a very timely and highly stimulating contribution to the discourse on EMNCs as FDI in Europe from emerging countries, especially from the BRICs (Brazil, Russia, India, China), has grown to record highs in recent years.

The collaborative research process

This book is based on EU COST Action IS0905, which encompasses a twenty-six nation research network addressing EMNCs and their impact on Europe and its stakeholders. This four-year international and interdisciplinary research collaboration makes this book distinctive. The collaboration was thoughtfully conceived and nurtured productive enquiry in this underexplored area over the past four years. The contributors to this book have already participated in various academic activities such as workshops and conferences funded by EU COST Action IS0905 between 2010 and 2014. Thus, most of the authors have draft chapters emanating from these meetings and received feedback from the discussants and participants.

As a result, the book offers fresh theoretical and empirical insights, interdisciplinary and comparative perspectives with up-to-date data; it is informed by a broad spectrum of international scholars; and it is a coherent research project rather than a compilation of various weakly connected chapters on EMNCs in Europe.

The focus of the book

This edited volume examines the various aspects of EMNC investment in Europe. Characteristics of EMNCs; their drivers, motivations, and strategies; country-specific EMNC activities; and country and industry studies represent the four key areas addressed in the book. The chapters in these sections deal with theoretical, conceptual, and empirical aspects of EMNCs in Europe.

This book represents a novel and innovative contribution. The strength of the book is that it provides diverse perspectives on EMNCs from different disciplines, including business, economics, political science, development studies, and regional studies. It covers not only emerging investment patterns and profiles of EMNCs and their internationalization strategies in Europe, but also their sectoral, industrial, and investment policy-related impacts, so that the reader has deeper understanding of EMNCs from this collection. The book's major contribution lies in providing fresh insights into EMNC activities and their impact in Europe. One of the central theses of this book is that EMNCs combine various country-specific advantages, existing firm-specific advantages (FSAs; exploitation), and/or new FSAs (exploration) in their market-seeking and resource-seeking FDI. There is considerable heterogeneity across EMNCs, even those from the same Southern economy. Further, there are also considerable country-level variations due in part to differences in local industry strengths and weaknesses, institutional environment, and government policy that affect patterns of outward FDI and behavior/ motivations of MNCs. European FDI policies and their implementation should consider this divergent EMNC behavior across Europe. Thus, this book will fill a significant gap in the existing literature and serve to motivate further studies on the subject.

The major themes covered by the book are:

- Characterising and quantifying EMNCs in Europe.
- Drivers, motivations, and strategies of EMNCs in Europe.
- Country-specific EMNCs in Europe.
- Country and industry studies.

Internationalization of emerging-/developing-country multinationals (EMNCs) is part of the economic globalization process whereby EMNCs start to play an increasingly important role (UNCTAD 2006). The emergence of MNCs from emerging/developing economies raises a wide range of challenges for scholars, business professionals, and policymakers alike. Specifically, explaining the rather sudden rise of these companies has become a major concern among scholars over the last few years (Goldstein 2007; Ramamurti and Singh 2009; Sauvant et al. 2010; Brennan 2011; Panibratov 2012; Marinov and Marinova 2013; Williamson et al. 2013; Kumar 2015). However, there are considerable shortcomings in the previous literature on EMNCs. First, many are country-specific MNC studies (e.g., Chinese MNCs), ignoring comparative analysis and synthesis. Second, although FDI in Europe from emerging markets, especially the BRICs, reached a record high in 2013 (Ernst and Young 2014: 6), they do not fully take into account the geographical and sectoral distribution of these investments, and the motivations, strategies, patterns, and impacts of these EMNCs investing in Europe. By contrast this proposed volume addresses those considerations and sheds new light on the operations of EMNCs in Europe. It also serves to complement *The Emergence of Southern Multinationals: Their Impact on Europe* (Palgrave 2011), edited by Louis Brennan, as our book is current in terms of the quantification of EMNCs in Europe and the issues and challenges that arise from their growing presence in Europe.

The content of the book

Following this introductory section, the second section of the book offers a characterisation and quantification of EMNCs in Europe. The first chapter in this section, by Filip De Beule and Andreja Jaklič, provides an overview of Southern multinationals in Europe. The chapter offers a comparative overview of all Southern investments in Europe. The chapter compares the extent (number), sectors, business activities, and corporate parents of European subsidiaries from various Southern multinationals by analysing in detail the firm-level investments made in Europe. The second chapter in this section, by Andreja Jaklič and Filip De Beule, addresses the challenges of tracing EMNCs and FDI in European countries with consideration of the extent of data coverage and data deficiencies. The authors assess how the existing data coverage, data deficiencies, and changes influence data analysis and consider the policy implications.

The third section of the book, which contains four chapters, addresses the drivers, motivations, and strategies of EMNCs. The first chapter in the section, by Jagjit Singh Srai, considers the drivers and motivations of EMNCs into the EU. In particular, the author seeks to explore the drivers and motivations of EMNCs that have sought to establish a key element of their value chain within the European market. The second chapter in this section, by Sebastian Weusthoff and Reinhard Meckl, considers the motivations, success, and implications of mergers and acquisitions by EMNCs in developed countries with a specific focus on Europe. The third chapter, by Codruța Dura and Imola Drigă, addresses the drivers, motivations, and strategies of EMNCs from Russia. The final chapter in this section, by Nükhet Vardar, focuses on Turkish EMNCs with investments in the EU and assesses the impact of their motivations on their degree of internationalization and performances.

Part IV of the book, which focuses on country-specific EMNCs in Europe, consists of four chapters. The first, by Françoise Hay, analyses Chinese investors in Europe and their idiosyncrasies. The second chapter, by Caner Bakir and Nuran Acur, looks at the trends, motivations, and strategies of Turkish MNCs' green-field and acquisition investments. The chapter by Christian Milelli addresses the characteristics, competitive advantages, and strategies of Indian firms in Europe. The final chapter in this section, by Stefano Elia, Lucia Piscitello, and Vittoria G. Scalera, also considers Chinese MNCs and analyses, utilising a database of European subsidiaries of high-tech Chinese MNEs, the role of cultural and insti-tutional distances on collaborative innovation within Chinese MNCs' international networks in Europe.

The fifth section of the book incorporates country and industry studies. Per Heum and Armando J. Garcia Pires focus on Norway in the first chapter of this section and explore the question of investments from BRIC countries in in the context of Norway. The second chapter, by Michał Zdziarski, Jagjit Singh Srai, and Rasha Rezk, presents overview of network approach to internationalization, and its application to analysis of emerging versus established multinationals' embed-dedness in the global value chain of the white goods industry. The third chapter, by Marjan Svetličič, takes an industry perspective. The chapter explores the embed-dedness of supply chains of emerging vs. developed market white goods MNCs in a global value chain. The fourth and final chapter in this section, by Michał Zdziarski, selects the BRIC countries that are increasingly active in global FDI flows and explore the patterns of investments among these countries and a group of Visegrad region countries in Central Europe.

The final section of the book provides a concluding chapter by Caner Bakir and Louis Brennan. It offers a summary and assessment of the main findings of the book.

Applicability of the book

This is a research book that is distinctive in that it is based on a four-year interna-tional research network (EU COST Action IS0905) and brings together scholars with diverse backgrounds from many countries. It is aimed at postgraduates, researchers, and academics, as well as managers and policy communities around the world having an interest in investments in Europe and the EU region and more generally in emerging market multinationals. Academic disciplines in which it would fit include international business, international relations, economics, eco-nomic geography, political science, and political economy. This book will have appeal for graduate courses in the fields of European integration studies, and Euro-pean business programs. It will also be appealing not only to researchers, academ-ics, managers, and policymakers in Europe but to those from emerging markets who have an interest in the European region. Since the contributors to this volume explore the emerging patterns of EMNC investments, internationalization strategies, and impacts in Europe, it will be attractive for academics teaching courses on international business and multinational corporations, the European economy, and FDI policy.

References

Brennan, L. ed. (2011). *The Emergence of Southern Multinationals: Their Impact on Europe*. London/New York: Palgrave Macmillan.

Ernst and Young (2014). *EY's Attractiveness Survey Europe 2014: Back in the Game*. Available at www.ey.com/Publication/vwLUAssets/EY-2014-European-attractiveness-survey/$FILE/EY-2014-European-attractiveness-survey.pdf

Goldstein, A. (2007). *Multinational Companies from Emerging Economies*. London/New York: Palgrave Macmillan.

Kumar, N. (2015). *India's Emerging Multinationals*. London: Routledge.

Marinov, M. and Marinova, S. (2013). *Successes and Challenges of Emerging Economy Multinationals*. London/New York: Palgrave Macmillan.

Panibratov, A. (2012). *Russian Multinationals: From Regional Supremacy to Global Lead*. London/New York: Routledge.

Ramamurti, R. and Singh, J. (2009). *Emerging Multinationals in Emerging Markets*. Cambridge: Cambridge University Press.

UNCTAD (2006). *World Investment Report 2006. FDI from Developing and Transition Economies: Implications for Development*. New York/Geneva: United Nations.

Williamson, P. J., Ramamurti, R., Fleury, A. and Fleury, M.T.L. (2013). *The Competitive Advantage of Emerging Market Multinationals*. Cambridge: Cambridge University Press.

Part II

Characterizing and quantifying EMCs in Europe

2 Southern multinationals in Europe

An overview

Filip De Beule and Andreja Jaklič

Introduction

Ten years ago, Battat and Aykut (2005: 4) asked the question of how Southern MNCs would affect the global economy: "Would we see major differences in strategies and behavior among Southern MNCs, and if so, would they be driven by nationalities, sectors, or other factors? Much of the growing effort of learning about this phenomenon has been to attempt to map it out – find out who is doing what, where, and test a few hypotheses here and there."

They went on to say that "[t]his initial effort has been challenged by the lack of data. In general, complete and reliable inward FDI data from developing countries is hard to find, and even more so for their outward FDI. This new and growing phenomenon is bound to affect the economic development of [. . .] countries, home and host to FDI. It is in the interest of those countries to learn more about it and deal with it, and for that they need to enhance their FDI data collection and management systems."

Furthermore, Brennan (2010) indicated that the rise of Southern multinationals was an increasingly important phenomenon and that their impact on Europe deserved more research attention. He noted as one of the research implications the need to improve our knowledge of the phenomenon and its implications.

This chapter is an effort to try to answer these questions and shortcomings by analyzing a range of interesting data with regard to Southern multinationals and drawing inference from them. In particular, this chapter will give an overview of Southern multinationals in Europe. Most research either tackles Southern multinationals, or rather, multinationals from emerging countries as a whole, or focuses on one specific country. Brazil, India, Russia, and China, in particular, have attracted the major share of research attention, given that these countries are some of the most prolific Southern investors. However, the phenomenon is more diversified than anecdotal evidence would suggest.

The term "Southern multinationals" has thereby been selected over "emerging multinationals" because some multinationals come from countries which have already emerged, some countries are indeed emerging, while others are still in developing stages. Southern multinationals include all companies that come from countries that are non-triad countries. This volume and especially this chapter have therefore opted for a more inclusive strategy. The chapter will give a comparative overview of all Southern investments in Europe. It will thereby compare the extent (numbers), sectors, business activities, and corporate parents of European subsidiaries from various Southern multinationals by analyzing in detail the firm-level investments made in Europe. In order to facilitate the analysis, some countries have been grouped given their common characteristics, location, or economic background. Also bear in mind that not all variables are available for all observations. As such, there are small differences in the numbers among the various tables.

The chapter will end by drawing conclusions from these descriptive statistics in order to catalogue the phenomenon of Southern multinationals in Europe and – in the end – make recommendations for European and Southern policymakers in order to attract, assist, and improve the overall extent and impact of Southern investments in Europe.

Theoretical background

Southern multinationals are a new and powerful force in global competition and are challenging the incumbency of much older global companies from the developed world. Southern multinationals now account for half of foreign investment in the world and are a prolific source of innovation. Despite this, traditional theories of international business do not provide a satisfactory explanation of their behavior or performance.

Southern MNC outward FDI drivers are threefold: access to resources, access to markets, and access to strategic assets (Deng 2004; Kaartemo 2007; Pradhan 2008). Efficiency-seeking has not been a major driver. Experiencing sustained high economic growth in recent years, a few emerging countries are under pressure to secure raw materials, including oil and gas. They often seek to diversify their sources from a wide range of countries, including those where there is no strong presence of developed market multinationals. China and India are two cases in point, with growing investment in energy and mining in sub-Saharan Africa, Central Asia, and Latin America. Of the deals in the extractive sector that China's state-owned enterprises are making worldwide, about half of China's outward FDI went to natural resources projects in Latin America. Similarly, India's Oil and Natural Gas Corporation closed deals in the Russian Federation and in Angola. The search for new sources of raw materials has also taken Southern MNCs to developed countries such as Australia and Canada (De Beule and Duanmu 2012).

Access to markets is the second most important driver of outward FDI from emerging countries. Southern MNCs, similar to those from the North, search for higher returns and lower risks through portfolio diversification. Using the experience acquired in their home market and taking advantage of globalization and trade liberalization, particularly regional integration, a large number of firms in emerging markets are venturing into foreign markets, often close to home but increasingly beyond. They exploit a number of assets they have developed at home:

products and production processes appropriate to emerging markets; the ability to manage regulatory processes, particularly in infrastructure; ability to network in neighboring countries; knowledge of cultures and markets; and low cost structures.

For example, multinationals in the information technology (IT) and telecommunication sectors from India, South Africa, Mexico, Malaysia, and China have expanded their market abroad. Both sectors are growing globally, and in both cases Southern firms have developed a strong base at home. In the case of telecommunication, they have also developed the ability to efficiently manage the regulatory process, particularly in their neighboring countries. In market segments where the level of competition has increased domestically and profit margins have diminished, firms have also sought growth abroad. Chinese firms in consumer electronics and home appliances have seen the domestic market approaching saturation and have invested in Asia and beyond, including in developed markets. For similar reasons, Indian firms in metals and minerals and Malaysian firms in utilities are also seeking investment opportunities abroad.

In their quest to expand internationally, many Southern MNCs have invested abroad to acquire strategic assets. With very few internationally recognized brand names of their own, Chinese firms such as Lenovo and TCL have acquired well-known Western brand names such as Thompson, RCA, and IBM. Haier's attempt to buy Maytag was not only for its brand name, but also for its distribution channel. Compared with other Southern MNCs, Chinese MNCs seem to have made more attempts to acquire well-known brand names. This strategy was not followed by Japanese and Korean budding MNCs that developed their own brand names in the second half of the last century. A small but increasing number of investments, mainly from Asia, are being made in R&D to tap technology in a wide range of sectors in developed countries. Almost all Indian IT firms have such an investment in developed countries.

Until recently, when the question "what are the competitive advantages of firms from emerging economies in the global market?" was posed to either scholars or Western executives, it typically elicited a simple response: "None." To the extent that these firms from emerging countries were winning market share abroad, this was explained by the fortuitous access to so-called country-specific advantages (CSAs), such as a pool of low-cost labor in their home base (Rugman and Verbeke 2001). They were generally thought to lack ownership of proprietary, intangible assets that theory argued was required for multinationals to be an efficient organizational form (Caves 1986). Dunning (2001) termed the benefits of these intangible assets "ownership advantages" – a term chosen to emphasize the idea that the transaction costs involved in transferring these assets (and hence their associated advantages) across borders using market mechanisms are higher than the costs of transferring them internally within an organization under the same ownership. Without these intangible assets, there was no reason why their products and resources should not be exchanged internationally through trade in an open market. According to a strict interpretation of this theory, therefore, the existence of EMFs must simply be the result of market distortions such as trade barriers or government support.

The above conceptualization assumes positioning of the Southern multinationals in the global value chain to occupy positions not willing to be taken by the firms from developed economies (e.g. Mathews 2002, 2006). Explicit is the assumption that Southern multinationals compete in dated technologies or low-cost or otherwise undesirable sectors by the firms from developed economies. In regard to the nature of firm-specific advantages (FSAs) (Dunning 1981; Dunning and Lundan 2008), they are assumed to be based on the Southern multinationals' ready access to their home country's locational advantages (Rugman and Li 2007; Narula 2012), such as oil/gas in Russia or minerals in Brazil (Rugman and Li 2007) or some Southern multinational-specific FSAs (Cuervo-Cazurra and Genc 2008), such as emerging market customer understanding or operating in institutionally underdeveloped environments. Therefore, they ventured often into other emerging markets or lesser-developed markets in order to exploit these competitive advantages (Luo and Tung 2007; Cuervo-Cazurra and Genc 2008; Ramamurti and Singh 2009).

This received wisdom has begun to look increasingly implausible because Southern multinationals have continued to expand globally, while they invested directly in building their subsidiaries overseas, both in the developing and developed world – in many cases successfully taking market share from multinationals headquartered in developed markets that benefit from global capabilities and networks built over many decades (Verma et al. 2011). Similarly, EMFs also started taking over companies in developed markets in search of strategic assets, resources, and capabilities (Dunning and Lundan 2008; Hennart 2012), frequently via joint ventures or purchase of subunits from multinationals from developed economies that undergo strategic refocusing (Luo and Tung 2007). Scholars and pundits questioned Southern multinationals' ability to take advantage of or even manage these acquisitions.

However, evidence abounds on how Southern multinationals, which are disadvantaged by the latecomer status (Luo and Tung 2007) and experience the lack of knowledge-based FSAs (Mathews 2006; Lessard and Lucea 2009; Rugman 2009), can successfully compete with developed market multinationals (Lessard and Lucea 2009; Ramamurti and Singh 2009; Dikova et al. 2015). They also seem to be able to take advantage of developed market acquisitions despite their supposed lack of absorptive capacity through a linkage, leverage, and learning effect (Mathews 2006).

Southern multinationals do not always seem to expand their international operations incrementally starting with regions with low psychic distance from their home market to regions with higher psychic distance (Vahlne and Wiedersheim-Paul 1973; Zaheer 1995). Instead, they often appear to establish subsidiaries or make acquisitions in locations with high psychic distance from their home base. This suggests a difference from established theory: that Southern multinationals appear to emphasize the role of internationalization as a means to access new locational advantages rather than to exploit ownership advantages. Yet prevailing theories suggest that strategies based purely on exploration will not be competitive against incumbent multinationals that have existing ownership advantages

(Dunning 2001) because the latter can already transfer them around the world more efficiently than the newcomers.

It is clear, therefore, that our theories about the emergence of multinationals and the drivers of FDI have been shaped by a rather particular set of national and historical contexts (even if these influences are seldom acknowledged or perhaps even recognized). If these contexts differ in important ways from the environment that prevails today, then we might expect the Southern multinationals of the twenty-first century to behave differently and achieve different results from multinational firms that expanded their international reach and competitiveness in earlier eras and from different home institutional country settings. Put differently, extant research is limited in identifying and examining how institutional or industry conditions of the emerging markets can enable (rather than inhibit) the Southern multinationals to compete not only in the host emerging market but internationally based on knowledge-based resources and capabilities transferred from the host emerging market.

These differences between the current environment and the context that shaped much of our existing theory, along with observations about the rise of EMFs and the nature of their international expansion that seem paradoxical when viewed through established theoretical lenses, at least requires us to reassess the explanatory power of existing theories.

Data and methodology

The data for this chapter come from two sources. One source is the fDi Markets database that monitors cross-border investments. Launched in 2003 by the *Financial Times*, fDi Markets is a central bank of information on the globalization of business. The service tracks cross-border greenfield investments across all sectors and countries worldwide. A second source is the Orbis database, commercially exploited by Bureau Van Dijk. The Orbis database contains comprehensive financial and ownership information on companies worldwide.

The first section will analyze greenfield investments made by Southern multinationals in Europe for the period 2003 through 2012. Greenfield investments have been selected specifically because these investments demonstrate intent given that locations have been weighed one against the other before making the investment. Acquisitions rather reflect the strength of the competitive advantages of the target companies rather than the country-level characteristics.

All multinationals from non-triad countries have been taken up in the analysis. A distinction has been made among the various regions or countries of origin of these Southern multinationals in order to allow a cross-country of origin comparative analysis. The regions or countries of origin have been classified according to their geographical location and/or developmental stage. The BRICS countries have been included separately as it does not make sense geographically or economically to group them together. Table 2.1 indicates the different regions of origin that have been used for any further analysis. Africa conglomerates all African countries except South Africa, which has been taken up separately. Greater Russia

Table 2.1 Regional classification of Southern multinationals

Region of Origin	Member Countries
Africa	All African countries except South Africa
Greater Russia	Armenia, Azerbaijan, Belarus, Georgia, Kazakhstan, Kyrgyzstan, Tajikistan, Turkmenistan, Ukraine, Uzbekistan
Central and eastern Europe (CEE)	Albania, Bosnia Herzegovina, Bulgaria, Croatia, Czech Republic, Estonia, Hungary, Kosovo, Latvia, Lithuania, Macedonia, Moldova, Montenegro, Poland, Romania, Serbia, Slovakia, Slovenia
Newly industrialized countries (NICs)	Korea, Macau, Taiwan, Singapore, Hong Kong
MMT	Malaysia, Mexico, Turkey
South America	All South American countries except Brazil
Central America	All Central American countries
Middle East	Bahrain, Jordan, Iran, Iraq, Saudi Arabia, Lebanon, Kuwait, Israel, Yemen, UAE, Syria, Qatar, Palestine, Oman
Southeast Asia 1 (SEA1)	Bangladesh, Indonesia, Philippines, Thailand, Vietnam
Southeast Asia 2 (SEA2)	Burma, Brunei Darussalam, Cambodia, Laos, Nepal, Sri Lanka, Pakistan

Notes: The classification will also include Brazil, Russia, India, China, and South Africa, separately. If a country is not included in one of the groups, then the country does not conduct any FDI (or simply has not been classified into one of the groups).

includes all CIS countries except Russia, which has again been taken up separately. Similarly, South America excludes Brazil. Other country groupings are listed in Table 2.1. The only odd group is MMT, based on their developmental and industrial backgrounds.

The second section will analyze the same greenfield investments from these various countries or regions of origin in the EU on the basis of the sectors of investment. In a first instance, the analysis will focus on the differences among primary, industrial, and service sector investments. In a second instance, the analysis will become comparative for manufacturing sector investment and will assess whether any differences can be determined in the sectoral distribution among the various Southern investors.

The third section will analyze the business activities of the foreign subsidiaries of these Southern multinationals. This analysis attempts to flesh out whether any differences can be distinguished in the activities of the subsidiaries on the basis of the region of origin.

The three above-mentioned analyses will not only tackle the countries or regions of origin, sectors of investment, or business activities, but also make a distinction in the investment location. In particular, a difference will be made whether the investment has been carried out in western Europe or central and eastern Europe. This means that CEE is both a region of destination as well as a region of origin of investment. Remember that western Europe as a source of investment has been excluded, since multinationals from that region do not qualify as Southern investors. The analysis will attempt to find out whether there are any discriminating differences between investment in western Europe and CEE. Given the developmental and institutional differences in these two regions, useful conclusions can hopefully also be drawn to inform us of practical investment (promotion) policies.

A fourth and final analysis will make the connection between the subsidiary-level investment made in the EU and the headquarters in the various countries or regions of origin. It will focus on some commonly used financial characteristics, such as profits, turnover, assets, and employment, but also on measures of competitive advantage, such as patents and trademarks. Through this analysis, the question as to whether these multinationals still draw on the comparative advantage of their home country or whether they have already developed competitive advantages is addressed.

Descriptive analysis

Geographical analysis

Table 2.2 illustrates the number of Southern investments in western Europe and in CEE, divided among the different countries or regions of origin. In general, the number of investments clearly demonstrates that western Europe is a more attractive investment location than central and eastern Europe, especially taking into account that CEE investments into CEE have also been taken up. Although this might seem like a straightforward conclusion – Southern multinationals invest mostly in western Europe – it is not. Many studies have clearly indicated that Southern multinationals normally prefer similar countries to their own to invest in, while economic and institutional differences deter investments (Buckley et al. 2007; De Beule and Duanmu 2012; De Beule and Van Den Bulcke 2012; Duanmu and Guney 2013).

In terms of the importance of the different countries or regions of origin, there are a number of clear frontrunners. China has been the most prolific Southern country in Europe, with over 725 greenfield investments in the last decade, or about 12.5 percent of total Southern investments. India and Russia have been distant seconds with 574 and 445 investments, respectively.

However, a number of other less conspicuous investors emerge from the analysis. The newly industrialized countries (NICs) have made 836 investments, while Middle Eastern countries have also made substantial investments, and Malaysia, Mexico, and Turkey feature prominently. At first glance, economic size and success are clear drivers of outward FDI for Southern multinationals. Other countries or regions of origin stand out far less. Brazil and South Africa, for instance, have made only a limited number of investments, 99 and 83, respectively.

Table 2.2 Number of greenfield investments by Southern multinationals in western Europe and central and eastern Europe, by country or region of origin, 2003–2012

		Country or Region of Origin																Total
		Africa	Brazil	Russia	India	China	South Africa	CEE	Central America	Central Asia	MMT	Middle East	NIC	SEA1	SEA2	South America	
Western Europe	Count	61	95	228	510	632	71	346	138	57	260	475	548	68	18	77	3584
	% of Row	1.7%	2.7%	6.4%	14.2%	17.6%	2.0%	9.7%	3.9%	1.6%	7.3%	13.3%	15.3%	1.9%	0.5%	2.1%	100%
	% of Column	87.1%	96.0%	51.2%	88.9%	87.2%	85.5%	23.4%	87.9%	43.5%	63.0%	70.5%	65.6%	85.0%	94.7%	100%	61.1%
Central & Eastern Europe	Count	9	4	217	64	93	12	1134	19	74	153	199	288	12	1	0	2279
	% of Row	0.4%	0.2%	9.5%	2.8%	4.1%	0.5%	49.8%	0.8%	3.2%	6.7%	8.7%	12.6%	0.5%	0.0%	0.0%	100%
	% of Column	12.9%	4.0%	48.8%	11.1%	12.8%	14.5%	76.6%	12.1%	56.5%	37.0%	29.5%	34.4%	15.0%	5.3%	0.0%	38.9%
Europe	Count	70	99	445	574	725	83	1480	157	131	413	674	836	80	19	77	5863
	% of Row	1.2%	1.7%	7.6%	9.8%	12.4%	1.4%	25.2%	2.7%	2.2%	7.0%	11.5%	14.3%	1.4%	0.3%	1.3%	100%
	% of Column	100%	100%	100%	100%	100%	100%	100%	100%	100%	100%	100%	100%	100%	100%	100%	100%

Region of Destination

Source: Cross-Border Investment Monitor, *Financial Times*

In terms of a comparison between the attraction of western Europe vs. central and eastern Europe, a number of interesting conclusions stand out. While the predominance of western Europe as an investment region is clear for most countries and regions of origin, there are a few notable exceptions. First, Russia and Central Asia invest equally in CEE as they do in western Europe. A number of possible explanations are suggested: this might be due to their former ideological background, the heritage of the Non-Aligned Movement, cultural and institutional proximity, or the sectoral composition of their investments (see later).

This cultural explanation has in fact been used to explain much of the South-South investment that has been witnessed the last few decades. In their search for new opportunities, Southern multinationals tended to invest close to their home country and where they have acquired a certain familiarity through trade or ethnic and cultural ties. As a result, there is a significant regional aspect to most South-South FDI flows. For instance, following trade liberalization in Latin America, multinationals from Chile, Brazil, and Argentina expanded their operations mainly in other developing countries in the region. Russian investments abroad have primarily been in the countries of the former Soviet Union and former socialist countries. Turkey has also been actively investing regionally, particularly in West and Central Asia and Russia. Further, South African investments in other developing countries are almost completely in the Southern part of Africa, and companies from India and China have been particularly active in Asian countries.

As such, the predominance of most Southern multinationals to invest more in western Europe goes against this former trend and seems to suggest that Southern multinationals have moved beyond the first stages of internationalization. However, culture does seem to continue to matter to some extent, also in western Europe. There are indications that strong economic and cultural ties play a role when these companies invest in developed countries. For example, there are strong tendencies for Brazilian investors to use Portugal as a springboard and for other South American investors to go to Spain. Furthermore, the UK receives a lot of Indian and African – mainly South African – investments.

A second exception – with regard to location choice, although less pronounced – can be witnessed for NICs, and Malaysian, Mexican, and Turkish investors that also have a more balanced approach towards western Europe and CEE. A possible explanation might be that given their industrial background, they might be looking for some production sites, which might favor CEE (see sectoral analysis).

Sectoral analysis

Tables 2.3 and 2.4 illustrate the sectoral distribution of investments in western and central and eastern Europe, respectively. A distinction has thereby been made among the primary sector (including agriculture but also oil and gas), industry, and services. On average, the industrial sector and the service sector have attracted an equal number of investments, or about 45 percent each. Western Europe has thereby attracted slightly less industry (44.6 percent) than services (48.8 percent), while the reverse is true of CEE. More than half of the investments in CEE are

Table 2.3 Greenfield investments by Southern multinationals by sector in western Europe, by country or region of origin, 2003–2012

SECTOR		Africa	Brazil	Russia	India	China	South Africa	CEE	Central America	Central Asia	MMT	Middle East	NIC	SEA1	SEA2	South America	Total
Industry	Count	8	48	42	139	431	28	103	28	12	143	139	341	18	9	20	1509
	% within R	0.5%	3.2%	2.8%	9.2%	28.6%	1.9%	6.8%	1.9%	0.8%	9.5%	9.2%	22.6%	1.2%	0.6%	1.3%	100%
	% within C	13.3%	54.5%	18.8%	28.6%	74.2%	41.8%	31.8%	20.4%	21.4%	60.9%	30.2%	67.4%	27.7%	50.0%	26.3%	44.6%
	% of Total	0.2%	1.4%	1.2%	4.1%	12.7%	0.8%	3.0%	0.8%	0.4%	4.2%	4.1%	10.1%	0.5%	0.3%	0.6%	44.6%
Primary	Count	2	15	45	43	29	3	20	0	8	14	15	18	2	0	7	221
	% within R	0.9%	6.8%	20.4%	19.5%	13.1%	1.4%	9.0%	0.0%	3.6%	6.3%	6.8%	8.1%	0.9%	0.0%	3.2%	100%
	% within C	3.3%	17.0%	20.2%	8.8%	5.0%	4.5%	6.2%	0.0%	14.3%	6.0%	3.3%	3.6%	3.1%	0.0%	9.2%	6.5%
	% of Total	0.1%	0.4%	1.3%	1.3%	0.9%	0.1%	0.6%	0.0%	0.2%	0.4%	0.4%	0.5%	0.1%	0.0%	0.2%	6.5%
Services	Count	50	25	136	304	121	36	201	109	36	78	306	147	45	9	49	1652
	% within R	3.0%	1.5%	8.2%	18.4%	7.3%	2.2%	12.2%	6.6%	2.2%	4.7%	18.5%	8.9%	2.7%	0.5%	3.0%	100%
	% within C	83.3%	28.4%	61.0%	62.6%	20.8%	53.7%	62.0%	79.6%	64.3%	33.2%	66.5%	29.1%	69.2%	50.0%	64.5%	48.8%
	% of Total	1.5%	0.7%	4.0%	9.0%	3.6%	1.1%	5.9%	3.2%	1.1%	2.3%	9.0%	4.3%	1.3%	0.3%	1.4%	48.8%
Total	Count	60	88	223	486	581	67	324	137	56	235	460	506	65	18	76	3382
	% within R	1.8%	2.6%	6.6%	14.4%	17.2%	2.0%	9.6%	4.1%	1.7%	6.9%	13.6%	15.0%	1.9%	0.5%	2.2%	100%
	% within C	100%	100%	100%	100%	100%	100%	100%	100%	100%	100%	100%	100%	100%	100%	100%	100%
	% of Total	1.8%	2.6%	6.6%	14.4%	17.2%	2.0%	9.6%	4.1%	1.7%	6.9%	13.6%	15.0%	1.9%	0.5%	2.2%	100%

Notes: Primary sector, including agriculture oil and gas.
Number, distribution by sector (% within row), distribution by region of origin (% within column)

Source: Cross-Border Investment Monitor, Financial Times

Table 2.4 Greenfield investments by Southern multinationals by sector in central and eastern Europe, by country or region of origin, 2003–2012

SECTOR		Country or Region of Origin															Total
		Africa	Brazil	Russia	India	China	South Africa	CEE	Central America	Central Asia	MMT	Middle East	NIC	SEA1	SEA2	South America	
Industry	Count	4	2	43	22	74	4	551	3	20	87	50	221	5	1	4	1091
	% within R	0.4%	0.2%	3.9%	2.0%	6.8%	0.4%	50.5%	0.3%	1.8%	8.0%	4.6%	20.3%	0.5%	0.1%	0.4%	100%
	% within C	44.4%	50.0%	21.0%	34.9%	84.1%	36.4%	52.1%	15.8%	30.8%	62.6%	26.7%	87.0%	45.5%	100%	100%	51.5%
	% of Total	0.2%	0.1%	2.0%	1.0%	3.5%	0.2%	26.0%	0.1%	0.9%	4.1%	2.4%	10.4%	0.2%	0.0%	0.2%	51.5%
Primary	Count	1	0	83	4	1	0	80	1	23	11	2	12	0	0	0	218
	% within R	0.5%	0.0%	38.1%	1.8%	0.5%	0.0%	36.7%	0.5%	10.6%	5.0%	0.9%	5.5%	0.0%	0.0%	0.0%	100%
	% within C	11.1%	0.0%	40.5%	6.3%	1.1%	0.0%	7.6%	5.3%	35.4%	7.9%	1.1%	4.7%	0.0%	0.0%	0.0%	10.3%
	% of Total	0.0%	0.0%	3.9%	0.2%	0.0%	0.0%	3.8%	0.0%	1.1%	0.5%	0.1%	0.6%	0.0%	0.0%	0.0%	10.3%
Services	Count	4	2	79	37	13	7	426	15	22	41	135	21	6	0	0	808
	% within R	0.5%	0.2%	9.8%	4.6%	1.6%	0.9%	52.7%	1.9%	2.7%	5.1%	16.7%	2.6%	0.7%	0.0%	0.0%	100%
	% within C	44.4%	50.0%	38.5%	58.7%	14.8%	63.6%	40.3%	78.9%	33.8%	29.5%	72.2%	8.3%	54.5%	0.0%	0.0%	38.2%
	% of Total	0.2%	0.1%	3.7%	1.7%	0.6%	0.3%	20.1%	0.7%	1.0%	1.9%	6.4%	1.0%	0.3%	0.0%	0.0%	38.2%
Total	Count	9	4	205	63	88	11	1057	19	65	139	187	254	11	1	4	2117
	% within R	0.4%	0.2%	9.7%	3.0%	4.2%	0.5%	49.9%	0.9%	3.1%	6.6%	8.8%	12.0%	0.5%	0.0%	0.2%	100%
	% within C	100%	100%	100%	100%	100%	100%	100%	100%	100%	100%	100%	100%	100%	100%	100%	100%
	% of Total	0.4%	0.2%	9.7%	3.0%	4.2%	0.5%	49.9%	0.9%	3.1%	6.6%	8.8%	12.0%	0.5%	0.0%	0.2%	100%

Note: Primary sector, including agriculture oil and gas.
Number, distribution by sector (% within row), distribution by region of origin (% within column)

Source: Cross-Border Investment Monitor, *Financial Times*

industrial (51.5 percent), as against 38.2 percent for services. CEE has also attracted somewhat more primary investments (10.3 percent) than western Europe (6.5 percent).

In western Europe, the most important industrial multinationals come from China and the NICs, which represent 28.6 percent and 22.6 percent of industrial investments, respectively. Furthermore, these industrial investments also represent 74.2 percent and 67.4 percent of their respective investments in western Europe. A second batch of industrial investors in Europe comes from India, MMT, and the Middle East. Investments in the primary sector come mainly from Russia (20.4 percent) and India (19.5 percent) with China a distant third (13.1 percent). In the service sector, most investments come from India (18.4 percent) and the Middle East (18.5 percent). These investments also represent two thirds of investments from these regions, which is higher than the average for all Southern multinationals (48.8 percent).

In eastern Europe, the most prolific Southern investors are obviously multinationals from CEE itself. The second most important group of investors come from the NICs and Russia, which have made 254 and 205 investments, respectively. Central and East European investors are mainly industrial companies (52.1 percent). Investments in the primary sector come mainly from Russia (38.1 percent) and again CEE (36.7 percent). Russian investment in the primary sector is predominant for it, representing about 40 percent of its investments in the region. Investments from Central Asia are mainly (35.4 percent) in the primary sector, although of limited impact (10.6 percent of investment in the region). Service sector investments are of limited importance for eastern Europe, except for CEE investors (426 investments).

Tables 2.5 and 2.6 go into more detail about investments in manufacturing. A distinction has been made among the following manufacturing sectors: chemicals, electronics, food and beverages, machinery, metals, minerals, paper and wood, pharmaceuticals, rubber, textiles, and transport equipment.

In western Europe, the most important manufacturing sector by far is electronics. This sector alone has attracted almost half (47.2 percent) of all investments. This is carried out primarily by multinationals from China (26.9 percent), the NICs (21.7 percent), and India (16.7 percent). In turn, electronics are an important sector for these countries as it represents about half of the investments made by China (51.8 percent), the NICs (53.8 percent), and India (50.2 percent). Other sectors of importance are machinery (10.5 percent), textiles (9.7 percent), and transport equipment (7.1 percent). Machinery is driven by investments from China (39.7 percent) and the NICs (23.3 percent). The most important investors in the chemical and rubber industry are Middle Eastern, with 29.9 percent and 35.4 percent of investments, respectively. Indian multinationals take up almost half of investments in the pharmaceutical industry (48.1 percent), while Chinese investors are most important in transport equipment, together with the NICs. As far as less advanced investors are concerned, such as Southeast Asian countries, they invest relatively more in textiles but also electronics. Although their numbers of investments are not very high, the relative importance of these investments for them is

Table 2.5 Greenfield investments by Southern multinationals in western Europe in selected manufacturing sectors, 2003–2012

SECTOR			Africa	Brazil	Russia	India	China	South Africa	CEE	Central America	Central Asia	MMT	Middle East	NIC	SEA1	SEA2	South America	Total
	Chemicals	Count	0	5	3	5	18	8	3	1	2	2	26	12	0	0	2	87
		% within R	0.0%	5.7%	3.4%	5.7%	20.7%	9.2%	3.4%	1.1%	2.3%	2.3%	29.9%	13.8%	0.0%	0.0%	2.3%	100%
		% within C	0.0%	6.9%	3.1%	1.5%	3.5%	21.1%	1.7%	1.6%	11.1%	1.6%	14.5%	3.0%	0.0%	0.0%	5.9%	4.2%
		% of Total	0.0%	0.2%	0.1%	0.2%	0.9%	0.4%	0.1%	0.0%	0.1%	0.1%	1.3%	0.6%	0.0%	0.0%	0.1%	4.2%
	Electronics	Count	7	12	51	164	264	15	90	47	5	28	63	213	5	2	15	981
		% within R	0.7%	1.2%	5.2%	16.7%	26.9%	1.5%	9.2%	4.8%	0.5%	2.9%	6.4%	21.7%	0.5%	0.2%	1.5%	100%
		% within C	0.0%	6.9%	3.1%	50.2%	51.8%	39.5%	51.7%	77.0%	27.8%	21.7%	35.2%	53.8%	21.7%	22.2%	44.1%	47.2%
		% of Total	0.3%	0.6%	2.5%	7.9%	12.7%	0.7%	4.3%	2.3%	0.2%	1.3%	3.0%	10.2%	0.2%	0.1%	0.7%	47.2%
	Food & Beverages	Count	5	12	2	16	10	2	10	7	5	16	8	8	4	4	7	116
		% within R	3.4%	8.1%	1.4%	13.8%	8.6%	1.7%	8.6%	6.0%	4.3%	13.8%	6.9%	6.9%	3.4%	3.4%	6.0%	100%
		% within C	38.5%	16.7%	2.1%	4.9%	2.0%	5.3%	5.7%	11.5%	27.8%	12.4%	4.5%	2.0%	17.4%	44.4%	20.6%	5.6%
		% of Total	0.2%	0.6%	0.1%	0.8%	0.5%	0.1%	0.5%	0.3%	0.2%	0.8%	0.4%	0.4%	0.2%	0.2%	0.3%	5.6%
	Machinery	Count	1	4	6	26	87	4	14	0	0	12	14	51	0	0	0	219
		% within R	0.7%	2.7%	4.1%	11.9%	39.7%	1.8%	6.4%	0.0%	0.0%	5.5%	6.4%	23.3%	0.0%	0.0%	0.0%	100%
		% within C	7.7%	5.6%	6.2%	8.0%	17.1%	10.5%	8.0%	0.0%	0.0%	9.3%	7.8%	12.9%	0.0%	0.0%	0.0%	10.5%
		% of Total	0.0%	0.2%	0.3%	1.3%	4.2%	0.2%	0.7%	0.0%	0.0%	0.6%	0.7%	2.5%	0.0%	0.0%	0.0%	10.5%

Country or Region of Origin

(Continued)

Table 2.5 (Continued)

		Country or Region of Origin															Total
		Africa	Brazil	Russia	India	China	South Africa	CEE	Central America	Central Asia	MMT	Middle East	NIC	SEA1	SEA2	South America	
Metals	Count	0	14	14	38	24	1	11	0	2	8	2	8	2	0	3	127
	% within R	0.0%	9.5%	9.5%	29.9%	18.9%	0.8%	8.7%	0.0%	1.6%	6.3%	1.6%	6.3%	1.6%	0.0%	2.4%	100%
	% within C	0.0%	19.4%	14.4%	11.6%	4.7%	2.6%	6.3%	0.0%	11.1%	6.2%	1.1%	2.0%	8.7%	0.0%	8.8%	6.1%
	% of Total	0.0%	0.7%	0.7%	1.8%	1.2%	0.0%	0.5%	0.0%	0.1%	0.4%	0.1%	0.4%	0.1%	0.0%	0.1%	6.1%
Minerals	Count	0	0	4	0	2	1	0	0	0	0	2	1	0	0	0	10
	% within R	0.0%	0.0%	2.7%	0.0%	20.0%	10.0%	0.0%	0.0%	0.0%	0.0%	20.0%	10.0%	0.0%	0.0%	0.0%	100%
	% within C	0.0%	0.0%	4.1%	0.0%	0.4%	2.6%	0.0%	0.0%	0.0%	0.0%	1.1%	0.3%	0.0%	0.0%	0.0%	0.5%
	% of Total	0.0%	0.0%	0.2%	0.0%	0.1%	0.0%	0.0%	0.0%	0.0%	0.0%	0.1%	0.0%	0.0%	0.0%	0.0%	0.5%
Paper & Wood	Count	0	2	1	0	6	3	8	5	0	3	1	3	2	0	0	34
	% within R	0.0%	1.4%	0.7%	0.0%	17.6%	8.8%	23.5%	14.7%	0.0%	8.8%	2.9%	8.8%	5.9%	0.0%	0.0%	100%
	% within C	0.0%	2.8%	1.0%	0.0%	1.2%	7.9%	4.6%	8.2%	0.0%	2.3%	0.6%	0.8%	8.7%	0.0%	0.0%	1.6%
	% of Total	0.0%	0.1%	0.0%	0.0%	0.3%	0.1%	0.4%	0.2%	0.0%	0.1%	0.0%	0.1%	0.1%	0.0%	0.0%	1.6%
Pharma	Count	0	1	2	37	8	0	8	0	0	1	12	7	0	0	1	77
	% within R	0.0%	0.7%	1.4%	48.1%	10.4%	0.0%	10.4%	0.0%	0.0%	1.3%	15.6%	9.1%	0.0%	0.0%	1.3%	100%
	% within C	0.0%	1.4%	2.1%	11.3%	1.6%	0.0%	4.6%	0.0%	0.0%	0.8%	6.7%	1.8%	0.0%	0.0%	2.9%	3.7%
	% of Total	0.0%	0.0%	0.1%	1.8%	0.4%	0.0%	0.4%	0.0%	0.0%	0.0%	0.6%	0.3%	0.0%	0.0%	0.0%	3.7%
Rubber	Count	0	2	3	10	10	3	5	0	0	3	28	12	3	0	0	79
	% within R	0.0%	1.4%	2.0%	12.7%	12.7%	3.8%	6.3%	0.0%	0.0%	3.8%	35.4%	15.2%	3.8%	0.0%	0.0%	100%
	% within C	0.0%	2.8%	3.1%	3.1%	2.0%	7.9%	2.9%	0.0%	0.0%	2.3%	15.6%	3.0%	13.0%	0.0%	0.0%	3.8%
	% of Total	0.0%	0.1%	0.1%	0.5%	0.5%	0.1%	0.2%	0.0%	0.0%	0.1%	1.3%	0.6%	0.1%	0.0%	0.0%	3.8%

Sector	Measure																Total
Textiles	Count	0	14	10	9	31	0	13	0	2	44	19	44	7	3	6	202
	% within R	0.0%	9.5%	6.8%	4.5%	15.3%	0.0%	6.4%	0.0%	1.0%	21.8%	9.4%	21.8%	3.5%	1.5%	3.0%	100%
	% within C	0.0%	19.4%	10.3%	2.8%	6.1%	0.0%	7.5%	0.0%	11.1%	34.1%	10.6%	11.1%	30.4%	33.3%	17.6%	9.7%
	% of Total	0.0%	0.7%	0.5%	0.4%	1.5%	0.0%	0.6%	0.0%	0.1%	2.1%	0.9%	2.1%	0.3%	0.1%	0.3%	9.7%
Transport	Count	0	6	1	22	50	1	12	1	2	12	4	37	0	0	0	148
	% within R	0.0%	4.1%	0.7%	14.9%	33.8%	0.7%	8.1%	0.7%	1.4%	8.1%	2.7%	25.0%	0.0%	0.0%	0.0%	100%
	% within C	0.0%	8.3%	1.0%	6.7%	9.8%	2.6%	6.9%	1.6%	11.1%	9.3%	2.2%	9.3%	0.0%	0.0%	0.0%	7.1%
	% of Total	0.0%	0.3%	0.0%	1.1%	2.4%	0.0%	0.6%	0.0%	0.1%	0.6%	0.2%	1.8%	0.0%	0.0%	0.0%	7.1%
Total	Count	13	72	97	327	510	38	174	61	18	129	179	396	23	9	34	2080
	% within R	0.6%	3.5%	4.7%	15.7%	24.5%	1.8%	8.4%	2.9%	0.9%	6.2%	8.6%	19.0%	1.1%	0.4%	1.6%	100%
	% within C	100%	100%	100%	100%	100%	100%	100%	100%	100%	100%	100%	100%	100%	100%	100%	100%
	% of Total	0.6%	3.5%	4.7%	15.7%	24.5%	1.8%	8.4%	2.9%	0.9%	6.2%	8.6%	19.0%	1.1%	0.4%	1.6%	100%

Source: Cross-Border Investment Monitor, *Financial Times*
Number, distribution by sector (% within row), distribution by region of origin (% within column)

Table 2.6 Greenfield investments by Southern multinationals in central and eastern Europe in selected manufacturing sectors, 2003–2012

SECTOR		Africa	Brazil	Russia	India	China	South Africa	CEE	Central America	Central Asia	MMT	Middle East	NIC	SEA1	SEA2	South America	Total
Chemicals	Count	0	0	10	1	2	0	20	0	0	1	5	2	0	0	0	41
	% within R	0.0%	0.0%	24.4%	2.4%	4.9%	0.0%	48.8%	0.0%	0.0%	2.4%	12.2%	4.9%	0.0%	0.0%	0.0%	100%
	% within C	0.0%	0.0%	0.8%	1.1%	2.2%	0.0%	3.3%	0.0%	0.0%	1.4%	8.6%	0.8%	0.0%	0.0%	0.0%	3.2%
	% of Total	0.0%	0.0%	0.8%	0.1%	0.2%	0.0%	1.6%	0.0%	0.0%	0.1%	0.4%	0.2%	0.0%	0.0%	0.0%	3.2%
Electronics	Count	0	2	15	20	38	2	141	6	5	11	12	151	0	0	0	403
	% within R	0.0%	0.5%	3.7%	5.0%	9.4%	0.5%	35.0%	1.5%	1.2%	2.7%	3.0%	37.5%	0.0%	0.0%	0.0%	100%
	% within C	0.0%	0.4%	1.2%	22.0%	41.8%	10.5%	23.0%	85.7%	14.7%	15.3%	20.7%	57.9%	0.0%	0.0%	0.0%	31.8%
	% of Total	0.0%	0.2%	1.2%	1.6%	3.0%	0.2%	11.1%	0.5%	0.4%	0.9%	0.9%	11.9%	0.0%	0.0%	0.0%	31.8%
Food & Beverages	Count	0	0	7	0	5	0	189	0	7	17	16	6	1	0	0	248
	% within R	0.0%	0.0%	2.8%	0.0%	2.0%	0.0%	76.2%	0.0%	2.8%	6.9%	6.5%	2.4%	0.4%	0.0%	0.0%	100%
	% within C	0.0%	0.0%	0.6%	0.0%	5.5%	0.0%	30.8%	0.0%	20.6%	23.6%	27.6%	2.3%	16.7%	0.0%	0.0%	19.6%
	% of Total	0.0%	0.0%	0.6%	0.0%	0.4%	0.0%	14.9%	0.0%	0.6%	1.3%	1.3%	0.5%	0.1%	0.0%	0.0%	19.6%
Machinery	Count	1	0	10	2	9	1	37	0	2	2	2	5	0	0	0	71
	% within R	1.4%	0.0%	14.1%	2.8%	12.7%	1.4%	52.1%	0.0%	2.8%	2.8%	2.8%	7.0%	0.0%	0.0%	0.0%	100%
	% within C	5.0%	0.0%	0.8%	2.2%	9.9%	5.3%	6.0%	0.0%	5.9%	2.8%	3.4%	1.9%	0.0%	0.0%	0.0%	5.6%
	% of Total	0.1%	0.0%	0.8%	0.2%	0.7%	0.1%	2.9%	0.0%	0.2%	0.2%	0.2%	0.4%	0.0%	0.0%	0.0%	5.6%
Metals	Count	1	0	19	3	1	0	28	1	9	7	2	10	0	0	0	81
	% within R	1.2%	0.0%	23.5%	3.7%	1.2%	0.0%	34.6%	1.2%	11.1%	8.6%	2.5%	12.3%	0.0%	0.0%	0.0%	100%
	% within C	5.0%	0.0%	1.6%	3.3%	1.1%	0.0%	4.6%	14.3%	26.5%	9.7%	3.4%	3.8%	0.0%	0.0%	0.0%	6.4%
	% of Total	0.1%	0.0%	1.5%	0.2%	0.1%	0.0%	2.2%	0.1%	0.7%	0.6%	0.2%	0.8%	0.0%	0.0%	0.0%	6.4%
Minerals	Count	0	0	2	0	0	0	0	0	0	0	0	0	0	0	0	2
	% within R	0.0%	0.0%	100.0%	0.0%	0.0%	0.0%	0.0%	0.0%	0.0%	0.0%	0.0%	0.0%	0.0%	0.0%	0.0%	100%
	% within C	0.0%	0.0%	0.2%	0.0%	0.0%	0.0%	0.0%	0.0%	0.0%	0.0%	0.0%	0.0%	0.0%	0.0%	0.0%	0.2%
	% of Total	0.0%	0.0%	0.2%	0.0%	0.0%	0.0%	0.0%	0.0%	0.0%	0.0%	0.0%	0.0%	0.0%	0.0%	0.0%	0.2%

Paper & Wood	Count	1	0	0	0	3	2	20	0	0	10	0	0	0	0	0	36
	% within R	2.8%	0.0%	0.0%	0.0%	8.3%	5.6%	55.6%	0.0%	0.0%	27.8%	0.0%	0.0%	0.0%	0.0%	0.0%	100%
	% within C	5.0%	0.0%	0.0%	0.0%	3.3%	10.5%	3.3%	0.0%	0.0%	13.9%	0.0%	0.0%	0.0%	0.0%	0.0%	2.8%
	% of Total	0.1%	0.0%	0.0%	0.0%	0.2%	0.2%	1.6%	0.0%	0.0%	0.8%	0.0%	0.0%	0.0%	0.0%	0.0%	2.8%
Pharma	Count	1	0	3	7	3	0	34	0	0	3	9	0	0	0	0	60
	% within R	1.7%	0.0%	5.0%	11.7%	5.0%	0.0%	56.7%	0.0%	0.0%	5.0%	15.0%	0.0%	0.0%	0.0%	0.0%	100%
	% within C	5.0%	0.0%	0.2%	7.7%	3.3%	0.0%	5.5%	0.0%	0.0%	4.2%	15.5%	0.0%	0.0%	0.0%	0.0%	4.7%
	% of Total	0.1%	0.0%	0.2%	0.6%	0.2%	0.0%	2.7%	0.0%	0.0%	0.2%	0.7%	0.0%	0.0%	0.0%	0.0%	4.7%
Rubber	Count	0	1	1	3	1	0	22	0	1	5	4	26	2	0	0	66
	% within R	0.0%	1.5%	1.5%	4.5%	1.5%	0.0%	33.3%	0.0%	1.5%	7.6%	6.1%	39.4%	3.0%	0.0%	0.0%	100%
	% within C	0.0%	0.2%	0.1%	3.3%	1.1%	0.0%	3.6%	0.0%	2.9%	6.9%	6.9%	10.0%	33.3%	0.0%	0.0%	5.2%
	% of Total	0.0%	0.1%	0.1%	0.2%	0.1%	0.0%	1.7%	0.0%	0.1%	0.4%	0.3%	2.1%	0.2%	0.0%	0.0%	5.2%
Textiles	Count	0	0	2	0	0	1	80	0	4	12	6	9	3	1	0	118
	% within R	0.0%	0.0%	1.7%	0.0%	0.0%	0.8%	67.8%	0.0%	3.4%	10.2%	5.1%	7.6%	2.5%	0.8%	0.0%	100%
	% within C	0.0%	0.0%	0.2%	0.0%	0.0%	5.3%	13.0%	0.0%	11.8%	16.7%	10.3%	3.4%	50.0%	0.0%	0.0%	9.3%
	% of Total	0.0%	0.0%	0.2%	0.0%	0.0%	0.1%	6.3%	0.0%	0.3%	0.9%	0.5%	0.7%	0.2%	0.1%	0.0%	9.3%
Transport	Count	1	0	12	8	14	0	43	0	6	4	2	52	0	0	0	142
	% within R	0.7%	0.0%	8.5%	5.6%	9.9%	0.0%	30.3%	0.0%	4.2%	2.8%	1.4%	36.6%	0.0%	0.0%	0.0%	100%
	% within C	5.0%	0.0%	1.0%	8.8%	15.4%	0.0%	7.0%	0.0%	17.6%	5.6%	3.4%	19.9%	0.0%	0.0%	0.0%	11.2%
	% of Total	0.1%	0.0%	0.9%	0.6%	1.1%	0.0%	3.4%	0.0%	0.5%	0.3%	0.2%	4.1%	0.0%	0.0%	0.0%	11.2%
Total	Count	5	3	81	44	76	6	614	7	34	72	58	261	6	1	0	1268
	% within R	1.6%	40.9%	96.5%	7.2%	7.2%	1.5%	48.4%	0.6%	2.7%	5.7%	4.6%	20.6%	0.5%	0.1%	0.0%	100%
	% within C	100%	100%	100%	100%	100%	100%	100%	100%	100%	100%	100%	100%	100%	100%	100%	100%
	% of Total	1.6%	40.9%	96.5%	7.2%	7.2%	1.5%	48.4%	0.6%	2.7%	5.7%	4.6%	20.6%	0.5%	0.1%	0.0%	100%

Source: Cross-Border Investment Monitor, *Financial Times*
Number, distribution by sector (% within row), distribution by region of origin (% within column)

quite high, at about 30 percent and 20 percent respectively. The most important investors in the textile industry are MMT, the NICs and China.

This seems to suggest that home country sectoral capabilities are an important driver of investments abroad. There is a clear link between home country comparative and competitive strengths in particular sectors and the outward investments from these countries.

As far as eastern Europe is concerned, the most important – albeit less so than in the case of western Europe – sector is again electronics (31.8 percent). The most important investors in this sector come from the NICs. In fact, more than a third of investments originate from this region (37.5 percent), and represent more than half (57.9 percent) of their investments in CEE. Other sectors of importance are food and beverage, transport equipment, and textiles. Furthermore, the NICs are the most important investors in the rubber (39.4 percent) and the transport sector (36.6 percent).

Business activity comparison

In terms of business activities (see Tables 2.7 and 2.8), the analysis indicates huge differences between western Europe on the one hand and central and eastern Europe on the other. In western Europe, the most important activity carried out by the subsidiaries is marketing and sales (43.3 percent), followed by business services (22.6 percent). Production activities represent a mere 13.8 percent of all Southern greenfield investments in the region. Western Europe is clearly quite attractive as a destination for headquarters, given that Southern multinationals have set up 286 there. Retailing has attracted 230 investments (8 percent of all), while fifty-nine R&D labs have been set up.

With regard to the home country or region, a number of significant differences can be observed. As far as business services are concerned, India is clearly the most important investor in western Europe. One in five investments in business services is carried out by Indian multinationals, which focus to a large extent on this sector, as one in three investments from India are in business services. China and the NICs are the most prolific investors of headquarters for the European market, investing 84 and 59 HQs, respectively.

In terms of production activities, the most important investors are India (18.7 percent), the NICs (14.6 percent), China (14.4 percent), MMT (13.4 percent), and the Middle East (13.1 percent). It should come as no surprise that Indian multinationals have developed substantial competitive advantages in sectors such as electrical engineering and pharmaceuticals and are aggressively tackling the European market. The NICs are investing in manufacturing activities in their strongest sectors, such as electronics, machinery, and transport equipment. Similarly, China also clearly focuses on electronics, machinery, and transport equipment. Middle Eastern investments are in chemicals, petrochemicals, rubber, and pharmaceuticals. There is a clear linkage between home country comparative and competitive advantages and these manufacturing investments.

Marketing and sales activities follow a similar geographical pattern to production activities. The same Southern investors are the most important, although

Table 2.7 Greenfield investments by Southern multinationals in western Europe by subsidiary business activity, 2003–2012

ACTIVITY			Country or Region of Origin																Total
			Africa	Brazil	Russia	India	China	South Africa	CEE	Central America	Central Asia	MMT	Middle East	NIC	SEA1	SEA2	South America	
Business Services	Count		34	15	59	141	61	10	89	48	24	20	56	25	31	7	27	647
	% within R		5.3%	2.3%	9.1%	21.8%	9.4%	1.5%	13.8%	7.4%	3.7%	3.1%	8.7%	3.9%	4.8%	1.1%	4.2%	100%
	% within C		59.6%	17.2%	31.9%	34.9%	11.3%	18.5%	30.0%	43.2%	44.4%	9.2%	18.4%	6.2%	48.4%	41.2%	37.5%	22.6%
	% of Total		1.2%	0.5%	2.1%	4.9%	2.1%	0.3%	3.1%	1.7%	0.8%	0.7%	2.0%	0.9%	1.1%	0.2%	0.9%	22.6%
HQ	Count		5	9	15	36	84	7	20	9	1	13	23	59	2	1	2	286
	% within R		1.7%	3.1%	5.2%	12.6%	29.4%	2.4%	7.0%	3.1%	0.3%	4.5%	8.0%	20.6%	0.7%	0.3%	0.7%	100%
	% within C		8.8%	10.3%	8.1%	8.9%	15.6%	13.0%	6.7%	8.1%	1.9%	6.0%	7.6%	14.7%	3.1%	5.9%	2.8%	10.0%
	% of Total		0.2%	0.3%	0.5%	1.3%	2.9%	0.2%	0.7%	0.3%	0.0%	0.5%	0.8%	2.1%	0.1%	0.0%	0.1%	10.0%
Production	Count		3	25	14	74	57	13	21	7	4	53	52	58	7	3	5	396
	% within R		0.8%	6.3%	3.5%	18.7%	14.4%	3.3%	5.3%	1.8%	1.0%	13.4%	13.1%	14.6%	1.8%	0.8%	1.3%	100%
	% within C		5.3%	28.7%	7.6%	18.3%	10.6%	24.1%	7.1%	6.3%	7.4%	24.4%	17.1%	14.5%	10.9%	17.6%	6.9%	13.8%
	% of Total		0.1%	0.9%	0.5%	2.6%	2.0%	0.5%	0.7%	0.2%	0.1%	1.9%	1.8%	2.0%	0.2%	0.1%	0.2%	13.8%
Marketing & Sales	Count		14	24	84	133	305	18	133	44	23	80	137	191	21	6	27	1240
	% within R		1.1%	1.9%	6.8%	10.7%	24.6%	1.5%	10.7%	3.5%	1.9%	6.5%	11.0%	15.4%	1.7%	0.5%	2.2%	100%
	% within C		24.6%	27.6%	45.4%	32.9%	56.6%	33.3%	44.8%	39.6%	42.6%	36.9%	45.1%	47.6%	32.8%	35.3%	37.5%	43.3%
	% of Total		0.5%	0.8%	2.9%	4.6%	10.7%	0.6%	4.6%	1.5%	0.8%	2.8%	4.8%	6.7%	0.7%	0.2%	0.9%	43.3%
R&D	Count		0	1	4	12	20	1	3	1	0	1	7	9	0	0	0	59
	% within R		0.0%	1.7%	6.8%	20.3%	33.9%	1.7%	5.1%	1.7%	0.0%	1.7%	11.9%	15.3%	0.0%	0.0%	0.0%	100%
	% within C		0.0%	1.1%	2.2%	3.0%	3.7%	1.9%	1.0%	0.9%	0.0%	0.5%	2.3%	2.2%	0.0%	0.0%	0.0%	2.1%
	% of Total		0.0%	0.0%	0.1%	0.4%	0.7%	0.0%	0.1%	0.0%	0.0%	0.0%	0.2%	0.3%	0.0%	0.0%	0.0%	2.1%

(Continued)

Table 2.7 (Continued)

		Africa	Brazil	Russia	India	China	South Africa	CEE	Central America	Central Asia	MMT	Middle East	NIC	SEA1	SEA2	South America	Total
																Country or Region of Origin	
Retail	Count	1	13	9	8	12	5	29	2	2	49	29	58	3	0	10	230
	% within R	0.4%	5.7%	3.9%	3.5%	5.2%	2.2%	12.6%	0.9%	0.9%	21.3%	12.6%	25.2%	1.3%	0.0%	4.3%	100%
	% within C	1.8%	14.9%	4.9%	2.0%	2.2%	9.3%	9.8%	1.8%	3.7%	22.6%	9.5%	14.5%	4.7%	0.0%	13.9%	8.0%
	% of Total	0.0%	0.5%	0.3%	0.3%	0.4%	0.2%	1.0%	0.1%	0.1%	1.7%	1.0%	2.0%	0.1%	0.0%	0.3%	8.0%
Total	Count	57	87	185	404	539	54	297	111	54	217	304	401	64	17	72	2863
	% within R	2.0%	3.0%	6.5%	14.1%	18.8%	1.9%	10.4%	3.9%	1.9%	7.6%	10.6%	14.0%	2.2%	0.6%	2.5%	100%
	% within C	100%	100%	100%	100%	100%	100%	100%	100%	100%	100%	100%	100%	100%	100%	100%	100%
	% of Total	2.0%	3.0%	6.5%	14.1%	18.8%	1.9%	10.4%	3.9%	1.9%	7.6%	10.6%	14.0%	2.2%	0.6%	2.5%	100%

Source: Cross-Border Investment Monitor, *Financial Times*
Number, distribution by sector (% within row), distribution by region of origin (% within column)

Table 2.8 Greenfield investments by Southern multinationals in central and eastern Europe by subsidiary business activity, 2003–2012

ACTIVITY			Country or Region of Origin																Total
			Africa	Brazil	Russia	India	China	South Africa	CEE	Central America	Central Asia	MMT	Middle East	NIC	SEA1	SEA2	South America	
Business Services		Count	1	0	37	3	10	0	115	1	12	9	19	3	4	0	0	214
		% within R	0.5%	0.0%	17.3%	1.4%	4.7%	0.0%	53.7%	0.5%	5.6%	4.2%	8.9%	1.4%	1.9%	0.0%	0.0%	100%
		% within C	14.3%	0.0%	21.5%	8.3%	13.0%	0.0%	13.7%	20.0%	19.0%	7.8%	20.7%	1.2%	40.0%	0.0%	0.0%	12.8%
		% of Total	0.1%	0.0%	2.2%	0.2%	0.6%	0.0%	6.9%	0.1%	0.7%	0.5%	1.1%	0.2%	0.2%	0.0%	0.0%	12.8%
	HQ	Count	0	0	2	1	1	0	5	0	0	0	3	4	0	0	0	16
		% within R	0.0%	0.0%	12.5%	6.3%	6.3%	0.0%	31.3%	0.0%	0.0%	0.0%	18.8%	25.0%	0.0%	0.0%	0.0%	100%
		% within C	0.0%	0.0%	1.2%	2.8%	1.3%	0.0%	0.6%	0.0%	0.0%	0.0%	3.3%	1.6%	0.0%	0.0%	0.0%	1.0%
		% of Total	0.0%	0.0%	0.1%	0.1%	0.1%	0.0%	0.3%	0.0%	0.0%	0.0%	0.2%	0.2%	0.0%	0.0%	0.0%	1.0%
	Production	Count	5	1	60	18	56	4	208	1	21	68	31	182	3	1	0	659
		% within R	0.8%	0.2%	9.1%	2.7%	8.5%	0.6%	31.6%	0.2%	3.2%	10.3%	4.7%	27.6%	0.5%	0.2%	0.0%	100%
		% within C	71.4%	100.0%	34.9%	50.0%	72.7%	40.0%	24.8%	20.0%	33.3%	59.1%	33.7%	73.7%	30.0%	0.0%	0.0%	39.3%
		% of Total	0.3%	0.1%	3.6%	1.1%	3.3%	0.2%	12.4%	0.1%	1.3%	4.1%	1.9%	10.9%	0.2%	0.1%	0.0%	39.3%
	Marketing & Sales	Count	1	0	43	11	8	6	210	3	19	14	27	31	1	0	0	374
		% within R	0.3%	0.0%	11.5%	2.9%	2.1%	1.6%	56.1%	0.8%	5.1%	3.7%	7.2%	8.3%	0.3%	0.0%	0.0%	100%
		% within C	14.3%	0.0%	25.0%	30.6%	10.4%	60.0%	25.0%	60.0%	30.2%	12.2%	29.3%	12.6%	10.0%	0.0%	0.0%	22.3%
		% of Total	0.1%	0.0%	2.6%	0.7%	0.5%	0.4%	12.5%	0.2%	1.1%	0.8%	1.6%	1.9%	0.1%	0.0%	0.0%	22.3%
	R&D	Count	0	0	0	1	2	0	1	0	0	0	0	3	0	0	0	7
		% within R	0.0%	0.0%	0.0%	14.3%	28.6%	0.0%	14.3%	0.0%	0.0%	0.0%	0.0%	42.9%	0.0%	0.0%	0.0%	100%
		% within C	0.0%	0.0%	0.0%	2.8%	2.6%	0.0%	0.1%	0.0%	0.0%	0.0%	0.0%	1.2%	0.0%	0.0%	0.0%	0.4%
		% of Total	0.0%	0.0%	0.0%	0.1%	0.1%	0.0%	0.1%	0.0%	0.0%	0.0%	0.0%	0.2%	0.0%	0.0%	0.0%	0.4%

(Continued)

Table 2.8 (Continued)

		Country or Region of Origin															Total
		Africa	Brazil	Russia	India	China	South Africa	CEE	Central America	Central Asia	MMT	Middle East	NIC	SEA1	SEA2	South America	
Retail	Count	0	0	29	1	0	0	300	0	11	23	12	24	2	0	0	402
	% within R	0.0%	0.0%	7.2%	0.2%	0.0%	0.0%	74.6%	0.0%	2.7%	5.7%	3.0%	6.0%	0.5%	0.0%	0.0%	100%
	% within C	0.0%	0.0%	16.9%	2.8%	0.0%	0.0%	35.8%	0.0%	17.5%	20.0%	13.0%	9.7%	20.0%	0.0%	0.0%	24.0%
	% of Total	0.0%	0.0%	1.7%	0.1%	0.0%	0.0%	17.9%	0.0%	0.7%	1.4%	0.7%	1.4%	0.1%	0.0%	0.0%	24.0%
Total	Count	7	1	172	36	77	10	839	5	63	115	92	247	10	1	0	1675
	% within R	0.4%	0.1%	10.3%	2.1%	4.6%	0.6%	50.1%	0.3%	3.8%	6.9%	5.5%	14.7%	0.6%	0.1%	0.0%	100%
	% within C	100%	100%	100%	100%	100%	100%	100%	100%	100%	100%	100%	100%	100%	100%	0.0%	100%
	% of Total	0.4%	0.1%	10.3%	2.1%	4.6%	0.6%	50.1%	0.3%	3.8%	6.9%	5.5%	14.7%	0.6%	0.1%	0.0%	100%

Source: Cross-Border Investment Monitor, *Financial Times*
Number, distribution by sector (% within row), distribution by region of origin (% within column).

China (24.6 percent) is most important, followed by the NICs (15.4 percent), the Middle East (11.0 percent), India (10.7 percent), and CEE (10.7 percent). Many of these investors clearly follow a trade-supporting approach to internationalization. They set up marketing and sales subsidiaries in support of their productive capacity back home in order to better supply the European market.

In a similar vein, retail activities are subsequently the most important for the NICs and MMT. Companies from these countries have already developed some familiar brand names in consumer but also in industrial products that require a more pronounced European distribution network with an extensive dealer network.

Last but not least, China (33.9 percent), India (20.3 percent), the NICs (15.3 percent), and the Middle East (11.9 percent) have invested in some R&D labs in western Europe. Although this represents only 2.1 percent of greenfield investments in Europe, there is a clear battle to attract these types of high-end investment projects across western European countries.

In central and eastern European countries, the distribution of business activities is quite different from the business activities invested in western Europe. In CEE, the most important business activity is clearly manufacturing, representing 39.3 percent of all investment projects in the region. This is followed by retailing (24.0 percent) and marketing and sales (22.3 percent). Business services have attracted only 12.8 percent of the investment projects, while there are almost no headquarters and R&D projects in CEE, especially if we exclude CEE projects in their own region.

In general, companies from CEE are the most prolific investors in their own region. It should come as no surprise that intraregional investment is the most predominant. The prevalence of central and eastern European investors is most outspoken for retailing, marketing and sales, and business services. As far as production activities are concerned, the NICs (27.6 percent), MMT (10.3 percent), Russia (9.1 percent), and China (8.5 percent) are quite important. Furthermore, CEE has attracted almost no headquarters or R&D labs.

All in all, Southern investors are clearly more attracted to western Europe than to central and eastern Europe. With the exception of intraregional CEE investment, among the few noteworthy types of Southern investments in the region are in manufacturing. The usual suspects, such as the NICs (182 plants), MMT (68 plants), China (56 plants), but also Russia have invested in 60 plants in CEE.

Conclusions and implications

The presence and the impact of Southern multinationals in Europe have increased in the recent decade. However, they vary across European countries. Southern multinationals are not concentrated only in Western or more developed European countries but dispersed across less developed or emerging European countries. While the aggregate data (from the national statistical offices of European economies or Eurostat) hardly show any pattern from Southern multinationals, the *Financial Times* data analyzed in this chapter offers some insights into the activities and geographical and sectoral spread, as well as the functional variability and strategic diversity.

It is not only that the attractiveness of Europe as a location for FDI varies largely for Southern direct investors, but Southern multinationals themselves are quite heterogeneous investors, with many different strategies and approaches. Southern multinationals pursue relatively more/quite diversified strategies (compared with Western MNEs) and are often long-term oriented. Their creation and use of synergies from host and home country location advantages, exploiting and looking for firm-specific advantages varies and has yet to be explored in detail. They do not exploit only South-South type of cooperation (relying on cost competitiveness in similarly or less developed technological environments) but develop also South-North strategies (with strategic alliances, intensive learning, and technology upgrading).

The existing theoretical frameworks and research offer limited insights on how institutional or industry conditions of the emerging markets enable the Southern multinationals to compete not only in the host emerging market but internationally. The context today is different than at the time of the development of dominant theoretical frameworks, and Southern multinationals are pursuing different strategies and motives at different locations. Central and eastern Europe is seen as a location for manufacturing as well an organizational and sales platform, and western Europe a strategic assets seeking location, appropriate for headquarters, development of business services, and R&D activity. Existing analyses, however, show that they not only draw on the comparative advantage of their home country, but are intensively developing their own competitive advantages by seeking firm-specific advantages of host country firms and integrating them into their "whole".

Many Southern multinationals deliberately plan their entry and market share in Europe; especially so after the crises. While several European countries did not make any strategic effort to attract Southern multinationals or even reluctantly host them initially, their presence in Europe was a result of firm-strategic plans. The global economic and financial crisis that hit the EU the hardest was another incentive for investment activities. On the one hand, western Europe is seen as a hub for business services, headquarters, and R&D. China and India are interested in western European technology, brands, and moving up in value chains. Central and eastern Europe is, on the other hand, seen as a window of opportunity and not as a strategic opportunity. The institutional, historical, and ideological proximity (especially with Hungary and the former Yugoslavia) and the level of industrialization may be seen as an advantage; the sea access is also seen as an advantage and could be exploited further. For instance, the 16+1 platform is a pragmatic platform initiated by China – and not Europe – with the 16 central and eastern European countries. China is committed to build trade volume, may see the New Silk Route and CEE as a pipeline/door to Western markets, and is motivated to be present in infrastructural projects as well. However, in spite of many CEE countries being integrated into the EU, they are often not seen as a unified political framework.

The implications for investment policies in the EU are several. Further activities in the area of investment promotion policy and programs for attracting FDI require comprehensive analysis, more complete data monitoring, and updated quality analyses. Existing data point to the fact that Europe – in spite of intensive integration processes – is still seen as "a set of regions" with regional specifics playing an important role in FDI decision processes. Global value chain analysis – which in recent years gave further insights into the creation of value – show that integration with Southern multinationals offers opportunities for all involved. These analyses have also shown that Southern foreign direct investors are not homogeneous and need a differentiated approach. Efforts initiated through intensive cultural diplomacy might also be exploited for greater understanding and development of economic cooperation. European countries cannot ignore rising cooperation with Southern multinationals, and their countries of origin should be factored into trade and investment strategies, as above all, these economies value stability and consistency in their partners.

References

Battat, J., and Aykut, D. (2005) *Southern Multinationals: A Growing Phenomenon*, Washington, DC: World Bank.

Brennan, L. (2010) 'Southern Multinationals and their Impact on Europe: What Have We Learnt?', in Brennan, L. (Ed.) *The Emergence of Southern Multinationals: Their Impact on Europe*, London: Palgrave Macmillan, pp. 367–377.

Buckley, P. J., Clegg, J., Cross, A. R., Liu, X., Voss, H., and Zheng, P. (2007) 'The determinants of Chinese outward foreign direct investment', *Journal of International Business Studies*, 38, 4: 499–518.

Caves, R. (1986) *Multinational Enterprise and Economic Analysis*, Cambridge, UK: Cambridge University Press.

Cuervo-Cazurra, A., and Genc, M. (2008) 'Transforming disadvantages into advantages: Developing-country MNEs in the least developed countries', *Journal of International Business Studies*, 39, 6: 957–979.

De Beule, F., and Duanmu, J. (2012) 'Locational determinants of internationalization: A firm-level analysis of Chinese and Indian acquisitions', *European Management Journal*, 30, 3: 264–277.

De Beule, F., Elia, S., and Piscitello, L. (2014) 'Entry and access to competencies abroad: Emerging market firms versus advanced market firms', *Journal of International Management*, 20, 2: 137–152.

De Beule, F., and Van Den Bulcke, D. (2012) 'Locational determinants of outward foreign direct investment: An analysis of Chinese and Indian greenfield investments', *Transnational Corporations*, 21, 1: 1–34.

Deng, P. (2004) 'Outward investment by Chinese MNCs: Motivations and implications', *Business Horizons*, 47, 3: 8–16.

Dikova, D., Jaklic, A., Burger, A., and Kunčič, A. (2015) 'What is beneficial for first-time SME-exporters from a transition economy: A diversified or a focused export-strategy?', *Journal of World Business*, 51, 4: 185–199.

Duanmu, J., and Guney, Y. (2013) 'Heterogeneous effect of ethnic networks on international trade of Thailand: The role of family ties and ethnic diversity', *International Business Review*, 22, 1: 126–139.

Dunning, J. H. (1981) *International Production and the Multinational Enterprise*, London: Allen & Unwin.

Dunning, J. H., and Lundan, S. M. (2008) 'Institutions and the OLI paradigm of the multinational enterprise', *Asia Pacific Journal of Management*, 25, 4: 573–593.

Hennart, J. F. (2012) 'Emerging market multinationals and the theory of the multinational enterprise', *Global Strategy Journal*, 2, 3: 168–187.

Kaartemo, V. (2007) *The Motives of Chinese Foreign Investments in the Baltic Sea Region*. PEI Electronic Publications, No. 7/2007, Turku, Finland: Pan-European Institute.

Lessard, D. R., and Lucea, R. (2009) '10 Mexican Multinationals: Insights from CEMEX', in Ramamurti, R., and Singh, J. V. (Eds.) *Emerging Multinationals in Emerging Markets*, Cambridge: Cambridge University Press, pp. 280–311.

Luo, Y., and Tung, R. L. (2007) 'International expansion of emerging market enterprises: A springboard perspective', *Journal of International Business Studies*, 38, 4: 481–498.

Mathews, J. A. (2002) 'Competitive advantages of the latecomer firm: A resource-based account of industrial catch-up strategies', *Asia Pacific Journal of Management*, 19, 4: 467–488.

Mathews, J. A. (2006) 'Dragon multinationals: New players in 21st century globalization', *Asia Pacific Journal of Management*, 23, 1: 5–27.

Narula, R. (2012) 'Do we need different frameworks to explain infant MNEs from developing countries?', *Global Strategy Journal*, 2, 3: 188–204.

Nestmann, T., and Orlova, D. (2008) *Russia's Outward Investment*, Frankfurt am Main: Deutsche Bank Research.

Pradhan, J. P. (2008) *Overcoming Innovation Limits through Outward FDI: The Overseas Acquisition Strategy of Indian Pharmaceutical Firms*. MPRA Paper, No. 12362, Germany: University Library of Munich.

Ramamurti, R., and Singh, J. V. (Eds.) (2009) *Emerging Multinationals in Emerging Markets*, Cambridge, UK: Cambridge University Press.

Rugman, A. M. (Ed.) (2009) *The Oxford Handbook of International Business*, Oxford, UK: Oxford Handbooks Online.

Rugman, A. M., and Li, J. (2007) 'Will China's multinationals succeed globally or regionally?', *European Management Journal*, 25, 5: 333–343.

Rugman, A. M., and Verbeke, A. (2001) 'Subsidiary-specific advantages in multinational enterprises', *Strategic Management Journal*, 22, 3: 237–250.

Vahlne, J. E., and Wiedersheim-Paul, F. (1973) 'The internationalization process of the firm: A model of knowledge development and increasing foreign market commitments', Journal of International Business Studies, 8, 1: 23–32.

Verma, S., Sanghi, K., Michaelis, H., Dupoux, P., Khanna, D., and Peters, P. (2011) *Companies on the Move. Rising Stars from Rapidly Developing Economies Are Reshaping Global Industries*, Boston: The Boston Consulting Group.

Zaheer, S. (1995) 'Overcoming the liability of foreignness', *Academy of Management Journal*, 38, 2: 341–363.

3 Tracing emerging market MNEs and FDI in European countries

Data coverage, deficiencies and implications

Andreja Jaklič and Filip De Beule

Introduction

The task to estimate the volume and impact of Chinese, Turkish, or Zimbabwean investment (or investment of any other Southern multinationals) in selected European countries in the last decade may seem easy at first glance but is not at all routine and trouble free. The data may vary among different international and national sources, and variations are also large among European countries. Researchers can see large and sometimes increasing variation among sources as well as several other problems that require caution with interpretation. The asymmetry between inward and outward FDI bilateral data in official statistical sources, complex structures used by multinational enterprises that can obscure the ultimate source of FDI into countries, substantial differences in information among different surveys and incomplete coverage for SMEs are such examples.

Data compilers, researchers and analysts all over the world, as well as strategists and policymakers, are aware of deficiencies in FDI data. The increased cross-country analytics and comparative studies, and especially the rise of FDI inflows from emerging economies (Brennan 2010a) have been revealing constantly new challenges for all data users. Recent literature emphasizes the differential impact of FDI determinants for emerging/nontraditional sources, as opposed to those for developed countries (Bevan and Estrin 2004; Sauvant 2008; Brennan 2010a; De Beule and Duanmu 2012; De Beule and Van Den Bulcke 2012). The researchers within the COST Action IS0905 project "The Impact of Southern Multinationals on Europe" were confronted with data restrictions, limitation and challenges at the very beginning; therefore the first working group was devoted to data compilation and data challenges. Most often used data providers such as the Organisation for Economic Co-operation and Development (OECD) and the Statistical Office of the European Union (Eurostat) in Europe are focused on statistical monitoring of their members and the activities of their entities. Southern multinationals have been often neglected and out of this focus. They are a relatively new and rapidly growing phenomenon, and besides, they were created in a different context than multinationals from the past. The contexts of existing and dominant theoretical frameworks differ in several ways from the environment today. Therefore, we might expect the behaviour, strategies and impact of the Southern multinationals of the twenty-first century on developed European economies to be different from multinational firms that expanded in earlier times and came from different home country institutional settings. The awareness that good and reliable data are thus extremely important is rising, especially after global economic crises, as even with a good database, estimating the impact of FDI remains a great challenge.

Data gathering should respond to economic and financial developments, changes in analytical interests and accumulation of experience by compilers. Yet, rapid growth of foreign direct investment, intra-firm transactions and international production for the last two decades (already before the global economic crises in 2008 and afterwards) brought about many new challenges, especially for FDI data compilers. As such, researchers and policymakers are seeking not only more complete coverage and more accurate estimations of volume but also improved understanding of multinational operation, behaviour and strategies. The ascent of emerging economies (developing economies became majority FDI hosts in 2010) and the boom of their multinational enterprises, but also challenges due to special purpose entities[1] (SPEs) and multi-economy corporate structures, have been just a few of the problems.

This chapter gives an overview of existing sources of statistical data on FDI and foreign affiliates that could be used for analysing the phenomenon of Southern multinationals, highlight deficiencies and difficulties that may influence conclusions as well as summarize the initiatives that have been recently implemented in order to overcome the above-mentioned deficiencies.

Most widely used data sources, availability and their gaps

Strategies and decisions for foreign direct investment are generated within multinational enterprises themselves; however, we are monitoring their activities mainly by aggregate macro-level and not firm-level data. FDI data are still among the best available indicators for following the activities of multinational enterprises and globalization trends, though efforts for improving statistical indicators of multinational enterprise groups and activities of foreign affiliates and their transactions are on the rise.

The major providers of FDI information for governments, economists and other clients worldwide are the United Nations Conference on Trade and Development (UNCTAD), OECD and Eurostat. The International Monetary Fund (IMF) and the World Bank also provide a wide range of data, including information on FDI. The statistical units of these organizations offer a wide range of statistical information, which are to a large extent free of charge. Aggregate data of FDI flows and stocks are available by all sources, while the availability of breakdowns by country, by industry and by type or instrument of investment differs among providers.

These organizations all provide an online query tool in order to export the data ready for use. However, these query tools typically differ among organizations, while some interfaces are better than others. For instance, the possibility to download data in a panel format, which can be used for further analysis, is not always straightforward. Given the intricate nature of the data, they provide predefined queries in order to facilitate researchers in their data search. Most predefined queries are limited, although the OECD provides a good array of available datasets. The list of main datasets and predefined queries (as presented by OECD) is presented in Table 3.1.

Besides the differences in disclosure policy, there is a large difference in the coverage of countries. UNCTAD provides the most complete country coverage dataset, while OECD and Eurostat have a narrowed range of countries (mostly limited to their members). OECD and Eurostat datasets have consequently greater deficiencies for capturing BRICS and the impact of Southern multinationals, though they provide more detailed and combined breakdowns by industry and by country. Both

Table 3.1 List of main datasets and predefined queries

FDI Financial Flows	FDI Income	FDI Positions
FDI financial flows, main aggregates BMD4*	**FDI income by partner country BMD4**	**FDI positions, main aggregates BMD4**
Predefined queries:	**Predefined queries:**	**Predefined queries:**
FDI liabilities and inward FDI flows	Inward and outward FDI by partner country	FDI assets and outward FDI positions
FDI assets and outward FDI flows	Inward FDI by instrument and by partner country	FDI liabilities and inward FDI positions
	Outward FDI by instrument and by partner country	
FDI financial flows by partner country BMD4	**FDI income by industry BMD4**	**FDI positions by partner country BMD4**
Predefined queries:	**Predefined queries:**	**Predefined queries:**
Inward and outward FDI by partner country	Income on inward FDI (payments) and income on outward FDI (receipts) by industry	Inward and outward FDI by partner country
Inward FDI by instrument and by partner country		Inward FDI by instrument and by partner country
Outward FDI by instrument and by partner country	Income on inward FDI (payments) by instrument and by industry	Outward FDI by instrument and by partner country
	Income on outward FDI (receipts) by instrument and by industry	Inward FDI positions by immediate and by ultimate investor
FDI financial flows by industry BMD4		**FDI positions by industry BMD4**
Predefined queries:		**Predefined queries:**
Inward and outward FDI by industry		Inward and outward FDI by industry
Inward FDI by instrument and by industry		Inward FDI by instrument and by industry
Outward FDI by instrument and by industry		Outward FDI by instrument

Note * BMD4 – Benchmark Definition of Foreign Direct Investment, fourth edition.

OECD and UNCTAD also provide bilateral FDI stock datasets; however, UNCTAD has not been free of charge. OECD covers member countries for the period from 1985 (latecomers may have shorter time series), while UNCTAD's Data Extract Service covers a wider set of developed, various emerging and developing countries and covers the period from 1980 onwards. UNCTAD thus offers the most holistic insight into FDI activity of emerging and developing economies. However, UNCTAD only allows for downloads of data of unilateral inward and outward FDI flows and stocks. Although they provide predefined groupings of countries, there is a major problem with their definition of developing countries. In UNCTAD's definition, developing countries are all countries not specified in developed or transition economies. According to UNCTAD, developed countries are the member countries of the OECD (other than Chile, Mexico, the Republic of Korea and Turkey), plus the new European Union member countries which are not OECD members (Bulgaria, Croatia, Cyprus, Latvia, Lithuania, Malta and Romania), plus Andorra, Bermuda, Liechtenstein, Monaco and San Marino. Transition countries/regions are Southeast Europe, the Commonwealth of Independent States and Georgia. However, this means that Singapore and South Korea, for instance, are included among the developing countries. In contrast, the World Bank and the IMF have better definitions of developed and developing countries. UNCTAD should therefore either adopt these groupings or stick to geographic areas. Besides, the FDI data of the IMF are much more intricate and detailed, yet more difficult to use.

Furthermore, there are always differences between and among the data from National Statistical Offices and the international organizations. As such, the bilateral data between two countries will differ depending on the data from which National Statistical Office you use. These data will also typically differ from the same bilateral data provided by international organizations, despite the fact that these international organizations rely on the National Statistical Offices to provide them with the necessary raw data. These raw data are, however, sometimes adapted as a result of differences in FDI definitions, sources and collection methods.

In fact, the two major references used as a benchmark for analyzing differences in FDI definition, data sources and collection methods – the OECD Benchmark Definition of Foreign Direct Investment) and the IMF Balance of Payments Manual – were revised. The third edition of the OECD Benchmark Definition of Foreign Direct Investment was replaced by the fourth edition – BMD4 – while the fifth edition of the IMF Balance of Payments and International Investment Position Manual was replaced by the sixth edition – BPM6 – and the new standards have resulted in significant changes since 2014 (BSP Implementation of the Balance of Payments and International Investment Position). While BPM6 provides guidance on the compilation of FDI statistics for the general balance of payments framework, it refers to BMD4 for more detailed guidance on the compilation of FDI statistics by country and by industry. These detailed statistics are particularly useful for the analysis of the economic impact of FDI. Another important initiative for improved FDI statistics is the EuroGroups Register, initiated in 2008, which aims to complement aggregate data, register the multinational groups present in Europe and provide a harmonized picture on groups for statistical purposes.

Most of the countries, however, have only recently introduced the OECD's BMD4 and the IMF's BPM6. Implementations have started since September 2014 and the revised databases are still being built (the Joint IMF/OECD Survey of Implementation of Methodological Standard for Direct Investment Report to the IMF Committee on Balance of Payments Statistics). The OECD FDI Statistics database featuring the new statistics was launched in March 2015, and National Statistical Offices started to provide updated data in 2015, while the EuroGroups Register does not provide publicly available data.

Being oriented towards the impact of Southern multinationals in Europe, we have examined closer the data sources in the EU. Besides FDI statistics, Eurostat also provides Foreign Affiliates Trade Statistics (FATS). While FDI statistics give an idea of the total amount of capital invested by foreigners in the EU economy, FATS add to that more detailed information on the economic impact of those investments in terms of job creation, value creation, share of foreign-owned firms, etc.

To collect the FATS, all sources that are considered to be relevant and appropriate can be used. However, despite the fact there are different ways to collect data, it is usually the case that business registers, statistical surveys or already existing data from administrative sources are the main data sources in the FATS. Information on foreign control and the country of the Ultimate Controlling Institutional Unit, which is frequently (although less accurately) referred to as the "parent company", may be obtained by linking with other available data sources: annual reports, internet, or by surveying enterprises. Using data from administrative sources helps to reduce the response burden on businesses.

FATS encompass inward and outward data. For the purpose of evaluating the impact of Southern multinationals, the inward FATS data are appropriate, as they describe the overall activity of foreign affiliates resident in the compiling economy – for example, how many jobs, how much turnover, etc. are generated by foreign investors in a given European host economy.

Transmitting the conclusions of the study for one member state to another member state should be done with caution, as the exposure to Southern multinationals differs. Variation in the share of foreign-controlled enterprises across European Union member states is high (Figure 3.1), in spite of the single European market. In some selected central European economies, such as Estonia, Romania and Slovakia, the foreign-controlled companies play a substantial role in the economic performance of their economies. Some member states have a comparatively large proportion of companies that are foreign-controlled by a non-EU country (Luxembourg, the United Kingdom and Slovenia over 50 percent, while Netherlands, Germany and Cyprus over 40 percent).

The impact on the labour market differs from country to country, however. The general trend is that in Europe, the majority of persons are employed by EU-controlled companies and not by those controlled from outside the EU.[2] Taking into account only affiliates controlled from outside the EU, the proportion of people employed by foreign affiliates ranged from 17 percent for Luxembourg and 11 percent for the United Kingdom to around 1.5 percent for both Croatia and Cyprus.[3]

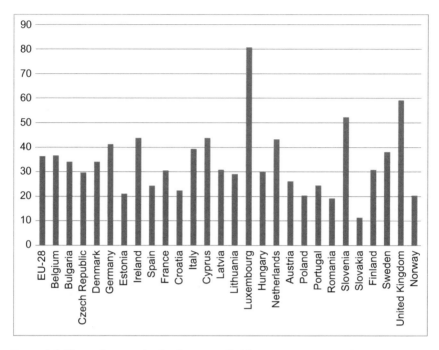

Figure 3.1 Share of companies foreign-controlled by a non-EU country, in %
Source: Eurostat FATS

As indicated, FATS rely on statistical registers. Statistical Business Registers fulfil a crucial function, as they provide a basis for identifying the relevant enterprises to be surveyed. This is because they may offer important information about control and ownership of foreign affiliates listed in these registers. Business registers themselves are generally fed from a number of different sources, such as tax registers, social security sources or other public sector data. Another advantage is that there is a considerable degree of harmonization of Statistical Business Registers among the European member states.

Problems with regard to this are relatively incomplete coverage or modest time series for more recent EU member states, i.e. countries that joined European Union since 2004. Their national statistical sources most commonly have normally been complete and included all information on FDI, yet the organization and the structure of data have not been completely harmonized with EU standards and have sometimes dropped out of survey.

Sometimes harmonization of statistical standards even reduced reporting requirements. In Slovenia, for example, FDI statistics dropped the reporting for entities with fewer than ten employees, which represents a significant share (in terms of number of enterprises) among direct investors abroad (see, for example, Jaklič and Svetličič 2003: 46). SME coverage in FDI statistics and FATS has thus several deficiencies. A good complementary source to Eurostat for younger member states is the Vienna Institute for International Economic Studies, the WIIW FDI Report, based upon the WIIW FDI database covering twenty-three countries of central, eastern and southeastern Europe. It analyzes the major features of FDI developments in and out of the countries of the region and is published annually at the beginning of June.

The next important support to FATS comes from the EuroGroups Register (EGR). The EuroGroups Register is a network of business registers coordinated by Eurostat. It is expected to become a single platform supporting the production of statistics on globalization, as it provides an EU-wide register on multinational groups and their affiliates.

EGR has produced four yearly cycles up to 2013. The reference years of the EGR cycles are 2008, 2009, 2010 and 2011. The latest EGR cycle with 2011 data was completed in March 2013. The EGR 2011 data include information on the characteristics and internal relationships of more than 15,000 multinational enterprise groups and their 700,000 constituent legal units. The coverage of enterprise groups outside the EU and EFTA countries included in the EGR has been improving, especially in 2011. Also the number of legal units in and outside the EU and EFTA countries monitored in the EGR has been rising over the years, and coverage of smaller groups significantly improved in 2011.

Part of the EGR program for large and complex MNEs is the profiling (ESSnet on profiling large and complex MNEs 2010). Profiling[4] as a method was developed to analyze the legal, operational and accounting structure of an enterprise group at national and world levels in order to establish the statistical units within that group and their links, and the most efficient structures for the collection of statistical data. Profiling aims to improve the consistency and the relevance of business statistics. Profiling a group of firms involves defining the most appropriate entity for the statistical observation of the group and its constituent enterprise units. The main stakeholders for profiling are the statisticians in the Structural Business Statistics, FATS, National Accounts and Balance of Payments, since the definition and use of profiled units may have an impact on the statistics they produce.

The reason for implementing profiling is the increasing "globalization", in which the operational structures of businesses deviate from the administrative legal structures more and more frequently and create a deepening gap between managerial organizations and data reporting systems. In statistics this amplifies several problems; as the intra-group flows become higher and higher, the transfer flows and prices need to be recognized as such or suppressed; imports and exports change their nature, often becoming intra-group and incorporating less traded goods; the attribution of value added (VA) among countries can become internal to enterprise groups; R&D and ancillary activities are often produced in one country for the whole group, etc. In the existing statistical monitoring of MNEs, their national parts are differently approached by the relevant national statistical institutes for the collection of similar data. If quality of the national economic statistics is affected, this also has a negative impact on the quality of European statistics compiled from these national statistics. Without efforts such as EGR and profiling, national as well as European statistics are rapidly losing their accuracy and validity (correctness).

The "profiling" method is welcomed as extremely useful. However, it needs the development of a common conceptual framework, methodology, rules and standards to carry out profiling. It also needs the development of process descriptions, tools, operational guidelines and quality assurance of profiling, as well as the development of models for the organization and financing of profiling in statistical institutes. The content, aim and wide range of partners being involved have made it a very demanding project, and the implementation (of the operational methods of the profiling model, the guidelines and testing and training of national statistical institutes) is not proceeding according to the initial plans.

The above-mentioned sources thus still do not provide micro-level statistics necessary for up-to-date analytics. Therefore, commercial/private statistical institutes and providers relying on surveys, such as *Amadeus* from Bureau Van Dijk, Reuters or *Financial Times*, which includes information and data related to around 20 million European companies, are highly used. The quality of the data is variable and requires a systematic screening when one wants to draw robust conclusions.[5] Besides the rapidly improving coverage in the number of countries and population of enterprises within the countries, the advantage of these surveys lies in the fact that they provide additional information on behaviour and strategies of multinational enterprises.

Explaining the recent changes and new features[6]

BPM6 and BMD4 make recommendations for compiling FDI statistics that result in more meaningful measures of FDI. These include:

- Presenting aggregate FDI statistics in a way comparable to other macroeconomic statistics, such as Balance of Payments statistics
- Separately identifying capital being channelled through SPEs
- Presenting statistics according to the country of the ultimate investor as well as the immediate investor

Under BPM6, direct investments are classified further according to the relationship between the investor and the recipient entity, as follows:

a) Investment by a direct investor in its direct investment enterprise (DIE) – where an entity or group of related firms is able to exercise control or a significant degree of influence over a direct investment enterprise
b) Reverse investment – where a DIE lends funds to or acquires equity in its direct investor, provided it does not own equity of 10 percent or more of the voting power in that direct investor
c) Investment between fellow enterprises – where enterprises are under the control or influence of the same immediate or indirect investor, but the fellow enterprises do not control or influence each other

Aggregate statistics are now reported on what is called the asset/liability basis instead of what is called the directional basis. Asset/liability-based direct investment statistics are organized according to whether the investment relates to an asset or a liability for the reporting country. On a directional basis, the direct investment flows and positions are organized according to the direction of the investment for the reporting economy – either inward or outward. The two presentations differ in their treatment of reverse investment (e.g. when an affiliate provides a loan to its parent).

With regard to indirect or transit investment flows the BMD4 recommends that countries compile FDI statistics in two ways, both including and excluding resident SPEs. This recommendation provides a more meaningful measure of the FDI of an economy by removing an FDI that involves funds passing through an SPE on their way to another destination (outward FDI) and those coming to the country through another economy's SPE (inward FDI). So far, FDI data were overestimated due to the risk of double counting, in some cases even as high as for 50 percent (Gestrin 2014).[7] *FDI in Figures*, issued by OECD in December 2014 (p. 1), reports that "new detail available on investment that is channelled through entities with little presence in the host economy reveals that the role of such entities in investment varies widely across countries, accounting for as much as 92 percent of inward investment for some countries to as little as 1 percent for other countries." Starting with 2013, the data on FDI exclude data on transactions by SPEs. By compiling FDI statistics that exclude resident SPEs, FDI statistics are not overstated by including funds that are simply being channelled through the SPEs, are easier to interpret for policymaking and other purposes and provide a better measure of FDI that is likely to have an economic impact in the host economy.

These changes currently make it difficult to interpret the statistics due to breaks in series and due to different measures being used by different countries during the transition period.

The above-mentioned aspects should also be kept in mind in interpreting FDI statistics when using different sources. While OECD has adopted new standards in their time series since 2013, UNCTAD will continue to report FDI data on the basis of the directional principle (World Investment Report 2015: 3). Although presentation on an asset/liability basis is appropriate for macroeconomic analysis (i.e. the impact on the balance of payments), the directional basis is more useful in formulating investment policies (which is one of UNCTAD's priorities) because they capture the source or destination countries of direct investment and access to specific markets by direct investors. To avoid double counting, UNCTAD removes SPE flows from its statistics where possible. For similar reasons, FDI flows through offshore financial centres are excluded from analyses where possible.

Helpful insights came from the efforts to avoid double counting in international trade that took place within the initiatives for mapping the global value chains (GVCs). The aim of these initiatives (started parallel and independently by UNCTAD/Eora, OECD/World Trade Organization, EU–The World Input-Output Database; IDE-JETRO and Purdue University) was to construct input-output tables illustrating how VA moves between countries within GVCs before final consumption of end-products.[8] The analysis of GVCs takes into account both foreign VA in exports (the upstream perspective) and the exported value added incorporated in third-country exports (the downstream perspective).

The OECD has recently also increased focus on FDI income allocation, and not only on the questions where the value is created: the question of "who gets what out of FDI" is becoming a crucial issue in an era of crises. Increasing importance in statistical monitoring has also been given to contractual arrangements (both by UNCTAD and OECD), as it has been observed that the contractual arrangement among enterprises can provide more control than very general management control provided by FDI (but are out of FDI definitions).

Conclusions and implications

Data users argue that intensified efforts for monitoring and compiling of FDI data in general and data on Southern multinationals in particular are necessary. The question of data availability and quality is of central importance for analysts and policymakers in the face of the rising activities of emerging multinationals from emerging economies and their international investments across many regions and sectors. Europe faced increased FDI inflow from Southern multinationals, especially after the global economic crises, and several initiatives for improved data compilation have been launched since then. Most compilers tried to improve data gathering and coverage, enhanced cross-country and cross-institutional cooperation and validation and implemented new methodologies and approaches.

Still, there has been a rising gap between business intelligence in terms of volume, quality of data and speed of updating, which is used in corporate strategies, and the quality of data supporting economic policies either at country level or at the EU level. Country-level statistics within National Statistical Offices and statistics by international organizations lag behind business intelligence. Efforts and revisions that have been taking place in the quantity and quality of FDI data, the revised standards for compiling FDI data on a macro level and several private initiatives and rising volume of surveys are therefore a welcome response.

According to the recent literature on emerging markets' outward FDI (Sauvant 2008; Ramamurti and Singh 2009; Brennan 2010a; De Beule and Duanmu 2012; De Beule and Van Den Bulcke 2012), Southern multinationals are quite heterogeneous, both by home country location advantages and by capacity to exploit host country advantages. Analysis based on macro-level aggregate data may often not reveal this heterogeneity and development. The recent tendency which is gaining some attention, i.e. signs of deglobalization (many countries have negative FDI inflows, volumes are decreasing) may in fact be a result of incomplete understanding of MNEs' behaviour and new ways of internationalization (rising importance of contractual arrangements). It is still difficult to make precise comparisons across countries due to the different measures of FDI being used by different countries. Surveys and profiling are essential complementary information needed to understand behaviour, growth and development of Southern multinational enterprises. Also multilateral cooperation and cross-country validation are needed. The results of initiatives such as the EuroGroups Register are therefore warmly welcomed and awaited.

Changes that have been introduced recently raised standards and improved data availability; however, challenges for further efforts in data compilation and data usage remain:

- Data providers do not adapt new standards set by BMD4 and BPM6 consistently and hence the datasets between UNCTAD and OECD have differed substantially from 2013 on. Nation states and their statistical offices have started the adoption in 2014 and novelties have been included and available in datasets since 2013. The same approach is taken by OECD and Eurostat, while UNCTAD continues to report FDI data on the basis of the directional principle and present FDI flows that exclude SPE flows and FDI flows through offshore financial centres from its statistics where possible.
- As a result of new standards, there are breaks in the time series for some countries. As countries are implementing the latest standards at different times, there is currently a mix of measures of FDI being used, which complicates the analysis of trends. A break-in-series between 2012 and 2013 thus requires that care be taken in interpreting the time series and making comparisons between 2013 and earlier years.
- Faster revision of data (especially firm-level and survey based data, such as FATS) and agile adoption of time series and clear methodological notes along all FDI sources should complement the change in data compilation and reduce difficulties due to breaks in time series.
- Further efforts are needed to complete the coverage, as the data are still not available for all countries in all details and many countries provide only aggregate and no firm-level data.
- Even for those providing firm-level datasets, the major weaknesses are seen in poor statistical coverage of SMEs. Though they may not be important in terms of volume, they are not negligible in terms of number and contractual cooperation and they can develop rapid internationalization patterns.
- Despite an improvement in tools, even expert users still face difficulties, and further potential for making economic data more user friendly remains through the introduction of user-friendly tools.
- Improved access to data, in particular micro-level data, and greater use of data among scholars and analysts add reliability to data and improvement due to regular feedback and application of new methodology or concepts.

Notes

1 SPEs are entities with little or no physical presence or employment in the host country but that provide important services to the MNE in the form of financing or of holding assets and liabilities. MNEs often channel investments through SPEs in one country before they reach their final destination in another country.
2 The only exception is the United Kingdom, where more than 2 million people work for affiliates owned by a non-EU country, while 1.2 million people work for the

EU-controlled foreign affiliates. Luxembourg has the highest proportion of people employed by foreign affiliates, accounting for 41 percent of the total employment in the country, closely followed by Estonia with 37 percent. At the other end of the scale, the ratio for Italy, Cyprus and Portugal was below 10 percent.

3 When looking at the labour market outside of the compiling economies, British affiliates were by far the biggest employer outside Europe, followed by France and Germany.

4 Profiling have been in use operationally in some nation states (for example, in the Netherlands and the United States for twenty years.

5 For example, some data or information provided by commercial suppliers (such as the value of the deal in the case of mergers and acquisitions, or the creation of jobs in green-field) could be either overevaluated or underevaluated; in some cases, data are missing. Researchers experienced mistakes in magnitude or currency transformation.

6 "New features are explained in a series of three OECD papers: "Analysing Asset/ Liability and Directional Presentation", "Examining How MNEs Channel Investments" and "Identifying the Ultimate Investing Country"."

7 According to the interview with Michael Gestrin from OECD in May 2014.

8 It starts from the point that conventional trade statistics may give a misleading perspective of the importance of trade to economic growth and income. Policymakers are increasingly aware of the necessity of complementing existing statistics with new indicators better tuned to the reality of global manufacturing, where products are 'Made in the World'. Therefore, we need to decompose gross trade flows into domestic value-added components and to imported components. In order to tackle the whole story in a context of highly fragmented production networks where circular trade takes place, one has to use an international input-output table.

References

Balance of Payments and International Investment Position Manual. Sixth Edition (BPM6). (2009). Washington D.C.: International Monetary Fund www.imf.org/external/pubs/ft/bop/2007/bopman6.htm

Bevan, A. A., and Estrin, S. (2004) 'The determinants of foreign direct investment into European transition economies', *Journal of Comparative Economics*, 32, 4: 775–787.

Brennan, L. (2010a) *The Emergence of Southern Multinationals: Their Impact on Europe*, New York: Palgrave Macmillan.

Brennan, L. (2010b) 'Southern Multinationals and Their Impact on Europe: What Have We Learnt?', in Brennan, L. (Ed.) *The Emergence of Southern Multinationals: Their Impact on Europe*, New York: Palgrave Macmillan, pp. 367–377.

De Beule, F., and Duanmu, J. (2012) 'Locational determinants of internationalization: A firm-level analysis of Chinese and Indian acquisitions', *European Management Journal*, 30, 3: 264–277.

De Beule, F., and Van Den Bulcke, D. (2012) 'Locational determinants of outward foreign direct investment: An analysis of Chinese and Indian greenfield investments', *Transnational Corporations*, 21, 1: 1–34.

'ESSnet on Profiling Large and Complex MNEs: 1st SGA'. Executive Summary. 22/12/2010. http://egr.istat.it/?q=node/244

EuroGroups Register (EGR). http://egr.istat.it/ Accessed March 15, 2015.

Eurostat. FATS. http://ec.europa.eu/eurostat/statistics-explained/index.php/Foreign_affiliates_statistics_-_FATS

Eurostat. http://ec.europa.eu/eurostat/

'FDI in Figures' December 2014. OECD, Paris. www.oecd.org/daf/inv/FDI-in-Figures-Dec-2014.pdf

Foreign_affiliates_statistics_-_FATS. http://ec.europa.eu/eurostat/statistics-explained/index.php/Foreign_affiliates_statistics_-_FATS

Gestrin, M. (2014) 'The great FDI crash of 2015', *EIBAzine: International Business Perspectives*, 14: 11–14.

Jaklič, A., and Svetličič, M. (2003) *Enhanced Transition through Outward Internationalization. Outward FDI from Slovenian Firms*, Burlington, VT: Ashgate.

The Joint IMF/OECD Survey of Implementation of Methodological Standard for Direct Investment Report to the IMF Committee on Balance of Payments Statistics. (1998). Prepared by the Statistics Department International Monetary Fund. Washington: International Monetary Fund.

Manual, Sixth Edition (BPM6) Compilation Framework. www.bsp.gov.ph/downloads/Publications/FAQs/bpm6.pdf

OECD (2014). Implementing the Latest International Standards for Compiling Foreign Direct Investment Statistics' Asset/Liability versus Directional Presentation. Paris: OECD. www.oecd.org/daf/inv/investment-policy/oecdimplementsnewinternationalstandardsforcompilingfdistatistics.htm

Ramamurti, R., and Singh, J. V. (Eds.) (2009) *Emerging Multinationals in Emerging Markets*, Cambridge, UK: Cambridge University Press.

Sauvant, K. (2008) *The Rise of Transnational Corporations from Emerging Markets*, Cheltenham, UK: Edward Elgar.

WIIW FDI Report 2015. (2015) Recovery in the NMS, Decline in the CIS. The Vienna Institute for International Economic Studies, Vienna.

The World Input-Output Database (WIOD). www.wiod.org/new_site/home.htm

World Investment Report 2015. (2015) Reforming International Investment Governance. UNCTAD, Geneva.

Part III

Drivers, motivations and strategies of emerging country multinationals

4 Drivers and motivations of emerging country multinationals entry into the EU

Jagjit Singh Srai

Introduction

This chapter explores the drivers and motivations of EMNEs that have sought to establish a key element of their value chain within the European market, and the potential policy implications thereof.

Firstly we examine EMNEs' integration into global value chains through EU acquisitions and alliances and the need to differentiate between those long-term investments that enrich the EU's supply base and the more predatory moves that seek to transfer out activities.

Second, we consider different patterns in innovation and technology developments of EMNEs, with more incremental product innovations, an appetite to invest in production processes, and business models that exploit home-country low cost labour advantages. Policymakers should recognise that the competitive innovation environment will challenge established firms whilst enriching competition.

Third, EMNEs' response to current reshoring activities of developed country MNCs may provide entry points for EMNEs into Europe. However, this may result in the decline of EMNEs in their home countries as MNCs reshore in favour of EU-located suppliers. Fieldwork studies suggest that policies that support reshoring will have the greatest impact where proximity to markets and technology encourage localisation strategies.

The chapter closes by the influence of 'product' and 'sectoral' considerations, which suggest EMNEs competitive advantages are most favourable where their home-country advantages of low cost labour and scale enable economic international supply. However, policymakers should consider where national strategic assets, such as infrastructure, defence, or supply security considerations require European safeguards. EMNEs that are considered national flagships by their home country, particularly state owned enterprises may, by their very scale and nature, possess competitive capabilities that will support global reach. However, their favourable home market conditions may provide these EMNEs with advantages that might fall outside traditional EU competition norms.

Product and sectoral changes are envisaged to impact global industry structures, most notably the geographic dispersion of manufacturing value chain activities. For example, the rapid growth in EMNE contract manufacturing activity in the supply of intermediate goods, in electronics, for example, has driven high levels of interdependency within global supply chains. Although this has driven production costs down, it has also resulted in new supply risks and vulnerabilities in global supply chains. Policymakers should consider carefully the supply security issues in these more globalised supply chains and consider whether economic and societal impacts of supply disruption require policy interventions, such as dual or local sourcing.

The themes set out in this introduction are now considered in more detail in the following sections.

EMNEs' integration into global value chains through EU acquisitions and alliances

In the examination of EMNE internationalisation patterns, and within the EU in particular, the established concept of the manufacturing value chain provides a basis for analysing the geographical distribution of activities, and which of these activities – from R&D/concept generation to final product/service delivery – provide entry points for EMNEs.

Figure 4.1 represents the manufacturing value chain in terms of the key activities undertaken from concept generation, product supply, and after-sales services. The diagram is of course somewhat simplified in nature, as within each stage of the value chain, a complex network of activities and actors exists, representing the multiple-tier structure of suppliers and support organisations that feed each of these critical value chain activities.

The literature on the internationalisation of value chains has predominantly reflected studies of MNE firms from developed economies that explore globalisation patterns in established industries. However, these studies have evolved in more recent times where academics consider rapidly changing markets, changes in industry structure resulting from the production of intermediate goods, the impact of disruptive technologies and, particularly relevant to this chapter, explicitly the EMNE context (Brennan 2011; Williamson and Fleury 2013; Economist Intelligence Unit 2015).

Early literature on the internationalisation of MNEs, while not explicitly addressing value chain perspectives, inevitably suggest that particular motives and investment patterns will result in changes to the activity scope of firms across the value chain. This, coupled with changes to the geographical dispersion of these broader set of activities and the changing role of overseas subsidiaries, introduces a spatial element, or 'value chain footprint' to these studies. Consequently, analysis

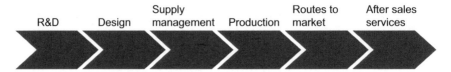

Figure 4.1 The manufacturing value chain (adapted from Srai 2007, p. 281)

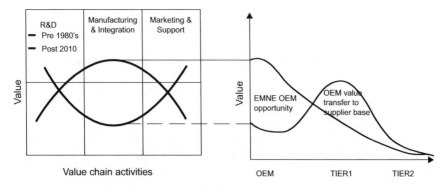

Figure 4.2 Smile curve representation and the transfer of value into the supply chain

of changing configuration patterns across the value chain can inform studies on the international evolution of MNEs. However, before proceeding further with this approach, it is necessary to draw on definitions of value chain configuration and how the existing literature contributes to this unit of analysis.

For manufacturing firms, studies typically consider 'upstream' and 'downstream' of the production task, the value-add at each stage of the chain (often depicted by the smile curve), the degree of coupling or nature of the linkages between stages, the importance of location/co-location, and degrees of vertical integration. More recent studies that consider interfirm perspectives explore how disaggregation or fragmentation of the value chain can impact value creation/appropriation, governance and coordination, and the relationship between actors.

Figure 4.2 sets out at a conceptual level how OEMs through the process of increased offshoring and outsourcing of manufacturing activities have opened up opportunities for EMNE firms, as competing OEMs or component suppliers, to enter the manufacturing activities of the value chain. The traditional 'smile curve' representation suggests the progressive erosion of the value of production within the manufacturing value chain. Although this depiction is controversial, at a firm level this may indeed reflect reality, as evidenced by increases in the percentage of input materials as a percentage of total product cost. The trend also represents the transfer of manufacturing-production value to the supply side of the supply chain. In the context of this chapter, this transfer (rather than the erosion) of production value represents potential entry points for EMNE firms, either as competing OEMs or as more significant component suppliers.

Industries have witnessed changing industry structures (Dicken 2007) with the fragmentation of their value chains as firms focus on internal advantages and exploit external capabilities. Drivers of this fragmentation can, however, be sector specific, as these include firm specialisation, e.g. in the computer industry (Jacobides 2005), location efficiency seeking in commodity markets, innovation control strategies in knowledge intensive industries (Mudambi 2008), changes facilitated by modularity in design (electronics), and the development of common standards and information exchange protocols (IT, telecoms). Mudambi (2008) uses the smile curve depiction of the value chain to explain the investment choices made by firms and their role in value addition.

The concept of configuration, first developed in the strategic management litera-ture, introduced concepts of structure and coherence and how particular archetype forms support particular firm-level capabilities (Mintzberg 1983; Miller 1986).The strategic and operational analysis of network configuration within the operations management community builds on these concepts, with intra-firm and interfirm case study research undertaken within international production (Shi and Gregory 1998), supply (Srai and Gregory 2008), and service networks (Srai 2011). Here, value chain configuration analysis involves structured methodologies to determine what activities firms undertake in-house, those that are best undertaken by third parties, where might these activities be ideally located, governance and coordina-tion mechanisms, partnering arrangements, and product architectures.

Case study data on value chain configuration patterns (Srai and Fleet 2010; Srai 2013; Williamson et al. 2013; Brennan et al. 2015) suggest that EMNEs are acquir-ing EU firms to enhance their R&D capability, production technologies, and capac-ity in Europe to more effectively serve regional volume. Their assessment of value contrasts the traditional value chain model with manufacturing-based investments seen as providing additional product functionality and quality, including access to EU customers, often through brand acquisition. However, tactical investments can be short term, with manufacturing ultimately moving out of the EU. These observations suggest that the traditional smile curve is not necessarily the norm for EMNEs as they invest in production assets for both quality and capacity.

From a policy standpoint, policymakers should differentiate between those long-term investments that enrich the EU's supply base and predatory moves that simply seek to transfer out activities where EU manufacturing is hollowed out to EMNE offshore locations. An example of a 'predatory' acquisition is a major EMNE global industrial motor manufacturer which had as one of its KPIs for a European acquisition the number of days to transfer production to its home country.

Changing patterns in innovation and technology developments

A key consideration when considering EMNE internationalisation patterns is the nature of their innovation and technology investments. Case studies suggest that EMNEs have traditionally focused on more incremental product innovations and that EU partnerships within R&D remain elusive. However, they do show an appetite to invest in production processes, for improved quality and brand build-ing (or co-branding), thereby expanding local production capacity for the EU market. However, EMNEs tend to do so where they can leverage business mod-els that continue to exploit home-country low cost labour through intermediate component supply. In this case, this may still result in a net offshoring of produc-tion away from the EU, despite these investments in final assembly within the EU, as the principal components/intermediates are sourced from EMNE home markets.

Within the automotive sector, the acquisition of the UK firm Jaguar Land Rover (JLR) by Indian conglomerate Tata is perhaps the best example of EMNE activity where the motivation is to move into a more innovation-intense sector of the automotive market, with the JLR acquisition providing advanced technology, innovation, and production capability. Perhaps, equally revealing is that despite the unexpected global recession after the financial crises, Tata continued investing in innovation and new product development. The more recent investment in a state-of-the-art engine plant facility in Wolverhampton demonstrates the long-term nature of UK/EU investments, including the willingness to invest in production facilities.

Policymakers should recognise the investment opportunities from EMNEs with a long-term strategic agenda and the competitive innovation environment they can contribute to. The UK automotive industry exemplifies how investment from both developing and emerging countries in R&D and production capabilities has resulted in a highly competitive industry with record car production volumes in recent years (Society of Motor Manufacturers). Equally interesting perhaps is how Tata JLR's internationalisation strategy will develop as its markets evolve beyond its traditional EU and North American consumer base to those rapidly growing markets in Southeast Asia and Latin America. Interestingly, the willingness to invest under EMNE leadership appears greater than under previous ownership, with different perspectives on return-on-investment and risk.

In other sectors, EMNE investments will challenge established national firms while enriching competition.

In pharmaceuticals, investment in both contract manufacturing and technology providers has both provided enhanced EU capability and increased competition for EU manufacturers. Other technology developments in the sector, such as the move to cell-based therapies or more continuous processing (Srai et al. 2015), suggest that future production models will involve advanced process and patient analytics that target more segmented patient populations. These technology disruptions will demand more technology-intense, tightly coupled value chains. From a manufacturing perspective, this may require potentially more distributed lower-scale production operations, perhaps making EMNE entry into developed markets more challenging.

Rezk et al. (2015) explore how product characteristics and disruptive technology change will influence value chain configurations across multiple sectors, drawing on examples from ICT, additive manufacturing, and continuous processing. They conclude that internationalisation strategy is largely driven by product attributes and knowledge characteristics, both factors constraining the geographic dispersion options available to firms.

EMNEs' response to current reshoring activities of developed-country MNCs

Outsourcing or offshoring agendas flow from the implementation of 'network design' approaches discussed earlier in the chapter. Historical analysis of the value chain configurations of firm networks can thus shed useful insights into firm strategies and motives, execution capabilities, and their ability to exploit and explore emerging opportunities.

Research on EMNEs' internationalisation patterns (e.g. in Brennan et al. 2010) and more specifically from the BRIC economies (e.g. in Williamson et al. 2013) suggest that EU reshoring trends in manufacturing production and services will provide entry points for EMNEs in Europe. However, these reshoring trends may result in the decline of EMNEs in their home countries as developed country MNCs reshore in favour of established EU located suppliers, or the motivation is driven by the need to re-internalise production.

Recent studies on reshoring trends in the EU, and in the UK and France in particular (Srai and Ane 2015, see Figure 4.3 below), appear to indicate that a complex set of motivations are behind EU-based firms' reshoring agendas.

These include 'asset rationalisation' strategies as part of reconfiguration plans where volume growth has been challenging post financial crises and firms are choosing to consolidate to their home base location. In some cases, a change of technology has demanded an investment decision in newer technologies where technical complexity requires co-location with technology centres, or reduced lead-time requirements that production be closer to market. Another main driver has been the need to be more responsive to volume uncertainties where proximity to market is the key criterion in production location decisions.

These studies suggest that policies that support reshoring of activity will have greatest impact where proximity to market and new technology investments encourage localisation strategies and that institutional support may extend to EMNEs willing to make these longer-term investments within the EU.

Product and sectoral considerations

Value chain configurational analysis suggests that there are likely to be significant variations to EMNE internationalisation patterns, depending on product characteristics and industry structure and dynamics. In terms of product characteristics, drivers of internationalisation are both physical qualities (e.g. value density [Srai 2013]) and knowledge attributes (e.g. tacit production skills [Rezk et al. 2015]) that enable or constrain geographical distribution. In terms of industry structure, the complexity and length of supply network tier structures, and in some sectors the development of an advanced intermediate goods supply, also provide new configuration options for EMNEs. Indeed, EMNEs competitive advantages also vary significantly sector-by-sector and have traditionally been most favourable where low cost labour and scale enable economic supply.

In this short chapter, it is not possible to develop a sector-by-sector specific treatment of the implications of changing industry contexts – such as emerging markets or new technologies – on EMNE internationalisation patterns. However, consideration of some representative sector types can provide some insights into possible developments. Process industries such as food processing and pharmaceuticals are very different from the discrete assembly operations seen typically in the automotive and aerospace sectors.

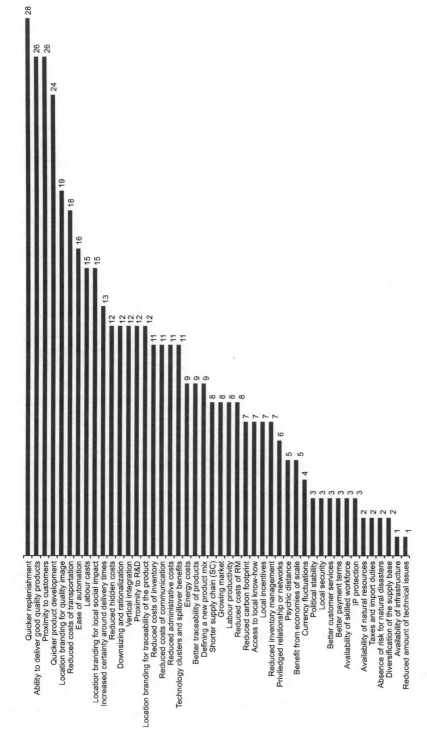

Figure 4.3 Identified reshoring drivers in the UK and France (adapted from Srai and Ane 2015)

In the food sector, industry mapping studies have compared developed world contexts with those from the developing world (e.g. Mukesh et al. 2013), where there are contrasting manufacturing and supply network structures and efficiency/ waste challenges upstream and downstream in the supply chain. Comparing food supply chains across two developed and developing market countries, namely India and the UK, we can observe common agendas as well as highly divergent operational practices and network configurations.

Within the food and beverage sector, common issues include the development of global markets that are largely immune to the costs of local supply, greater concerns on food security at national and global levels that may lead to more localised approaches to food supply, and greater awareness of the use of natural resources. Globalisation has introduced the supply of food products from EMNE producers to developed world markets, often involving scale operations that can have significant local impact. Examples include major beverage operations that have exacerbated water availability in developing world regions and have driven relocation strategies away from water-stressed environments.

However, these comparative studies (e.g. Lorentz et al. 2011; Mukesh et al. 2013) identify significant structural differences in the food supply networks of these EMNE firms when compared with their European counterparts. From a European perspective, EMNEs face a consolidated and highly cost sensitive retail sector compared with a highly fragmented and distributed food network in their home countries, a more efficient transport network enabling more remote supply, but greater demands of food traceability and quality.

Food importation levels in the UK are significant, in excess of 40 percent, suggesting that remote supply is now well established, but future concerns on food security, by the importing or exporting nations, may provide new on-shore opportunities.

Within MNE pharmaceuticals, traditionally multi-tier batch manufacturing operations have enabled development of large-scale centralised operations, which in the case of off-patent generic drug supply, also involve EMNE contract manufacturing organisations. However, new therapy and continuous processing developments (Srai et al. 2015) that target more niche patient populations will involve smaller-scale manufacturing with high levels of process analytics. Advances in smart/intelligent packaging and patient analytics may also enable far more integrated advanced digital supply chains that are more just-in-time than the current slow high-inventory models of today. In the UK, major research programmes involving pre-competitive industry-academic collaborations have been established to develop next-generation technologies, with government strategies to retain leadership in this area.

Within the automotive and aerospace industries, which have more discrete component and final assembly activities, there are many opportunities to enter these supply and value chains through individual component supply, production of modular intermediates, and final assembly operations, as already exemplified by the Tata JLR example discussed earlier.

Financial and political drivers

Where EMNE entry strategies involve state-owned enterprises (SOEs), policy-makers should consider where national strategic assets, such as infrastructure, defence, or supply security considerations, require European safeguards.

EMNEs that are considered national flagships by their home country, particularly SOEs from the major BRICs economies, may by their very scale and nature possess competitive capabilities that will also support global reach. However, their favourable home market conditions may provide these EMNEs with advantages that might fall outside traditional EU competition norms.

For the purposes of exemplification, we consider the development of SOEs within China, many of which have developed their international footprint including presence in developed markets.

One measure of the rapid development of Chinese SOEs can be seen by their increased number in the Fortune 500 list, where some 98 firms have a China (including Hong Kong) base in the 2015 summary (http://fortune.com/global500/), with the largest being SOEs predominantly in the infrastructural sectors of energy, banking, construction, and telecommunications. Whereas many of the Chinese SOEs are easily defined, with more than 120 organisations reporting to the central State-owned Assets and Supervision Administration Commission (SASAC), they represent only half of the SOE assets in China. These assets may be part of a complex set of subsidiaries where the state, provincial, or municipal governments have a significant stake. More household names such as computer manufacturer Lenovo and the appliance giant Haier are less clear-cut cases, in which the state is the dominant shareholder. A majority of the equity in the automaker Chery belongs to the municipal government of Wuhu.

State-owned companies of all kinds have gradually been losing some of the advantages once conferred by their relationship with the state. Since the 1980s, the Chinese government and the ruling party have followed a policy of *zhengqi fenkai*, which formally separates government functions from business operations. The policy has been applied gradually, first to the consumer goods industry, then to high-tech and heavy manufacturing, and, more recently, to banking, as officials have attempted to strengthen domestic businesses and the economy to prepare them for unfettered global competition. Nevertheless, sensitivities remain, in the US in particular, when awarding contracts to Chinese firms, as exemplified by recent controversies in the telecom sector, and the firm Huawei. Interestingly, a more open approach has been adopted by the UK with respect to Huawei, resulting in significant inward investment by the EMNE, suggesting that different national financial and political priorities can influence these relationships.

EMNEs' impact on changing industry structures

The massive growth in EMNE contract manufacturing activity in the supply of intermediate goods, in electronics, for example, has driven high levels of inter-dependency within global supply chains. Although this has driven production costs down, it has also resulted in new supply risks and vulnerabilities in global supply chains.

Sturgeon (2001) set out how the development of intermediate goods produced by global scale contract manufacturers has impacted the structure of global industries, in a range of industries, but most evidently in electronics and automotive parts. These modular product sectors are most amenable to the outsourcing of components to low cost manufacturing locations but may also encourage these contract manufacturers to enter developed world markets has they hone their skills in the home countries and seek increased share of global markets. As discussed earlier in the chapter, shorter product life cycles, and the need for just-in-time capability to respond to changes in volume and mix, and supply security are driving some OEMs to increasingly require local supply sources.

Policymakers should consider carefully the supply security issues in these more globalised supply chains and consider whether economic and societal impacts of supply disruption require policy interventions, such as dual or local sourcing.

Conclusion

In this chapter we have explored the drivers and motivations of EMNEs that have sought to establish a key element of their value chain within the European market. Specifically, we have examined emerging patterns of EMNE internationalisation and potential policy implications thereof. In conclusion, we observe that EMNEs strategies involve:

- Internationalisation activities that integrate into global value chains through EU acquisitions and alliances; policymakers should differentiate between those long-term investments that enrich the EU's supply base and those predatory moves that primarily seek to transfer out activities.
- Changing patterns in innovation and technology developments that are typified by more incremental product innovations, and an appetite to invest in production processes, and business models that exploit home-country low cost labour. Policymakers should recognise that the competitive innovation environment will challenge established firms while enriching competition.
- Responses to current reshoring activities of developed country MNCs, in manufacturing production and services will provide entry points into Europe. However, this may result in the decline of EMNEs in their home countries as MNCs reshore in favour of EU located suppliers. Policies that support reshoring will have greatest impact where proximity to markets and technology encourage localisation strategies.
- Are differentiated by product and sectoral considerations where their competitive advantages vary significantly sector by sector and are most favourable where low cost labour and scale enable economic supply. Policymakers should consider where national strategic assets, such as infrastructure, defence, or supply security considerations require European safeguards.

- Many firms that are considered national flagships by their EM home country, particularly SOEs which by their very scale and nature possess competitive capabilities that will support global reach. However, their favourable home market conditions may provide these EMEs with advantages that might fall outside traditional EU competition norms.
- Impact global industry structures, reflected by the massive growth in their contract manufacturing activity in the supply of intermediate goods, driving high-levels of interdependency within global supply chains. Although this has driven production costs down, it has also resulted in new supply risks and vulnerabilities in global supply chains. Policymakers should consider carefully the supply security issues in these more globalised supply chains and consider whether economic and societal impacts of supply disruption require policy interventions, such as dual or local sourcing.

References

Brennan, L. (Ed.) (2011) 'The Emergence of Southern Multinationals and their Impact on Europe'. New York: Palgrave.

Brennan, L., Ferdows, K., Godsell, J., Golini, R., Keegan, R., Kinkel, S., Srai, J. S., and Taylor, M. (2015) 'Manufacturing in the world: Where next?', *International Journal of Operations and Production Management* 35(9): 1253–1274.

Dicken, P. (2007) 'Global Shift: Mapping the Changing Contours of the World Economy', 5th edition. London: Sage.

Economist Intelligence Unit. (2015) 'Chain Reactions – How Trade between Emerging Markets Is Reshaping Global Supply Chains', Economist Intelligence Unit Report, May 2015.

Gereffi, G., Humphrey, J., and Sturgeon, T. (2005) 'The governance of global value chains', *Review of International Political Economy* 12: 78–104.

Jacobides, M. G. (2005) 'Industry change through vertical disintegration: How and why markets emerged in mortgage banking', *Academy of Management Journal* 48(3): 465–498.

Kumar, M., Srai, J. S., Pattinson, L., and Gregory, M. J. (2013) 'Mapping of the UK food supply chains: Capturing trends and structural changes', *Journal of Advances in Management Research* 10(2): 299–326.

Mudambi, R. (2008) 'Location, control and innovation in knowledge intensive industries', *Journal of Economic Geography* 8: 699–725.

Mudambi, R., and Venzin, M. (2010) 'The strategic nexus of offshoring and outsourcing decisions', *Journal of Management Studies, Special Issue: Offshoring and Outsourcing* 47(8): 1510–1533.

Rezk, R., Srai, J. S., and Williamson, P. (2016) 'International configuration revisited: Assessing the impact of product and knowledge attributes and changes in ICT on the choices available to firms', Journal of International Business Studies, published on-line 10 March 2016, doi:10.1057/jibs.2016.9

Srai, J. S. (2007) 'Exploring the Relationship between Capability and Configuration in International Supply Networks', PhD thesis, University of Cambridge, UK.

Srai, J. S. (2013) Value-chain configurations of emerging country multinationals. In 'The Competitive Advantage of Emerging Market Multinationals'. Ed. P. J. Williamson, R. Ramamurti, A. Fluery, & M. T. Fluery, Cambridge: Cambridge University Press, 180–190.

Srai, J. S., and Alinaghian, L. S. (2013) 'Value chain reconfiguration in highly disaggregated industrial systems: Examining the emergence of healthcare diagnostics', *Global Strategy Journal* 3: 88–108.

Srai, J. S., Badman, C., Krumme, M., Futran, M., and Johnston, C. (2015) 'Future supply chains enabled by continuous processing – Opportunities and challenges', *MIT White Paper Series, Journal of Pharmaceutical Sciences* 104(3): 840–849.

Srai, J. S., and Christodoulou, P. (2014) 'Capturing Value from Global Networks; Strategic Approaches to Configuring International Production, Supply and Service Operations', University of Cambridge IfM Publication, ISBN: 978–1–902546–30–8.

Srai, J. S., and Fleet, D. E. (2010) Exploring the configuration of emerging country multinationals. In 'The Emergence of Southern Multinationals and their Impact on Europe'. Ed. L. Brennan, New York: Palgrave, 261–280.

Srai, J. S., and Gregory, M. J. (2008) 'A supply network configuration perspective on international supply chain development', *International Journal of Operations Management* 28(5): 386–411.

Sturgeon, T. (2001) 'How Do We Define Value Chains and Production Networks?', Special Working Papers Series, MIT IPC Globalization Working Paper 00–010. Massachusetts Institute of Technology, Background Paper Prepared for the Bellagio Value Chains Workshop, September 25 – October 1, 2000, Rockefeller Conference Center, Bellagio, Italy.

Williamson, P., and Fleury, A. (Eds.) (2013) 'The Competitive Advantage of Emerging Market Multinationals'. Cambridge: Cambridge University Press.

5 M&A by EMNCs in developed countries

Motivation, success and implications

Sebastian Weusthoff and Reinhard Meckl

Introduction

The competitive position of emerging multinational corporations has been characterised by focusing on cost advantages. As the landscape changes towards knowledge-based competition, companies from emerging markets have to change as well. Grounding on a brief theoretical discussion, this chapter scrutinises the motivation behind M&A transactions by these firms and investigates their success. While intellectual capital strongly appears to be the predominant M&A driver, the study concerning M&A success does not reveal outstanding results. This underlines the strategic character of intellectual capital, which is not equally reflected in the market for corporate control. The chapter finally derives implications for both management and politics, suggesting a strong focus on emphasising and developing intellectual capital.

Internationalisation of EMNCs: an underinvestigated issue

As several waves of internationalisation have been identified in the literature (e.g. Dunning, van Hoesel and Narula 1998; Rasiah, Gammeltoft and Jiang 2010), internationalisation of EMNCs cannot be considered a brand new phenomenon. Nevertheless, the internationalisation of EMNCs has recently gained a lot of public attention, with an increase in M&A transactions by EMNCs observed in developed countries. Katkalo and Medvedev detect a "booming interest in Emerging Multinational Enterprises in international business (IB) and strategic management (SM) fields" (2013: 116). However, a missing understanding of motivational factors of EMNCs leads to uncertainty about appropriate evaluations and responses. As a result, individual and political action is dominated by rumors and stereotypes, whereas appropriate regulative and individual feedback could lead to beneficiary gains for all participants on macroeconomic and microeconomic levels. Consequently, research on the motivation of M&A, executed by EMNCs in developed countries, bears high potential to form an analytical basis that responds to a yet underinvestigated phenomenon in an appropriate way.

This chapter therefore addresses the question of the motivation behind M&A transactions by EMNCs in developed countries. After a concise review of relevant recent literature, this chapter focuses on the concept of intellectual capital as the main motivation of recent EMNC internationalisation using M&A. Theory and evidence-based hypotheses are scrutinised by samples using the calculated intangible value (CIV) and event study methodology. Finally, managerial and political implications are derived from the empirical results.

The concept of EMNC internationalisation

Literature review

Research on M&A motivations of EMNCs could broadly be classified into the well-known "seeking taxonomy" (e.g. Dunning 1993: 56–63; Weusthoff 2014: 145–150). Broadly summarizing previous research, a focus on exploring markets (e.g. Beule 2010; Pradhan 2010) and targeting strategic assets (e.g. Wang and Boateng 2008) can be noted. Rui and Yip point out that Chinese companies are trying "to gain sustainable competitive advantages by transforming themselves" (2008: 224) from cost-based manufacturers to market leaders with cutting edge technology. Moghaddam, Sethi, Weber and Wu prove that EMNCs "may best pursue their value creation goal through international expansion with upstream Knowledge Seeking and End-Customer-Market Seeking motives supplemented by international expansions with downstream Knowledge Seeking and Natural Resource Seeking motives" (2014: 12). Deng underlines in a case study that "acquisition of foreign firms may act as an effective escape response to the home country institutional constraints" (2009: 83). In this context especially experience, learning and absorptive capacity form the crucial factors of a successful internationalisation. "Gaining access to more advanced technologies may not be an utopian ambition" (Knoerich 2010: 190) if EMNCs combine the ability to absorb technology with existing knowledge (e.g. Madhok and Keyhani 2012: 37; Rabbiosi, Elia and Bertoni 2012: 207).

While agreeing on strategic motivations as the main driver of M&A by EMNCs in developed countries, there is almost no approach to investigating these factors using a quantitative method. While Rabbiosi et al. (2012) investigate general transactional and home-country characteristics, Moghaddam et al. (2014) perform a qualitative analysis with coding of interviewed respondents. This study involves the first examination of EMNCs' M&A motivations using objective accounting data of the companies involved.

Theoretical background

EMNCs are generally characterised as "latecomers" to the global economic stage (e.g. Mathews 2002). EMNCs base their late market entry mainly on cost advantages (e.g. Mathews 2002: 471) and face severe competitive disadvantages in a technology-oriented environment (e.g. Luo and Tung 2007: 485; Ramamurti 2010: 400). Internationalisation is therefore used as an instrument to compensate for disadvantages as part of a "catch-up-strategy" (Goldstein and Pusterla 2010: 294). Following Mathews, latecomers start internationalisation "from the resource-meager position of an isolated firm seeking some connection with the technological and business mainstream" (Mathews 2002: 471). This approach has found its theoretical formalisation in the "linkage, leverage, learning" model (LLL-Model) (e.g. Wells 1983, 1998; Mathews 2006: 19), which can be seen as an EMNC-specific evolution of the basic Uppsala model (e.g. Johanson and Vahlne 1977). Within the LLL-Model, firms try to gain access by linking with missing resources and leveraging their value by using them in their networks. Finally, learning processes ensure an internalisation of external knowledge to sustain a competitive advantage by compensating for weaknesses (e.g. Chen and Chen 1998: 446). "To escape such a situation, many EMNC firms seek to gradually go upmarket [. . .]. It is the access to opportunities and combination with the resources of others, in our context through acquisitions, which allows them to occupy new value space" (Madhok and Keyhani 2012: 37). Beyond the ongoing "Goldilocks debate" about a need for EMNC-specific theories (e.g. Cuervo-Cazurra 2012: 154), catching up and learning are consequently predominant motivations for M&A-based internationalisation of EMNCs.

While the traditionally competitive positioning of EMNCs was based on country-specific cost advantages at the manufacturing stage of the value chain (e.g. Fleury, Leme Fleury and Mendes Borini 2013: 108; Moghaddam et al. 2014: 1), "value-added is becoming increasingly concentrated at the upstream and downstream ends of the value chain" (Mudambi 2008: 706). To evolve from an easy imitable competitive positioning, it is crucial for EMNCs to develop into the more value-adding activities of the value chain (e.g. Mudambi 2008: 706). EMNCs are therefore supposed to catch up for their latecomer-based disadvantages by internationally acquiring capabilities in higher value-added downstream and upstream activities of the value chain (e.g. Knoerich 2010: 184; Williamson, Ramamurti, Fleury and Leme Fleury 2013: 310). The "smile of value creation" (Mudambi 2007: 206) represents the geographical focus of EMNC investment decisions (see Figure 5.1).

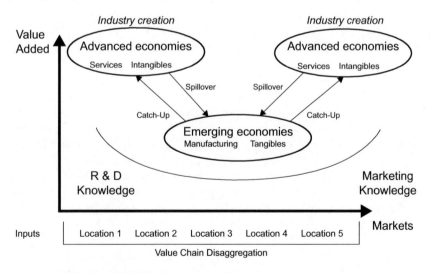

Figure 5.1 Activity-based site selection and value creation

Source: Mudambi 2008: 709

Intellectual capital as the main acquisition motivation

The ongoing change towards knowledge-based competition results in an increased importance of intangible values forming the sources of sustainable competitive advantage, because "investments in human resources, information technology, research and development, and advertising have become essential in order to maintain the firm's competitive position and ensure its future viability" (Canibano, García-Ayuso and Sánchez 2000: 102). Internationalisation into developed countries is therefore assumed to focus on a catch up in value-added activities fundamentally based on intellectual capital.

In consideration of the many definition approaches to intellectual capital (e.g. Dumay 2009; Sydler, Haefliger and Pruksa 2014), Sánchez and Canibano state that "almost every author classifies intangibles in a different way" (2001: 20). This study defines intellectual capital as "the possession of the knowledge, applied experience, organisational technology, customer relationships and professional skills" (Edvinsson and Malone 1997: 44). This definition leads to a segregation of the "Human Capital", "Organisational Capital" and "Relational Capital" (e.g. Saint-Onge 1996: 10; Sydler et al. 2014: 2).

Human capital consists of individual-related aspects such as knowledge or experience as well as competencies such as creativity, team orientation or motivation (e.g. Sydler et al. 2014: 3). As a basic element it reflects the starting point and source of intellectual based competitive advantages (e.g. Nonaka and Takeuchi 1995: 47–48; Hormiga, Batista-Canino and Sánchez-Medina 2011: 621). Empirical research shows that company performance mainly relies on managerial skills (e.g. Leverty and Grace 2012: 753). Considering "that turnover represents knowledge leaving the firm" (Hatch and Dyer 2004: 1172), there is a remarkable tendency of emerging market acquirers to keep existing management in charge (e.g. Child and Rodrigues 2005: 393; Bellmann and Range 2008: 1).

Unlike human capital, organisational capital is closely linked to the possessing organisation (e.g. Rosario Cabrita and Bontis 2008: 217), because "structural capital is the intellectual asset that remains when employees leave the company" (Sydler et al. 2014: 3). Tied to organisational structures, processes, informational flows or databases as explicit information (e.g. Nonaka and Takeuchi 1995: 69–70; Edvinsson and Malone 1997: 35), it is stored in large part in the organisational knowledge management (e.g. Edvinsson and Malone 1997: 35). Legally protected forms of organisational capital, such as patents, technologies or brands (e.g. Edvinsson and Malone 1997: 35, 36; Sydler et al. 2014: 3) form "the most refined part of the structural capital, as there could be a market for this and it can be bought and sold" (Jacobsen, Hofman-Bang and Nordby 2005: 573). Lists of technology-driven acquisitions are long, for there is always at least a partial reasoning that explains M&A by the opportunity to acquire cutting edge technology (e.g. Deng 2010: 511; Ramamurti 2013: 246; Williamson and Raman 2013: 264).

EMNCs suffer from the country-of-origin effect (e.g. Peterson and Jolibert 1995), because they traditionally offer limited quality at low price levels. However, research has shown that high valued brands improve company performance (e.g. Meckl and Graser 2011: 332; Chailan and Ille 2012: 325). As there are only a few internationally well-known brands from emerging markets (e.g. Child and Rodrigues 2005: 386; Buckley, Cross, Tan, Xin and Voss 2008: 739; Williamson and Zeng 2010: 99), EMNCs are thought to be attempting to substantially improve their brand positioning and perception by acquiring well known Western brands. Brand acquisition is consequently widely accepted as a driver for M&A transactions by EMNCs in developed countries (e.g. Child and Rodrigues 2005: 392, 399; Ramamurti 2013: 246).

Relational capital identifies "the value of a firm's relationships with people and organizations with which it conducts business" (Sydler et al. 2014: 3) and consists of its relations to important stakeholders, such as suppliers, customers' interacting groups outside of the transformation process itself (e.g. Marr, Schiuma and Neely 2004: 315; Hormiga et al. 2011: 621–622). It is widely accepted that a firm's market and customer orientation drives customer satisfaction, which finally leverages shareholder value (e.g. Srivastava, Shervani and Fahey 1998: 2, 8; Jyoti and Sharma 2012: 309). Geographical proximity hereby eases the necessary information flow from and to market partners, thereby facilitating spillover effects (e.g. Almeida and Kogut 1999: 906; Nachum and Zaheer 2005: 751). However, gaining and developing relational capital is both capital and time consuming (e.g. Rosenbloom and Larsen 1992: 95–96; Williamson and Zeng 2010: 103), meaning that acquisitions of existing distributional and intercompany networks save time and potentially money for market-entering EMNCs (e.g. Anderson, Havila and Salmi 2001: 579; Moghaddam et al. 2014: 8). Empirical evidence supports the hypothesis of acquisition of networks by EMNCs (e.g. Child and Rodrigues 2005: 393; Wu 2011: 87). EMNCs might therefore be motivated to conduct acquisitions of firms in established markets with the ojective of incorporating target company networks (e.g. Buckley et al. 2007: 505; Wu 2011: 85).

As a result, theoretical as well as empirical evidence shows that EMNCs are missing intellectual capital in a technology- and knowledge-oriented global competition. Search for intellectual capital in both upstream and downstream activities can be expected to be the main driver of M&A transactions by EMNCs in developed countries. Hence, target firms in M&A transactions conducted by EMNCs are expected to possess high intellectual capital. This leads to the following hypothesis:

> EMNC acquisition targets in developed countries possess a significant amount of intellectual capital.

As intellectual capital is assumed to form a substantial competitive advantage of firms, acquisition of intellectual capital should be reflected in successful M&A transactions increasing shareholder value of the acquiring firms. In general, research on intellectual capital shows a positive correlation between high values of intellectual capital and firm performance (e.g. Mention and Bontis 2013; Sydler et al. 2014). Furthermore, research has demonstrated a positive correlation between investments in intellectual capital and market value of firms (e.g. Aboody and Lev 1998; Chen, Cheng and Hwang 2005). Sydler et al. state that "market participants behave as if parts of R&D, labor and advertising expenditures were treated as assets that represent significant future economic benefits to the firm" (2014: 10). According to the results of Gubbi, Aulakh, Ray, Sarkar and Chittoor (2009), Jormanainen and Koveshnikov state that EMNCs "were found to create substantial value for acquirers through facilitating the internalisation of valuable tangible (i.e. strategic capabilities) and intangible (i.e. status and reputation) resources, especially in cases when the target firms are located in advanced economic and institutional environments" (2012: 707). This study therefore expects acquisitions of EMNCs undertaking M&A in developed countries to be successful.

Empirical study

Measuring intellectual capital

The basic problems of valuing intangible assets are enhanced when measuring intellectual capital as "it is not possible to measure social phenomena with anything close to scientific accuracy" (Sveiby 2010). Valuing intellectual capital is mainly influenced by techniques of daily business practice requirements and therefore quite a number of methods have been created (e.g. Andriessen 2004; Dumay 2009: 192; Sydler et al. 2014: 2). As there is no standard evaluation method, a procedure has to be selected which best fits the research requirements (e.g. Sydler et al. 2014: 4). As M&A are mainly undertaken to gain financial value, this study uses an accounting based approach. While direct methods gather useful data from non-public information (e.g. Brennan and Connell 2000: 226–234), an accounting-based valuation employs available public information to measure intellectual capital. Since summarizing individually identifiable assets of intellectual capital might neglect possible synergies between single elements (e.g. Mention and Bontis 2013: 288; Sydler et al. 2014: 3), this study uses a comparative approach, assuming firm profitability above the industry average to be due to the firm's individual intellectual capital. As common market comparing approaches, such as market-to-book ratios or Tobin's q, require market values based on capital markets listings, this study applies an approach based solely on accounting data, because EMNCs generally buy unlisted developed market firms.

The CIV views intellectual capital by comparing an adopted individual return on assets to an industry average (e.g. Stewart 1997: 228–230; Lev 1999; Andriessen 2004: 376–398). Similar to market-based procedures, the CIV assumes that intellectual capital generates an individual profitability above the comparable industry-specific average (e.g. Dzinkowski 2000: 36; Kujansivu and Lönnqvist 2007: 274), but unlike other accounting-based indicators, the CIV does not use external (Intellectual Capital Scoreboard, Lev 1999) or internal (Weightless Wealth Tool Kit, Andriessen 2004: 390) prognostic data. Relating to the return on assets (ROA), the CIV furthermore applies the "most popular financial ratio" (Hossari and Rahman 2005: 324). This study calculates the CIV as described in referenced literature (e.g. Stewart 1997: 228–229, Dzinkowski 2000: 36; Kujansivu and Lönnqvist 2007: 275) by employing the formula below. It basically assumes that firms are able to achieve earnings at the average industry profitability rate by exploiting tangible assets. Any excess returns therefore rely on the deployment of intellectual resources which are capitalized by the costs of capital to calculate the value of intellectual capital.

Equation 1: CIV calculation

$$CIV = \frac{\emptyset \sum_{t-3}^{t} pretax\ earnings_{Firm} - \left(\emptyset \sum_{t-3}^{t} tang.assets_{Firm} * \emptyset \sum_{t-3}^{t} ROA_{industry}\right) * \left(1 - \emptyset \sum_{t-3}^{t} taxrate_{firm}\right)}{\emptyset \sum_{t-3}^{t} costs\ of\ capital_{Firm}}$$

Source: Authors

To avoid any structural accounting bias, this study includes firms with comparable sales volume and sales structure to build the industry average. The capitalisation of annual data applies cost of capital estimations as previously proposed in the literature cited (e.g. Lev 1999; Andriessen 2004: 390). Even if there are shortcomings using the CIV, it represents "the only one of these [methods], which can be easily applied by someone external to the company without company specific (internal) information" (Kujansivu and Lönnqvist 2007: 274).

Analysis of M&A drivers

Data for this study were provided by Bureau van Dijk's databases "Zephyr" and "Amadeus". The statistical population was determined by majority stake achieving M&A transactions completed between January 1, 2005 and December 31, 2013 having an acquirer from a BRIC state and a target from the EU-25 area. By excluding industries with Standard Industrial Classification codes between 6000 and 6999, this study concentrates on strategic investments. The event population of 612 transactions contained 61 analysable datasets. The control group consisted of companies that were at least once included among Europe's top 500 companies with the highest ROA included in the Amadeus database. As the CIV increases in proportion to ROA, a strict control group selection increases the validity of results and led to a control population of 365 companies. Representative statuses of the random samples were investigated and approved. Further t-test requirements were verified. The applied t-test rejects the null hypothesis of equal CIVs on a highly significant level ($p < 0.000$). The hypothesis of high CIVs in target firms therefore cannot be rejected.

When EMNCs acquire developed country companies, they select firms with a significant CIV, hence a high intellectual capital (Table 5.1).

Analysis of M&A success

A subsequently conducted acquirers' analysis applying event study methodology used identical criteria to determine the sample. A population of 194 strategic M&A transactions from BRIC to EU-25 with a final majority stake was investigated. Neither the non-parametric GRANK t-test (e.g. Kolari and Pynnonen 2011), nor

Table 5.1 Statistical results of the *t*-test

Group	Obs	Mean	SD	t-Stat.	DoF	Sign.
0	43	1.502	0.643			
1	43	−0.392	0.747			
combined	86		1.178			
				12.607	84	
Ha: diff < 0						1.000
Ha: diff != 0						0.000
Ha: diff > 0						0.000

Source: Authors

Table 5.2 Results of the event study

[−d;d]	CAAR	Wilcoxon	GRANK t-Test		CUMRANK-Test	
		Sign.	t-Value	Sign.	z-Value	Sign.
−10;10	−0.002990	0.026	1.054	0.293	0.868	0.385
−5;5	0.007213	0.000	1.055	0.293	−0.857	0.391
−1;1	0.0027861	0.722	1.056	0.292	0.129	0.898
0;0	0.0038705	0.902	1.058	0.291	0.622	0.534

Source: Authors

the CUMRANK-test (e.g. Cowan 1992) showed significant results in any investigated event window. The results of the parametric Wilcoxon sign test are not mirrored by the robust non-parametric tests. They more likely derive from statistical and calculating inaccuracies than from substantial differences. In a nutshell, the event study did not deliver significant results. Event study results are shown in Table 5.2.

Conclusion and implications

Over the past decades, EMNCs could not develop necessary and useful skills to become well-known technology leaders, because they were positioned as the world's cost-efficient manufacturers. Additionally, due to a rather short global economic history, EMNCs have not yet gained much market and management experience. In fact, they lack the intellectual capital that is necessary nowadays for a globalised, technology-oriented, competitive environment. Research shows some evidence of the importance of intellectual capital for both firm performance and shareholder value, even if valuing intangible assets bears some problems concerning accurate measurement.

This study values intellectual capital on the basis of accounting data, eliminating individual opinions or assessments. Results prove that EMNCs select firms with high values of intellectual capital while entering developed markets by means of M&A. These findings are consistent with the theoretical background of traditional and EMNC-specific learning theories explaining M&A as instruments for acquiring missing skills.

This study does not reveal any statistically significant capital market reaction to M&A announcements. From this broadly accepted perspective of "M&A success", it does not reflect the positive evaluation of Gubbi et al. (2009: 412). However, these results do not prove unsuccessful M&A activities of EMNCs in developed markets. Considering the complexity of M&A transactions in general, measuring synergies, the increased intricacy of valuing intellectual capital, an accurate capital market evaluation can hardly be expected. Acquiring intellectual capital might more likely be seen as long-term investments by strategic investors, which is not reflected in short-term oriented capital markets.

Western firms considered as potential acquisition targets should emphasise company-bound intellectual capital during the transaction process. Furthermore, EMNCs might be prepared to pay high prices as they pursue long-term strategic goals as missing capital market pressure enables EMNCs to buy firms at a higher price. Consequently, Western companies that sell have some remarkable options for achieving high transaction gains.

Measurement complexity may attach great importance to flexible contract conditions such as earn-out clauses. Applying earn-out terms enables the selling party to signal confidence in firm-bound intellectual capital leading to a trustworthy negotiation position with higher returns, whereas fixed terms might include an unrealistic and unwanted discount simply due to a lack of authentic communication. On the other hand, acquirers face a seller willing to withstand uncertainty about the final price. This might increase the acquirer's trust and thus enhance the general possibility of an agreement being reached.

Public opinion generally expects the acquirer to dislocate big parts of the acquired company as a consequence of an international M&A transaction. However, a short-term dislocation with members of the workforce leaving the company or a reduction of personnel will weaken the competitive positioning and consequently counteract the transaction objectives. Some aspects of intellectual capital, such as distributional networks, are by no means an objective of relocation, as these components benefit from geographical proximity. Political and public communication should consider this when facing an increase of inbound M&A activity of EMNCs in coming years. However, in the long term, negative effects might appear anyway. A successful integration of acquired companies might loosen geographical ties and form options to relocate value-creating activities at later stages. Especially legally protectable intellectual capital, such as brands or patents, can be transferred globally within the owning EMNC. If these firms transfer intellectual capital to the companies' home emerging markets, developed markets might be facing a future knowledge and technology drain. Regulatory bodies at the European level should consider this optional development when creating future market conditions. However, legal measures are limited in protecting markets holistically, as they always provoke evasive reactions by market players. Regulatory bodies should therefore create appropriate incentives to encourage EMNCs to a long-term European commitment. This is primarily achieved by setting up an investment-favouring regulative body accompanied by structural investments. In doing so, physical and information infrastructure might form the economic basis, but investments in education, knowledge and personal competencies will ensure the European firms' competitive position.

References

Aboody, D. and Lev, B. (1998) 'The Value Relevance of Intangibles: The Case of Software Capitalization.', *Journal of Accounting Research*, 36: 161–191.

Almeida, P. and Kogut, B. (1999) 'Localization of Knowledge and the Mobility of Engineers in Regional Networks.', *Management Science*, 45, 7: 905–917.

Anderson, H., Havila, V. and Salmi, A. (2001) 'Can You Buy a Business Relationship?: On the Importance of Customer and Supplier Relationships in Acquisitions.', *Industrial Marketing Management*, 30, 7: 575–586.

Andriessen, D. (2004) *Making sense of intellectual capital: Designing a method for the valuation of intangibles.* Amsterdam, Boston: Elsevier.

Bellmann, E. and Range, J. (2008) Indian-Style Mergers: Buy a Brand, Leave It Alone. *The Wall Street Journal,* March 22.

Beule, F. de (2010) *Locational determinants of acquisitions from China and India: The role of human capital.* Annual Conference of IASSI and Knowledge Forum. IIT Bombay, Mumbai.

Brennan, N. and Connell, B. (2000) 'Intellectual Capital: Current Issues and Policy Implications.', *Journal of Intellectual Capital*, 1, 3: 206–240.

Buckley, P. J., Clegg, J., Cross, A. R., Liu, X., Voss, H. and Zheng, P. (2007) 'The Determinants of Chinese Outward Foreign Direct Investment.', *Journal of International Business Studies*, 38, 4: 499–518.

Buckley, P. J., Cross, A. R., Tan, H., Xin, L. and Voss, H. (2008) 'Historic and Emergent Trends in Chinese Outward Direct Investment.', *Management International Review*, 48, 6: 715–748.

Canibano, L., García-Ayuso, M. and Sánchez, P. (2000) 'Accounting for Intangibles: A Literature Review.', *Journal of Accounting Literature*, 19: 102–130.

Chailan, C. and Ille, F. (2012) 'Brand strategies of firms from emerging economies.', in M. Marinov (ed.), *Internationalization of emerging economies and firms* (pp. 320–342). Basingstoke, Hampshire: Palgrave Macmillan.

Chen, H. and Chen, T.-J. (1998) 'Network Linkages and Location Choice in Foreign Direct Investment.', *Journal of International Business Studies*, 29, 3: 445–467.

Chen, M.-C., Cheng, S.-J. and Hwang, Y. (2005) 'An Empirical Investigation of the Relationship between Intellectual Capital and Firms' Market Value and Financial Performance.', *Journal of Intellectual Capital*, 6, 2: 159–176.

Child, J. and Rodrigues, S. B. (2005) 'The Internationalization of Chinese Firms: A Case for Theoretical Extension?', *Management and Organization Review*, 1, 3: 381–410.

Cowan, A. (1992) 'Nonparametric Event Study Tests.', *Review of Quantitative Finance and Accounting*, 2, 4: 343–358.

Cuervo-Cazurra, A. (2012) 'Extending Theory by Analyzing Developing Country Multinational Companies: Solving the Goldilocks Debate.', *Global Strategy Journal*, 2, 3: 153–167.

Deng, P. (2009) 'Why do Chinese Firms Tend to Acquire Strategic Assets in International Expansion?', *Journal of World Business*, 44, 1: 74–84.

Deng, P. (2010) 'What Determines Performance of Cross-Border M&As by Chinese Companies? An Absorptive Capacity Perspective.', *Thunderbird International Business Review*, 52, 6: 509–524.

Dumay, J. C. (2009) 'Intellectual Capital Measurement: A Critical Approach.', *Journal of Intellectual Capital*, 10, 2: 190–210.

Dunning, J. H. (1993) *Multinational enterprises and the global economy. International business series.* Wokingham, England, Reading, MA: Addison-Wesley.

Dunning, J. H., van Hoesel, R. and Narula, R. (1998) 'Third world multinationals revisited: New developments and theoretical implications.', in J. H. Dunning (ed.), *Series in international business and economics: Globalization, trade and foreign direct investment.* Amsterdam, New York: Elsevier, pp. 255–286.

Dzinkowski, R. (2000) 'The Measurement and Management of Intellectual Capital: An Introduction.', *Management Accounting: Magazine for Chartered Management Accountants*, 78, 2: 32.

Edvinsson, L. and Malone, M. S. (1997) *Intellectual capital: Realizing your company's true value by finding its hidden roots.* New York: HarperBusiness.

Fleury, A., Leme Fleury, M. T. and Mendes Borini, F. (2013) 'Value-chain configurations of Brazilian EMNEs.', in P. J. Williamson, R. Ramamurti, A. Fleury and M. T. Leme Fleury (eds.), *The competitive advantage of emerging market multinationals.* Oxford: Cambridge University Press, pp. 97–115.

Goldstein, A. E. and Pusterla, F. (2010) 'Emerging Economies' Multinationals: General Features and Specificities of the Brazilian and Chinese Cases.', *International Journal of Emerging Markets*, 5, 3/4: 289–306.

Gubbi, S. R., Aulakh, P. S., Ray, S., Sarkar, M. B. and Chittoor, R. (2009) 'Do International Acquisitions by Emerging-Economy Firms Create Shareholder Value? The Case of Indian Firms.', *Journal of International Business Studies*, 41, 3: 397–418.

Hatch, N. W. and Dyer, J. H. (2004) 'Human Capital and Learning as a Source of Sustainable Competitive Advantage.', *Strategic Management Journal*, 25, 12: 1155–1178.

Hormiga, E., Batista-Canino, R. M., Sánchez-Medina, A. (2011) 'The Impact of Relational Capital on the Success of New Business Start-Ups.', *Journal of Small Business Management*, 49, 4: 617–638.

Hossari, G. and Rahman, S. (2005) 'A Comprehensive Formal Ranking of the Popularity of Financial Ratios in Multivariate Modeling of Corporate Collapse.', *Journal of American Academy of Business*, Cambridge, 6, 1: 321–327.

Jacobsen, K., Hofman-Bang, P. and Jr, Nordby, R. (2005) 'The IC Rating™.', *Journal of Intellectual Capital*, 6, 4: 570–587.

Johanson, J. and Vahlne, J. E. (1977) 'The Internationalization Process of the Firm – A Model of Knowledge Development and Increasing Market Commitment: New Empirical Evidence.', *Journal of International Business Studies*, 8: 23.

Jormanainen, I. and Koveshnikov, A. (2012) 'International Activities of Emerging Market Firms.', *Management International Review*, 52, 5: 691–725.

Jyoti, J. and Sharma, J. (2012) 'Impact of Market Orientation on Business Performance: Role of Employee Satisfaction and Customer Satisfaction.', *Vision*, 16, 4: 297–313.

Katkalo, V. S. and Medvedev, A. G. (2013) 'Value-chain configurations of Russian EMNEs.', in P. J. Williamson, R. Ramamurti, A. Fleury and M. T. Leme Fleury (eds.), *The competitive advantage of emerging market multinationals.* Cambridge: Cambridge University Press, pp. 116–131.

Knoerich, J. (2010) 'Gaining from the Global Ambitions of Emerging Economy Enterprises: An Analysis of the Decision to Sell a German Firm to a Chinese Acquirer.', *Journal of International Management*, 16, 2: 177–191.

Kolari, J. W. and Pynnonen, S. (2011) 'Nonparametric Rank Tests for Event Studies.', *Journal of Empirical Finance*, 18, 5: 953–971.

Kujansivu, P. and Lönnqvist, A. (2007) 'Investigating the Value and Efficiency of Intellectual Capital.', *Journal of Intellectual Capital*, 8, 2: 272–287.

Lev, B. (1999) 'Seeing Is Believing – A Better Approach to Estimating Knowledge Capital.', *CFO Magazine*, 15, February: 29–37.

Leverty, J. T. and Grace, M. F. (2012) 'Dupes or Incompetents? An Examination of Management's Impact on Firm Distress.', *Journal of Risk and Insurance*, 79, 3: 751–783.

Luo, Y. and Tung, R. L. (2007) 'International Expansion of Emerging Market Enterprises: A Springboard Perspective.', *Journal of International Business Studies*, 38: 481–498.

Madhok, A. and Keyhani, M. (2012) 'Acquisitions as Entrepreneurship: Asymmetries, Opportunities and the Internationalization of Multinationals from Emerging Economies.', *Global Strategy Journal*, 2, 1: 26–40.

Marr, B., Schiuma, G. and Neely, A. (2004) 'The Dynamics of Value Creation: Mapping Your Intellectual Performance Drivers.', *Journal of Intellectual Capital*, 5, 2: 312–325.

Mathews, J. A. (2002) 'Competitive Advantages of the Latecomer Firm: A Resource-Based Account of Industrial Catch-Up Strategies.', *Asia Pacific Journal of Management*, 19, 4: 467–488.

Mathews, J. A. (2006) 'Dragon Multinationals: New Players in 21st Century Globalization.', *Asia Pacific Journal of Management*, 23, 1: 5–27.

Meckl, R. M. and Graser, S. (2011) 'The impact of financial strategy on internationalization of EMNCs – A neglected factor?', in L. Brennan (ed.), *The emergence of southern multinationals: Their impact on Europe* (1st ed., pp. 331–341). Basingstoke: Palgrave Macmillan.

Mention, A.-L. and Bontis, N. (2013) 'Intellectual Capital and Performance within the Banking Sector of Luxembourg and Belgium.', *Journal of Intellectual Capital*, 14, 2: 286–309.

Moghaddam, K., Sethi, D., Weber, T. and Wu, J. (2014) 'The Smirk of Emerging Market Firms: A Modification of the Dunning's Typology of Internationalization Motivations.', *Journal of International Management*, 20, 3: 359–374

Mudambi, R. (2007) 'Offshoring: Economic Geography and the Multinational Firm.', *Journal of International Business Studies*, 38, 1: 206.

Mudambi, R. (2008) 'Location, Control and Innovation in Knowledge-Intensive Industries.', *Journal of Economic Geography*, 8, 5: 699–725.

Nachum, L. and Zaheer, S. (2005) 'The Persistence of Distance? The Impact of Technology on MNE Motivations for Foreign Investment.', *Strategic Management Journal*, 26, 8: 747–767.

Nonaka, I. and Takeuchi, H. (1995) *The knowledge-creating company: How Japanese companies create the dynamics of innovation.* New York: Oxford University Press.

Peterson, R. A. and Jolibert, A.J.P. (1995) 'A Meta-Analysis of Country-of-Origin Effects.', *Journal of International Business Studies*, 26, 4: 883–900.

Pradhan, J. P. (2010) 'Strategic Asset-Seeking Activities of Emerging Multinationals: Perspectives on Foreign Acquisitions by Indian Pharmaceutical MNEs.', *Organizations and Markets in Emerging Economies*, 2, 1: 9–31.

Rabbiosi, L., Elia, S. and Bertoni, F. (2012) 'Acquisitions by EMNCs in Developed Markets.', *Management International Review*, 52, 2: 193–212.

Ramamurti, R. (2010) 'What have we learned about emerging-market MNEs?', in R. Ramamurti and J. V. Singh (eds.), *Emerging multinationals in emerging markets*. Cambridge: Cambridge University Press, pp. 399–426.

Ramamurti, R. (2013) 'Cross-border M&A and competitive advantage of Indian EMNEs.', in P. J. Williamson, R. Ramamurti, A. Fleury and M. T. Leme Fleury (eds.), *The competitive advantage of emerging market multinationals*. Oxford: Cambridge University Press, pp. 239–259.

Rasiah, R., Gammeltoft, P. and Jiang, Y. (2010) 'Home Government Policies for Outward FDI from Emerging Economies: Lessons from Asia.', *International Journal of Emerging Markets*, 5, 3/4: 333–357.

Rosario Cabrita, M. d. and Bontis, N. (2008) 'Intellectual Capital and Business Performance in the Portuguese Banking Industry.', *International Journal of Technology Management*, 43, 1–3: 212–237.

Rosenbloom, B. and Larsen, T. L. (1992) 'How Foreign Firms View their U.S. Distributors.', *Industrial Marketing Management*, 21, 2: 93–101.

Rui, H. and Yip, G. S. (2008) 'Foreign Acquisitions by Chinese Firms: A Strategic Intent Perspective.', *Journal of World Business*, 43, 2: 213–226.

Saint-Onge, H. (1996) 'Tacit Knowledge the Key to the Strategic Alignment of Intellectual Capital.', *Strategy and Leadership*, 24, 2: 10–16.

Sánchez, P. and Canibano, L. (2001). *MEasuRing Intangibles To Understand and improve innovation Management (MERITUM)*. Brüssel, Madrid. Project funded by the European Community under the Targeted Socio- Economic Research (TSER).

Srivastava, R. K., Shervani, T. A. and Fahey, L. (1998) 'Market-Based Assets and Shareholder Value: A Framework for Analysis.', *Journal of Marketing*, 62, 1: 2–18.

Stewart, T. A. (1997) *Intellectual capital: The new wealth of organizations*. New York: Doubleday.

Sveiby, K. E. (2010) *Methods for Measuring Intangible Assets*. Retrieved from www.sveiby.com/articles, March 18, 2016.

Sydler, R., Haefliger, S. and Pruksa, R. (2014) 'Measuring Intellectual Capital with Financial Figures: Can We Predict Firm Profitability?', *European Management Journal*, 32, 2: 244–259.

Tobin, J. (1969) 'A General Equilibrium Approach to Monetary Theory.', *Journal of Money, Credit and Banking*, 1, 1: 15–29.

Wang, Q. and Boateng, A. (2008) 'Cross-Border M&As by Chinese Firms: An Analysis of Strategic Motivation and Performance.', *International Management Review*, 3, 4: 259–270.

Wells, L. T. (1983) *Third world multinationals: The rise of foreign investment from developing countries*. Cambridge, MA: MIT Press.

Wells, L. T. (1998) 'Multinationals and the Developing Countries.', *Journal of International Business Studies*, 29, 1: 101–114.

Weusthoff, S. (2014) *Motive und Erfolg von M&A durch emerging multinational corporations in entwickelten Staaten*. Bayreuth: Verlag für Nationalökonomie, Management und Politikberatung.

Williamson, P. J., Ramamurti, R., Fleury, A. and Leme Fleury, M. T. (2013) 'Conclusion: rethinking the implications of EMNEs' rise.', in P. J. Williamson, R. Ramamurti, A. Fleury and M. T. Leme Fleury (eds.), *The competitive advantage of emerging market multinationals*. Cambridge: Cambridge University Press, pp. 290–318.

Williamson, P. J. and Raman, A. P. (2013) 'Cross-border M&A and competitive advantage of Chinese EMNEs.', in P. J. Williamson, R. Ramamurti, A. Fleury and M. T. Leme

Fleury (eds.), *The competitive advantage of emerging market multinationals*. Cambridge: Cambridge University Press, pp. 260–277.

Williamson, P. J. and Zeng, M. (2010) 'Chinese multinationals: Emerging through new global gateways.', in R. Ramamurti and J. V. Singh (eds.), *Emerging multinationals in emerging markets* (pp. 81–109). Cambridge: Cambridge University Press.

Wu, C. (2011) 'Internationalization of China's enterprises and its implications for Europe.', in L. Brennan (ed.), *The emergence of southern multinationals: Their impact on Europe.* Basingstoke: Palgrave Macmillan, pp. 79–91.

6 Emerging multinational companies from Russia

Drivers, motivations and strategies

Codruţa Dura and Imola Drigă

Outward foreign direct investment from Russia

Although developed countries remain the leading source of outward foreign direct investment (OFDI), the importance of transition economies as investors has significantly increased over the last period. Various factors, such as the continuous liberalization of FDI regimes worldwide, competition among firms from all parts of the world, technological and logistical advancements, influence and support global OFDI flows from both developed and emerging markets (Gammeltoft 2008; Drigă and Dura 2013a). The crisis drew attention to the importance of the emerging markets of Brazil, Russia, India, China and South Africa. BRICS economies have emerged as important outward investors and, among them, Russian corporations have a meaningful international role in the world. Russia has stood out among transition economies as the country with the highest outward/inward FDI ratio and as a net capital exporting country from the beginning of the economic transition.

According to the *World Investment Report 2014* (UNCTAD 2014), in 2013 six developing and transition economies were among the top twenty investors. This trend is confirmed by UNCTAD's *World Investment Prospects Survey 2013–2015* which states that developing and transition economies are becoming important investors. Among the most promising investor countries, the majority of BRICS countries (China, India, and Russia, while Brazil fell out of the ranking) are seen as major developing country sources of FDI. Thus, 60 percent of IPA respondents (UNCTAD 2013a) ranked China as the most promising source of FDI due to fast increase of outward FDI from this country in late years, but India and the Russian Federation are also seen as major sources of FDI, ranked seventh and tenth, respectively (see Figure 6.1).

Statistical updates (see Figure 6.2 and 6.3) show that the sharp increase in FDI by BRICS in the last decade was driven by Russia and China. The two countries contributed to more than 70 percent of the BRICS countries' FDI growth between 2005 and 2008. However, in the following years (2009–2012) the rise of outward FDI flows from these economies came to a temporary halt (except China) when the financial crisis and recession had a strongly negative impact on them. In 2013, in the case of Brazil and India the value of FDI outflows continued to fall for the third and fourth consecutive years, while for China, Russia and South Africa they

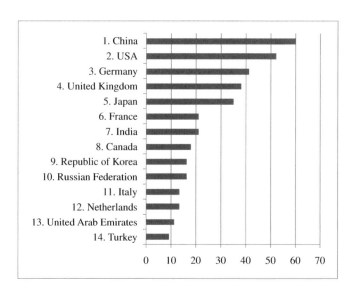

Figure 6.1 IPA's selection of the most promising investor home economies for FDI, 2013–2015

Source: Based on data from UNCTAD, *World Investment Prospects Survey 2013–2015*

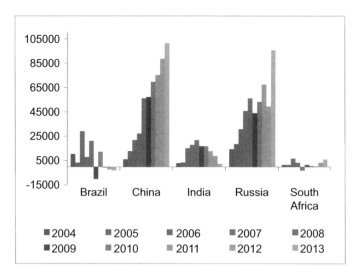

Figure 6.2 Outward foreign direct investment flows from BRICS countries, 2004–2013 (millions of USD)

Source: Based on data from UNCTAD's FDI database

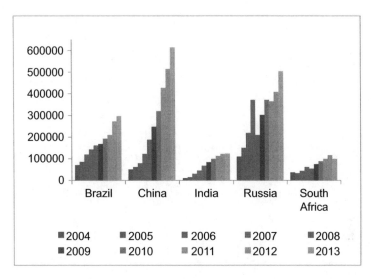

Figure 6.3 Outward foreign direct investment stock from BRICS countries, 2004–2013 (millions of USD)

Source: Based on data from UNCTAD's FDI database

increased (Drigă and Dura 2013b). Thus, FDI flows from transition economies reached record levels in 2013, China and the Russian Federation being the world's third and fourth largest investors.

From 2007, the Bank of Russia began to publish detailed statistics on the geographical distribution of Russian outward FDI flows in order to underline the priorities of Russian investors (Bank of Russia database, www.cbr.ru/eng/statistics) (see Table 6.1). The British Virgin Islands, together with Cyprus, Austria, Turkey, Switzerland, Spain, Germany, Luxembourg, United Kingdom and the United States have become in 2013 the most important host countries. Some small countries of the Commonwealth of Independent States (CIS), which are not very popular among foreign investors globally, attract significant OFDI from Russia (Belarus, Kazakhstan and Ukraine).

The geography of multinationals' expansion reflects that Europe is, by far, the main target zone for Russian OFDI, and the gap is even growing with other zones during the last period. Moreover, CIS countries and eastern Europe are preferred by the giant corporations from Russia when they conceive their strategies of expanding abroad (Kuznetsov and Kvashnin 2014). This trend is caused by the linkages already in place in the former Soviet Union area, common business practices and cultural values, developed industrial chains, business contacts and other advantages of the so-called neighbourhood effect and low competition from MNCs from elsewhere (Dura and Drigă 2012).

Table 6.1 Geographical distribution of Russian outward FDI flows in 2007–2013 (millions of USD)

	2007	2008	2009	2010	2011	2012	2013
CIS countries, of which:	3,642	3,563	3,890	1,338	4,431	2,340	2,238
Armenia	277	266	179	5	69	130	94
Azerbaijan	5	104	5	9	9	−6	37
Belarus	813	1,032	1,370	934	2,820	593	867
Kazakhstan	107	326	1,029	−225	674	845	671
Kyrgyz Republic	−11	0	0	11	21	−2	11
Moldova	43	15	110	21	−5	131	43
Tajikistan	45	23	14	8	48	38	−42
Turkmenistan	7	25	55	−60	0	2	23
Ukraine	1,667	146	678	485	703	600	496
Uzbekistan	355	414	217	151	92	9	−12
Non-CIS countries, of which:	41,158	52,100	39,392	51,277	62,422	46,482	84,474
Austria	230	253	458	847	512	1,035	5,265
British Virgin Islands	1,345	3,962	2,301	1,834	3,861	7,395	62,266
Cyprus	14,700	15,524	15,288	18,309	22,930	20,920	7,689
Germany	673	1,860	1,488	1,880	971	1,118	1,334
Luxembourg	497	2,633	765	2,483	2,005	−504	1,314
Netherlands	11,991	4,684	3,376	7,035	9,901	2,599	−3,022
Spain	258	458	375	490	812	980	1,356
Switzerland	1,404	2,426	1,806	1,750	3,719	76	1,358
Turkey	183	272	106	143	1,685	4,105	1,447
United Kingdom	2,454	3,886	1,997	1,232	1,474	632	1,294
United States	973	7,264	1,634	1,060	1,625	688	739
World	44,801	55,663	43,281	52,616	66,851	48,822	86,712

Source: Based on data from Bank of Russia database, www.cbr.ru/eng/statistics

Emerging multinational companies from Russia

Russian companies arose from small and medium-sized enterprises which had to struggle against the inflexible framework of a centrally planned economy, isolated from the external world, and had to face the challenging passage towards the post-communist era through privatization, reorganization, uncertainty and losses. The performances these corporations have reached today are worth mentioning (Dura and Drigă 2013a).

In the Boston Consulting Group (BCG, www.bcgperspectives.com) 2013 ranking of 100 companies from rapidly developing economies, some 31 Chinese, 20 Indian, 13 Brazilian and only 6 Russian companies were identified. These were

United Company Rusal (which operates in the metallurgy sector), Evraz Group (metallurgy), Gazprom (oil and gas), Lukoil (oil and gas), Severstal (metallurgy) and Vimpelcom (telecommunication services) (Dura and Drigă 2013b).

To have a more recent picture of Russian multinationals and their huge potential, as well as in order to provide the proper background to investigate the internationalization strategies adopted by these companies, Table 6.2 provides recent data on

Table 6.2 Russian companies ranked in the top 500 largest European companies in 2014

Europe Rank 2014	Europe Rank 2013	Company	Sector	Market Value (billions of USD)	Turnover (billions of USD)	Net Income (billions of USD)	Total Assets (billions of USD)
26	14	Gazprom	Oil and gas	91.3	159.8	35.5	408.9
41	25	Rosneft	Oil and gas	70.7	138.2	16.6	228.7
56	30	Sberbank	Banks	53.4	n/d	11.1	553.2
68	43	Lukoil	Oil and gas	47.4	115.9	7.6	108.8
106	68	Surgutneftegas	Oil and gas	31.9	25.5	8.5	72.6
110	87	Novatek	Oil and gas	30.3	9.1	3.3	18.2
129	84	Norilsk Nickel	Diversified metals and mining	26.4	10.8	0.8	18.8
148	149	Magnit	Food retail	21.8	17.7	1.1	8.2
175	142	MegaFon	Telecommunications services	17.4	9.0	1.6	13.0
191	148	Mobile Telesystems	Telecommunications services	15.9	12.5	2.4	14.7
210	161	VTB Bank	Banks	14.6	n/d	2.8	266.6
220	126	Uralkali	Chemicals	14.0	3.2	0.6	12.6
242	183	Tatneft	Oil and gas	12.4	13.8	2.1	20.4
255	219	Bashneft	Oil and gas	11.9	17.7	1.2	13.6
303	297	Sistema	Mobile telecommunications	9.8	1.1	0.1	1.3
364	314	Alrosa	Mining	7.6	4.2	1.1	12.7
370	256	Novolipetsk Steel	Industrial metals and mining	7.5	10.6	0.2	16.2
398	362	RusHydro	Electric utilities	6.8	9.5	0.6	25.9
420		Mosobl Bank	Banks	6.5	n/d	0.03	1.4
430	308	Severstal	Iron and steel	6.4	12.9	0.1	14.4
440	221	Rostelecom	Telecommunications services	6.3	8.8	0.7	17.0

Source: Financial Times (2014) FT Europe 500, www.ft.com

Note: Market values and prices as of 31 March 2014

the financial performance of some major Russian multinationals, ranked in the top 500 largest European companies by *Financial Times* in 2014.

The biggest Russian multinationals are concentrated in two industrial sectors related to the exploitation and processing of natural resources, a traditional source of competitive advantage for this country (Deloitte CIS 2008). The oil and gas sector is represented by Lukoil, Gazprom, Rosneft Oil, Surgutneftegas, etc., while the metallurgical sector includes companies like Severstal, UC Rusal and Norilsk Nickel. Nevertheless, new multinationals are developing in industrial sectors as diverse as food production and retail, IT and the Internet, banking, hospitality, telecommunications, electronics, etc. (Dura and Drigă 2013b).

Alongside other multinationals from BRICS countries, corporate giants from Russia started to emerge in the international rankings of global companies. While in 2011 the Forbes List of 2000 Global Companies (www.forbes.com) included 278 companies from BRICS (136 Chinese – including Hong Kong, 61 Indian, 33 Brazilian, 28 Russian and 20 South African corporations), by 2015 the list included 352 companies from these countries (232 Chinese – including Hong Kong, 56 Indian, 24 Brazilian, 27 Russian and 13 South African companies). Russia is represented by 27 companies (Forbes 2015), with an aggregate capitalization of 393 billions of USD, returns of 58.2 billions of USD and total assets valued at 1681 billions of USD (see Table 6.3).

Table 6.3 Forbes list of 2000 global companies, Russia rank, 2015

Global Rank	Company	Sector	Sales (billions of USD)	Profits (billions of USD)	Assets (billions of USD)	Market Value (billions of USD)
27	Gazprom	Oil and gas	158	24.1	356	62.5
59	Rosneft	Oil and gas	129	9	150	51.1
109	Lukoil	Oil and gas	121.4	4.7	111.8	43.5
124	Sberbank	Banks	58.1	7.6	420	26.9
209	Surgutneftegas	Oil and gas	26.6	8.8	74.6	24.2
555	Transneft	Oil and gas	22	4.1	56.8	3.6
576	Norilsk Nickel	Diversified metals and mining	11.9	1.9	13.1	29.2
615	VTB Bank	Banks	28.4	0.1	203.2	14.6
701	Magnit	Food retail	19.8	1.2	6.1	20.4
710	Tatneft	Oil and gas	12.3	2.4	12.2	12.1
748	Novatek	Oil and gas	9.3	1	11.7	26.3
984	IDGC Holding	Electric utilities	23.4	−3.2	58.4	1.7
1016	Novolipetsk Steel	Iron and steel	10.3	0.9	10.4	8.3
1033	MegaFon	Telecommunications services	8.2	1	7.6	10.8

Global Rank	Company	Sector	Sales (billions of USD)	Profits (billions of USD)	Assets (billions of USD)	Market Value (billions of USD)
1198	Sistema	Telecommunications services	28.6	−4.1	20.7	3
1202	RusHydro	Electric utilities	8.7	0.7	15.2	3.7
1255	UC Rusal	Aluminium	9.4	0.3	14.7	9.5
1327	Rostelecom	Telecommunications services	7.9	1	9.4	4
1530	Severstal	Iron and steel	10.1	−1.6	7.8	9.7
1584	X5 Retail Group	Food retail	16.3	0.3	6	4.3
1592	Inter Rao	Electric utilities	19.2	0.2	9.8	1.8
1595	Moscow Exchange	Diversified financials	0.8	0.4	25.4	3.1
1618	United Aircraft Corporation	Aerospace and defence	6.9	−0.4	20.9	1.1
1667	Nomos Bank	Banks	4.2	0.3	38.4	3
1918	Mechel	Iron and steel	8.6	−2.9	11.4	0.5
1927	Mail.ru Group Ltd. Sponsored GDR RegS	Computer services	0.9	0.8	2.9	4.4
1995	Alrosa	Diversified metals and mining	5.4	−0.4	6.5	9.7
Total	–	–	765.7	58.2	1681	393

Source: Forbes (2015) *The World's Biggest Public Companies. 2015 Ranking.* www.forbes.com

Oil and gas companies have strengthened their presence among Russian MNEs because this industry was affected by the global crisis less profoundly than, for instance, metal industries. However, steel and non-ferrous metals sectors are still important sources of Russian foreign assets. These industrial domains assume the role of the most active fields of Russian specialization in the world economy. Nevertheless, other Russian industries also have representatives among large MNEs (Dura and Drigă 2013b).

In the last few years, Russian multinationals turned into key players in the landscape of national economies of their neighbours – former Soviet republics and current member states of the CIS, as well as the European Union.

Drivers and motivations behind Russian multinationals

The purpose of identifying the main drivers and motivations behind the phenomena of Russian multinational rapid growth requires a retrospective analysis of mainstream theories regarding the internationalization of multinational enterprises (Dura and Drigă 2012). There were three main traditional approaches that dominated the literature on multinational companies in the last thirty years (Taylor and Nolke 2008): *the eclectic paradigm* or *the OLI model* – ownership, localization, internationalization (Dunning 1977, 1988, 2001, 2006; Dunning et al. 1998; Tolentino 2001; Salehizadeh 2007); *the international product cycle theory* (Verno 1966; Wells 1968; Buckley and Casson 1976) and *the LLL model* – linkage, leverage and learning – conceptualized by Mathews (2002, 2006a, 2006b).

- *The eclectic paradigm or the OLI model* was first conceptualized by Dunning (1977), starting from the three variables or advantages that might determine "the going abroad strategy" for a company: ownership, localization and internationalization. *Ownership advantages* mean that the company should possess a specific resource to be exploited, a new technology or a product that could successfully compete on the domestic market. *Location advantages* (L) are related to the characteristics of the host country and specific opportunities it offers to any potential investor. This kind of advantage is specific to each economic system and cannot be transferred elsewhere. *Internationalization advantages* (I) include the capability of developing and managing international production/distribution networks which should generate higher profits for the company as compared with the export of goods manufactured domestically. The most recent elaboration of the eclectic paradigm (Dunning and Lundan 2008) makes a differentiation between asset advantages (O_a) and transaction advantages (O_t), which could be extended to a fourth variable – *home country advantages* (H). The extended eclectic paradigm – OLIH – is explained at full length and then particularized in the case of Russia by Kalaman Kalotay, economic affairs officer at UNCTAD, in his research paper "Russian Transnationals and International Investment Paradigms" (Kalotay 2008, 2010; Narula 2010).
- *The international product cycle theory* assumes that enterprises are innovating as a reply to the demand increasing trend, given the factor prices from their home country. Following the launching of a new product, companies supply their home markets and begin subsequently to provide for other foreign markets that are similar to their own (of course, as long as that demand occurs in these locations). The company will serve these markets through exporting until the product reaches the maturity phase of its life cycle, the production process becomes standardized and the management of the company comes to the conclusion that it would be more profitable (in terms of lower costs, increasing rents and overcoming competition from the domestic firms) to establish production facilities in the host country. As product standardization spreads, other competitors will gain access to the knowledge and technology required to manufacture the product, and the competition between host and home countries will intensify, bringing prices to the fore (Nigam and Su 2010).
- *The linkage, leverage and learning or the LLL model* – Mathews (2006a, 2006b) proposes a model complementary to the OLI approach, which is more suitable for multinationals from emerging economies. Thus, the new

approach requests development economic theories of the 1960s (Gerschen-kron 1952, 1962; Akamatsu 1962) and puts forward the catch-up strategies that the latecomer companies can use in order to rise from global ranks. The fact that multinationals from emerging economies are newcomers in international markets can turn into an advantage for them because they can skip the standard initial steps of internationalization; hence, they get easier access to advanced technologies (through imitation) and fill the gap between them and the developed countries. Thus, multinationals from emerging economies have rapidly gone global *by linking up* with a partner from a developed country and yet having access not only to the foreign market, but to the knowledge and the technology of their ally. This strategy has offered the emerging multinationals the opportunity *to leverage* the knowledge and the technology they have been exposed to by their partner. In the process of leveraging, emerging multinationals have undergone several feedback loops to internally assimilate, strengthen and/or adjust resources acquired through linking. In short, this denotes the process of *learning*, whereby gaining knowledge represents the key factor that enables the emerging multinationals to successfully leverage the resources they procured through linking (Taylor and Nolke 2008). This model is different from the afore-mentioned OLI model because it entails a dynamic process of the develop-ment of multinationals, in contrast to the static OLI model.

However, the earlier theories of firms' internationalization were built for the purpose of identifying the main motivations and strategies that drove the fight of developed countries for supremacy in global markets. Therefore, they may not fully reflect the whole motivation behind overseas activities performed by MNCs from emerging countries.

The Uppsala model, introduced by Johanson and Vahlne (1977), perfectly fits in the pattern of the international evolution of Russian resource-based companies. The model postulates that the lack of knowledge about foreign markets leads mul-tinational companies to expand their activities in countries which are culturally and geographically nearer to them. The conquering of targeted markets follows incrementally, step by step, in an attempt to overcome the so-called psychological distance which imply many obstacles such as differences in languages, culture, political environment, business practices, the level of industrial development, etc. (Nigam and Su 2010).

Kalaman Kalotay (2008) has demonstrated that the Uppsala model can actually explain the behaviour of Russian resource-based multinationals. First, they began internationalization by exporting products; afterwards, they acquired foreign assets and set up subsidiaries, due to various motivations – seeking resources, seeking technologies, seeking markets, seeking efficiency or even avoiding export duties (Filippov 2011a). From a geographical point of view, statistical data pre-sented above trace the preference of Russian multinationals towards CIS coun-tries and eastern Europe in terms of their strategies of expanding abroad (Kudina and Jakubiak 2008).

A closer look at *the drivers of Russian multinationals' expansion abroad* puts forward *motives* that are considered quite traditional and typical for the companies belonging to developed market economies (Vahtra and Liuhto 2006). Authors in the international business literature agree upon four basic motivations that guide the internationalization process of corporations, regardless of their background – developed or emerging country. According to a research study conducted by Deloitte CIS Moscow in 2008 , *Russian Multinationals: New Players in the Global Economy*, these motivations hold true for the largest Russian companies with foreign assets.

These drivers of internationalization are as follows:

- *Seeking markets* – multinationals tend to extend their tentacles to markets that guarantee further development either through the great number of consumers or through their purchasing power. As far as Russian multinationals are concerned, there are plenty of examples of firm strategies that reflect such motivation. In line with the doctrine of the Uppsala model, multinationals from Russia have developed their geographical presence in the neighbouring markets of CIS and eastern European countries. The largest Russian oil and gas companies were driven by the need to penetrate new markets when they purchased processing entities, distribution networks and storage and transportation facilities across Europe and the US (Deloitte CIS 2008). We also highlight the fact that Russian giants have been successful in conquering markets from advanced developed economies, despite the high intensity of competition and/or regulatory impediments (Filippov 2010).
- *Seeking resources* – refers to investments which are pursued to gain a better access to raw materials. As we saw in the previous section, the rankings of Russian multinationals are highly populated by companies from resource-based sectors. But this fact should not lead to the conclusion that Russian multinationals tend to give up their plans of seeking new resources. On the contrary, the rich natural resources of Russia stimulate Russian companies to continue investments in order to ensure access to resources, given that most of the giant companies from Russia are highly integrated and they need to obtain low cost supplies from other countries.
- *Seeking efficiency* – this aims to improve the firm's efficiency by exploiting the advantages of economies of scale and scope, as well as the common ownership. If seeking markets is the basic motivation for "horizontal companies" which manufacture relatively standardized products, seeking efficiency is the prevailing investment motivation for "vertical companies" which geographically split the production process into several stages, based on the local levels of endowment with production factors (Voinea 2007).
- *Seeking technology* – generally speaking, multinationals from emerging countries show a preference for investments in developed countries, going in quest of sophisticated technologies, know-how, management and marketing abilities and thus counterbalancing their own competitive disadvantages. As Russian companies from the telecommunications, automotive industry,

high-tech and other more technologically complex sectors soar within the international business scene, the role of this driver of internationalization is expected to increase.

The entry modes

Traditionally, there are two approaches that a multinational can use in order to enter a host economy: *the acquisition of an existing firm or business facility* (brownfield investment) and *the setting up of a new affiliate* (greenfield investment). Another recent trend in the praxis of the internationalization of multinational companies, prefigured by the LLL model, is the creation of strategic alliances with partners from the host market.

In the case of Russian multinationals, statistical data regarding the dynamics of mergers and acquisitions (M&A), available for the period 1993–2014, show a gradual increasing trend in the 1990s (see Figure 6.4). Nevertheless, the number and the value of transactions are insignificant as compared with those registered during the decade to come. From 2001 up to 2007, the value of the M&A has developed substantially, surpassing the number of deals. Between 2006 and 2007 the number of transactions was 800 on average, but their financial value reached a historic peak: 160 billions of USD. During and after the 2008 financial crisis, the world underwent a slowdown in M&A activity, but the number of deals rose up to approximately 3,700 transactions in 2010. Nevertheless, the report *Trends in Cross-Border M&A*, released by Baker and McKenzie in April 2013, revealed that experts anticipate an increase in the level of cross-border M&A into and from high-growth markets over the next few years.

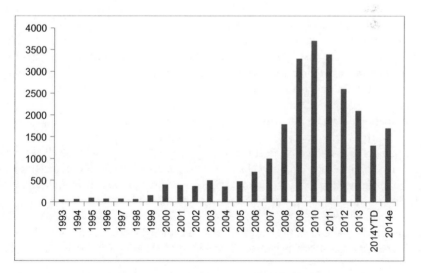

Figure 6.4 Announced mergers and acquisitions, Russia: 1993–2014e

Source: Thomson Financial, Institute of Mergers, Acquisitions and Alliances (IMAA), 2014

Note: YTD: January to September 30; e: expected full year.

Table 6.4 Top Russian greenfield FDI projects between 2009 and 2011

Year of Start	Company	Target Country	Target Industry	Project	Value of Investment at the End of 2011, US$ million
2009	Gazprom	Austria	Gas supply	Second part of gas holder Haidach	55
2009	UTair	Ukraine	Transport	Airlines from Lugansk and Kiev	50
2009	Rosneft	Abkhazia	Oil exploration	New subsidiary "RN-Shelf Abkhazia"	46
2011	Evraz	Kazakhstan	Steel	65% in the plant in Kostanay	40
2009	Gazprom	Germany	Gas supply	Gas holder Schweinrich	30

Source: *IMEMO-VCC Survey of Russian Multinationals,* 2013

Most Russian companies choose to merge with established companies or to acquire relatively low-priced production facilities. For instance, acquisitions of refineries in Europe by Rosneft and Lukoil and mergers of mines or steel plants by Mechel and NLMK all fall into the category of brownfields (Kuznetsov 2011). The practice of expanding abroad via brownfield investments became more popular in the case of Russian multinationals during the global downturn. Recent studies on the issue showed that there were few Russian greenfield significant projects between 2009 and 2011, some of them being initiated before the outbreak of the financial crisis (see Table 6.4). We can mention here the building of a new steel plant in Turkey by Russian giant MMK and the construction of gas-storage facilities by Gazprom in Germany and Austria.

In terms of innovation strategies, strategic alliances and partnerships with Western multinationals represented the main options that enabled Russian corporations to incorporate highly developed technologies between 1990 and 2000. Collaboration (strategic alliances) with Western companies is supposed to have played the role of a trigger in the recent process of raising the competitiveness of Russian multinationals. There are many examples of best practices in the literature (Filippov 2011b): the strategic alliance between Yukos and Schlumberger aiming at the implementation of quality, health, safety, environment management at all sites; the partnership between Yukos and Norwegian engineering firm Kvaerner for development of surface infrastructure at the western Siberian Priobskoye field; the alliance between Lukoil and US giant Conoco Philips that facilitated Lukoil's access to the latest technologies and capital; the partnership between the Russian telecommunications companies MTS and VimpelCom and Ericsson that allowed the Russians to incorporate fast-paced new telecommunications technologies which were developing in the West, etc.

As far as the internationalization strategies are concerned, a very important contribution to the field was brought by Panibratov (2010, 2014). Relying on several well-documented case studies of Russian multinationals which operate in various industries, Panibratov elaborated a synopsis of internalization strategies used by Russian multinationals in terms of geographical destinations, entry modes and expansion approach. It turned out that although companies tend to prefer a primary entry mode, the majority of them employ several different modes when they approach a new market (Zubrovskaya 2014). Thus, the main entry modes for Russian giants in the resource-based sector are exporting, acquisitions, joint-ventures and strategic partnerships. In particular, oil and gas companies also implement wholly owned subsidiaries. IT and Internet companies internationalize their business first by simple exporting; then the initial approach is often developed into strategic partnerships. Corporations from the banking sector usually open subsidiaries overseas and then undertake strategic acquisitions. In the telecommunications sector, acquisitions and strategic alliances are preferred, whereas the main paths employed in internationalization of companies from the electricity sector are acquisitions and greenfield investments. Therefore, there are obvious differences among various industrial branches in terms of their entry modes; that's why we emphasize that the internationalization strategies of Russian corporations should be analyzed with relation to the peculiarities of each sector.

Conclusion

Although they emerged relatively recently on the world economy scene, an examination of the magnitude and the outstanding growing trend of Russian multinationals demonstrates that they are becoming redoubtable competitors within the global business environment.

The study of Russian multinationals has highlighted that the drivers of foreign investments for these companies match the conventional group of motivations of multinationals from developed economies, namely market-seeking motives, resource-seeking reasons, technology-seeking drivers and efficiency-seeking incitements. But these motivations are strongly related to the models of the internationalization of multinational companies. Overall, internationalization theory has generated plenty of debates in the literature. We have reviewed the classical approaches that brought significant contributions to the theory – building in the field: the eclectic paradigm (or the OLI model), the international product cycle theory, the linkage, leverage, learning (LLL) model and the Uppsala model. From among them, we believe that the unprecedented expansion of Russian multinationals in the last fifteen years can be explained starting from the postulation of the LLL and Uppsala models. Thus, the position of "latecomers" was turned by Russian multinationals from a disadvantage to a significant advantage and allowed them to penetrate market niches that multinationals from developed countries have overlooked. Through the rapid assimilation of knowledge and new technologies from their business partners, Russian corporations managed to skip over several decades of multinational evolution as compared with their counterparts from developed economies. Moreover, the setting up of innovative strategies enabled the Russian giants to compete with the top companies from the developed economies, at the same scale (Dura and Drigă 2013a).

References

Akamatsu, K. (1962) 'A Historical Pattern of Economic Growth in Developing Countries', *Developing Economies*, 1: 3–25.

Bank of Russia Database [Online] Available from: www.cbr.ru/eng/statistics [Accessed: 20 May 2015].

Boston Consulting Group (2009) *The 2009 BCG 100 New Global Challangers. How Companies from Rapidly Developing Economies are Contending for Global Leadership*, January.

Boston Consulting Group [Online] Available from: www.bcgperspectives.com [Accessed: 20 May 2015].

Buckley, P. and Casson, M. (1976) *The Future of the Multinational Enterprise*, Basingstoke and London: Macmillan.

Deloitte CIS (2008) *Russian Multinationals: New Players in the Global Economy*, Moscow: Deloitte CIS.

Drigă, I. and Dura, C. (2013a) 'Restoring the Economic Power of Russia through OFDI Expansion', *Economia: Seria Management*, 16, 2: 227–41.

Drigă, I. and Dura, C. (2013b) 'New Trends Regarding OFDI from Russia', *Annals of the University of Petroşani: Economics*, 13, 2: 41–50.

Dunning, J. H. (1977) 'Trade, Location and Economic Activity and the Multinational Enterprise: A Search for an Eclectic Approach', in Ohlin, B., Hesselborn, P. and Wijkman, P. (eds.) *The International Allocation of Economic Activity*, London: Macmillan, pp. 395–418.

Dunning, J. H. (1988) 'The Eclectic Paradigm of International Production – A Restatement and Some Possible Extensions', *Journal of International Business Studies*, 19, 1: 1–31.

Dunning, J. H. (1998) *Globalisation, Trade and Foreign, Direct Investment*, Bingley: Emerald Group Publishing Limited; 1st edition.

Dunning, J. H. (2001) 'The Eclectic (OLI) Paradigm of International Production: Past, Present and Future', *International Journal of the Economic Business*, 8, 2: 173–90.

Dunning, J. H. (2006) 'Comment on Dragon Multinationals: New Players in 21st Century Globalization', *Asia Pacific Journal of Management*, 23, 2: 139–41.

Dunning, J. H. and Lundan, S. (2008) *Multinational Enterprises and the Global Economy*, 2nd edition, Cheltenham: Edward Elgar.

Dura, C. and Drigă, I. (2012) *Emerging Multinational Companies from Russia and their Impact on Host European Countries*, Working Paper Presented at Conference EPI 2012, June 18–19, University of Parma, Italy.

Dura, C. and Drigă, I. (2013a) 'The Rise of Emerging Multinationals from Russia – Models, Drivers and Internationalization Strategies', *Review of International Comparative Management*, 14, 3: 387–99.

Dura, C. and Drigă, I. (2013b) 'The Amazing Universe of Russian Multinationals: New Insights', *Annals of the University of Petroşani, Economics*, 13, 2: 51–60.

Filippov, S. (2010) 'Russian MNCs Companies: The Rise of New Multinationals', *International Journal of Emerging Markets*, 5, 3/4: 307–32.

Filippov, S. (2011a) 'Russia's Emerging Multinational Companies amidst the Global Economic Crisis', *Maastricht Economic and Social Research and Training Centre on Innovation and Technology*, UNU-MERIT, United Nations University, 3: 1–31.

Filippov, S. (2011b) 'Innovation and R&D in Emerging Russian Multinationals', *Economics, Management and Financial Markets*, 6, 1: 182–206.

Financial Times (2014) *FT Europe 500* [Online] Available from: www.ft.com/intl/cms/
    s/0/988051be-fdee-11e3-bd0e-00144feab7de.html#axzz3dPp7K29E [Accessed: 15 May
    2015].
Forbes (2015) *The World's Biggest Public Companies. 2015 Ranking* [Online] Available
    from: www.forbes.com/global2000/list/#country:Russia [Accessed: 29 May 2015].
Gammeltoft, P. (2008) *Emerging Multinationals: Outward FDI form the BRIC Countries*,
    paper presented at the 'IV Globelics Conference' at Mexico City, September 22–24: 1–15.
Gerschenkron, A. (1952) 'Economic Backwardness in Historical Perspective', in Hoselitz,
    B. (ed.) *The Progress of Underdeveloped Areas*, Chicago: University of Chicago Press.
Gerschenkron, A. (1962) *Economic Backwardness in Historical Perspective*, Cambridge,
    MA: The Belknap Press of Harvard University Press.
IMEMO-VCC (2013) *Survey of Russian Multinationals*, Moscow and New York, Primakov
    Institute of World Economy and International Relations, Russian Academy of
    Sciences.
Kalotay, K. (2008) 'Russian Transnationals and International Investment Paradigms',
    Research in International Business and Finance, 22: 85–107.
Kalotay, K. (2010) 'The Future of Russian Outward Foreign Direct Investment and the Eclec-
    tic Paradigm: What Changes after the Crisis of 2008–2009?', *Competitio*, 9, 1: 31–54.
Kudina, A. and Jakubiak, M. (2008) 'The Motives and Impediments to FDI in the CIS',
    CASE Network Studies & Analyses, CASE-Center for Social and Economic Research,
    Warsaw, 370: 6–31.
Kuznetsov, A. V. (2011) *Outward FDI from Russia and Its Policy Context, Update 2011*,
    Vale Columbia Center on Sustainable International Investment and Institute of World
    Economy and International Relations of Russian Academy of Sciences.
Kuznetsov, A. V. and Kvashnin, Y. D. (2014) *Monitoring of Mutual Investments in the CIS
    Countries 2014*, Saint Petersburg: EDB Centre for Integration Studies.
Liuhto, K. (2006) *Expansion or Exodus – Why Do Russian Corporations Invest Abroad?*
    London: Routledge; 1st edition.
Mathews, J. A. (2002) 'Competitive Advantages of the Latecomer Firm: A Ressource –
    Based Account of Industrial Catch-up Strategies', *Asia Pacific Journal of Management*,
    19: 467–88.
Mathews, J. A. (2006a) 'Catch-up Strategies and the Latecomer Effect in Industrial Devel-
    opment', *New Political Economy*, 11, 3: 313–35.
Mathews, J. A. (2006b) 'Dragon Multinationals: New Players in the 21st Century Globali-
    sation', *Asia Pacific Journal of Management*, 23, 1: 139–41.
Narula, R. (2010) *Keeping the Eclectic Paradigm Simple: A Brief Commentary and Impli-
    cations for Ownership Advantages*, MERIT-UNU Working Paper 2010–031, Maastricht:
    UNU-MERIT.
Nigam, R. and Su, Z. (2010) 'Flying Towards the Successful Skies: The Emerging Region
    Multinationals', *Journal of Emerging Knowledge on Emerging Markets*, 2: 159–79.
Panibratov, A. (2010) 'Russian Multinationals: Entry Strategies and Post-Entry Opera-
    tions', *Electronic Publications of Pan-European Institute*, 15: 1–59.
Panibratov, A. (2014) *Russian Multinationals: From Regional Supremacy to Global Lead*,
    New York: Routledge.
Salehizadeh, M. (2007), 'Emerging Economies' Multinationals: Current Status and Future
    Prospects', *Third World Quarterly*, 28, 6: 1151–66.
Taylor, H. and Nolke, A. (2008) *Regulatory Governance and the Rise of Non-Triad Multi-
    national Companies: A Modified "Varieties of Capitalism – Perspective on Indian*

Multinationals, Paper Prepared for the ECPR Standing Group on Regulatory Governance Conference '(Re)Regulation in the Wake of Neoliberalism: Consequences of Three Decades of Privatization and Market Liberalization, Utrecht, June 5–7.

Thomson Financial, Institute of Mergers, Acquisitions and Alliances (2014) [Online] Available from: www.imaa-institute.org/statistics-mergers-acquisitions.html [Accessed: 25 May 2015].

Tolentino, P. E. (2001) 'From Theory to a Paradigm: Examining the Eclectic Paradigm as a Framework in International Economics', *International Journal of the Economic of Business*, 8, 2: 191–209.

UNCTAD (2013a) *World Investment Prospects Survey 2013–2015*, United Nations, New York and Geneva.

UNCTAD (2013b) *World Investment Report 2013*, Global Value Chains: Investment and Trade for Development, United Nations, New York and Geneva.

UNCTAD (2014) *World Investment Report 2014*, Investing in the SDGs: An Action Plan, United Nations, New York and Geneva.

Vernon, R. (1966) 'International Investment and International Trade in the Product Cycle', *The Quarterly Journal of Economics*, 80, 2: 190–207.

Voinea, L. (2007) *Transnational Corporations and the Global Capitalism*, Iasi: Polirom Publishing House.

Wells, L. T. (1968) 'A Product Life Cycle for International Trade?', *Journal of Marketing*, 32: 1–6.

Zubkovskaya, A. and Michailova, S. (2014) 'The Development of Russian Multinational Enterprises from the 1990s to the Present', *Organizations and Markets in Emerging Economies*, 5, 2: 59–78.

7 Turkish EMNCs with foreign direct investments in the EU

Their motivations, degree of internationalization and company performances

Nükhet Vardar

Introduction

Outward foreign direct investment (OFDI) from emerging countries was observed to increase globally especially after the 1990s (Demirbag and Tatoglu 2008; Goldstein and Pusterla 2010; Lau et al. 2010; Rasiah et al. 2010). This shift in OFDI also encouraged academics to study the patterns of OFDI from emerging multinational companies (EMNCs) like China (Gammeltoft et al. 2010; Rios-Morales and Brennan 2010), Brazil (Cyrino et al. 2010) and Korea (Kwon 2010). Previous literature regarding EMNCs' OFDI moves indicate that their internationalization process follows a different pattern and that it is much quicker than that of developed country MNCs (Bonaglia et al. 2007). Therefore, our research aims to investigate the link between Turkish EMNCs' OFDI motivations into the EU, with their degree of internationalization and general as well as marketing performance levels.

Theoretical background

Undoubtedly as new players, the EMNCs have added momentum to the international business literature. Although EMNCs' internationalization has been investigated since the 1990s, no ad hoc theories have been developed (Rios-Morales and Brennan 2010). However, the dominance of EMNCs in international markets has led to a few existing theories' revision (Gammeltoft et al. 2010; Rasiah et al. 2010). Considering the nature of this edited book, only a brief literature review is supplied here, mainly focusing on internationalization and performance. A detailed review of Turkish MNCs' FDI motives was conducted by our team (Uray et al. 2012).

Previous research points out that EMNCs do not follow the traditional OLI (ownership–location–internationalization) theory introduced by Dunning (1981, 1988) or the Uppsala School's theory for developed country MNCs going abroad, which states that developed country MNCs start the internationalization process in nearby countries, gradually entering farther countries. EMNCs seem to be more aggressive, moving quickly and taking bigger steps in their internationalization efforts. Deng (2012) reasons that "EMNCs are increasingly embracing accelerated internationalization via aggressive overseas acquisitions as an effective mechanism to quickly catch up with the existing global players." He points out that EMNCs prefer a "dual international expansion path," as they tend to compete in both developed and developing economies. Furthermore it is generally stated that EMNCs engage in OFDI to enhance their competitiveness, rather than exploit their existing status (Bonaglia et al. 2007; Deng 2007; Schüler-Zhou and Schüller 2009). Thus, internationalization through FDI becomes a strategy aimed at strengthening the firm through the accumulation of resources previously not available (Amighini et al. 2010). As emphasized in the literature, developed country FDI exploits their strategic assets in developing countries, while developing country FDI explores those strategic assets especially from developed ones (Deng 2003, 2007). Wang and Suh (2009) explain that firms may expand into different countries or regions pursuing different strategies simultaneously, instead of utilizing one uniform approach in all their international expansions. Their model explains the internationalization process of latecomer MNEs in FDI, rapidly entering developed and developing countries, by following multiple routes that can coexist.

Focusing on country-specific examples, Parente et al. (2013) report Brazilian MNCs "increased their international investments to take advantage of economies of scale, expand their international portfolio, reduce the risk of dependency on the Brazilian market and exploit firm-specific resources and capabilities developed in the Brazilian market." Another study, on Russian MNCs, by Kalotay and Sulstarova (2010) state that they have a monopolistic/oligopolistic position in the domestic market, strong competitive positions in their sectors and significant export revenues for financing overseas operations. Finally, Maponga and Maxwell (2000), reporting on Australian mining companies' internationalization efforts since the 1980s, identify "juniors" as more market driven, as they lack strong working capital, making them take more risks. They conclude, "risk-taking mentality is a source of competitive advantage in internationalization" (2000). Wang and Suh (2009) also indicate that different internationalization routes taken by headquarters in different subsidiary countries yield different company performance levels. For instance, if the chosen internationalization route is more "market" and "both market and asset seeking" oriented, then MNCs will be more successful in achieving sales growth and market share.

All these examples indicate that rapid internationalization efforts of EMNCs make different contributions to company performance. In addition, they emphasize that even the same EMNCs do not act uniformly all the time. Rather, they make decisions according to given conditions in each and every country. Therefore, it is expected that empirical analysis of Turkish MNCs' underlying motives while entering the EU and their effects on MNCs' internationalization and performance levels will yield valuable insight.

Research methodology

In our research, both qualitative and quantitative methods were incorporated. Ten interviews were conducted through case study method, trying to identify

Turkey-specific marketing-related factors. The interviewed executives were from Turkish MNCs with OFDI in EU countries and EU countries' investment agencies. Subsequently, based on qualitative research findings, a quantitative research questionnaire was finalized. For the quantitative phase, the data obtained from the Turkish Treasury was filtered for Turkish MNCs with investments in the EU. Hence, primary data were collected from 100 Turkish MNCs with the help of face-to-face interviews via a research company. Findings were analyzed using the SPSS statistical package.

OFDI motivations included in our research (16 international market and 22 firm-related statements) were mostly taken from Deng (2003, 2007), Bonaglia et al. (2007), Demirbag and Tatoglu (2008), Kaya and Erden (2008), Schüler-Zhou and Schüller (2009) and Goldstein and Pusterla (2010), as well as being developed by the researchers. The subjective degree of internationalization (SDoI) was questioned by subjective measures (instead of objective) by asking managers their perceptions about their company's success in the internationalization process on an eleven-point scale (0 = no progress, 10 = advanced level of internationalization) based on Kaya and Erden (2008) and Eren-Erdogmus et al. (2010). The firm's general and marketing performance levels (PLs) were measured by asking managers' perceptions using twelve statements with a five-point Likert scale. The scale was developed based on Bonaglia et al. (2007), Demirbag and Tatoglu (2008), Kaya and Erden (2008), Khavul et al. (2010), Lau et al. (2010) and Rios-Morales and Brennan (2010). The research questions were:

- What are the imperative motives that make Turkish MNCs have FDI in the EU?
- How do these motives have an effect on the company's general and marketing performance levels?
- How do these motives have an effect on the company's degree of internationalization?
- How does the Turkish MNCs' degree of internationalization affect the company's general and marketing performance levels?

The model

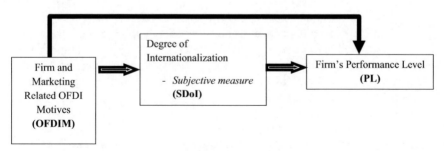

Findings

Turkish MNCs' major OFDI motives when investing in the EU

The factor analysis was run with thirty-eight firm and international market-related OFDI motives (OFDIM), asking respondents the importance degree of each factor. Analysis yielded eight factors, explaining 70 percent of the total variance.

The most critical factor is named *Developing New Products and Having Strong International Brands (OFDIM1)*. Companies seem to make a concerted efforts to have strong international brands, such as "wanting to have brands with European origin" or "having international trademarks and patents" or "following in the footsteps of innovation." Therefore, it is believed that having strong international brands will continue to be an important factor for EMNCs when going abroad.

The second largest factor is *Making Use of Niche Market Potential in the EU (OFDIM2)*. There are nearly five million consumers of Turkish origin in Europe. Market research indicates that they visit Turkey annually at least for two weeks, they continue watching Turkish series via satellite and talk to their relatives in Turkey at least fifteen minutes monthly. Therefore, Turkish MNCs cannot overlook the Turkish population in Europe.

The third factor is *Having an Effective International Value Chain (OFDIM3)*. As the world becomes smaller and the "produced by" concept evolves towards "produced for," the concept of value chain gains more significance. Therefore, becoming a global player means being able to access global sources more efficiently than competitors. We see the value chain's implications in Turkish EMNCs' OFDI motives, when they admit that "having their own distribution network in the EU" or "buying time for becoming an international company" are important factors, as coined by our team previously (Vardar et al. 2011).

In the fourth factor, *Making Use of Less Risky Markets (OFDIM4)*, we observe Turkish EMNCs' aversion to risk. Turkish EMNCs' OFDI decision is positively affected when perceived country risk is low, when there is a qualified workforce, when the investment is near to energy, to raw material and to semi-finished goods and when the international markets' growth potential is high. It could also be argued that Turkish EMNCs encounter many uncertainties in their domestic markets, so they have become risk aversive. Therefore, in OFDI, they assign higher importance to making international investments in lower risk-countries.

The fifth factor, *Increasing Company Value (OFDIM5)*, includes "wishing to be known and trusted in international markets," "wanting to increase global market shares" and "the importance assigned to the design attribute." All of these work towards increasing the company value. It is also worth noting that the "design" issue is grouped together with company value, instead of belonging to Factor 1. This could be interpreted that design is perceived more as a company-related factor than as a brand asset.

The sixth factor, *Having Financial and Cost Advantage (OFDIM6)*, and the seventh factor, *Making Use of Feasible Investment Opportunities (OFDIM7)*, are both related to finances and ranked after marketing-related factors.

Table 7.1 Degree of importance assigned to international market and firm-related motives (OFDIM) by Turkish companies with OFDI in EU countries

Factors	Statements	Factor Loadings	% of Variance Expl.	Cum. Exp. Variance	Reliability
Developing New Products and Having Strong International Brands	Wanting to have brands with European origin	0.8030	12.347	12.347	0.875
	Wanting to have international trademarks and patents	0.6810			
	Wanting to make best use of pioneering R&D efforts in international markets	0.6460			
	Wishing to improve quality standards of goods and services produced	0.6370			
	Wishing to keep pace with technological advancements and transfer technology	0.6200			
	Wanting to make use of international firms' managerial capabilities	0.5440			
	Wishing to have access to new private equity sources	0.5200			
	Wanting to go where the innovation is	0.4790			
Making Use of Niche Market Potential in EU	Wishing to market products for Turkish people living in the EU	0.8370	10.254	22.601	0.820
	Hindering backward immigration by creating new job opportunities for Turkish people living in EU	0.7960			
	Making the best use of Turkish TV series which became very popular in EU	0.7010			
	Making use of Turkish brands' existing awareness levels in the EU	0.6650			
Having Effective International Value Chain	Wanting to have its own distribution network in the EU	0.7340	8.968	31.569	0.715
	Wanting to buy time for becoming an international company	0.6580			
	Wanting to attain integration with global commerce	0.6400			
	Having alternative means (air freight/ship) for reaching international markets	0.5600			

(*Continued*)

Table 7.1 (Continued)

Factors	Statements	Factor Loadings	% of Variance Expl.	Cum. Exp. Variance	Reliability
Making Use of Less Risky Markets	Having 'less country risk' perception	0.8210	8.737	40.306	0.754
	Having qualified workforce	0.6960			
	Being near to energy, raw materials and semi-finished good sources	0.6830			
	International markets' growth potential (macro indicators such as consumption per capita, etc.)	0.4650			
Increasing Company Value	Wanting to be known and being trusted in international markets	0.7470	8.727	49.033	0.757
	Wanting to increase global market shares	0.7440			
	Wishing to increase company value	0.6970			
	Wishing to develop new products frequently	0.5210			
	Wishing to make use of design's power	0.3690			
Having Financial and Cost Advantages	Attainable prices of companies which are for sale	0.7730	7.588	56.621	0.772
	Cost advantage (workforce, raw material, transportation costs)	0.7370			
	Not having very fierce competitors	0.7170			
Making Use of Feasible Investment Opportunities	Wanting to make investments with the extra cash generated	0.7520	7.14	63.761	0.714
	Dispersing risk	0.7070			
	Attaining sustainable profitability and productivity	0.5310			
Making Use of Geographic and Psychic Proximity	Geographic proximity (being able to visit the international operation on the same day)	0.7760	6.44	70.205	0.610
	Cultural proximity (similarities in language, religion, race, sect, customs, etc.)	0.5860			

Varimax rotation with Kaiser normalization was employed and repeated six times; total variance explained 70.21% (KMO: 0.768; Barlett: 0.000).

The eighth factor, *Making Use of Geographic and Psychic Proximity (OFDIM8)*, is related to the marketing aspect of international business. Here observe the importance of cultural proliferation for Turkish EMNCs while marketing in the EU, similar to Factor 2.

Dimensions of subjective degree of internationalization based on manager perceptions

In this section, by questioning companies' levels of internationalization through managers' perceptions (SDoI), Turkish MNCs' subjective degree of internationalization is analyzed. In primary data collection, interviewees can be reluctant in

Table 7.2 Turkish MNCs' (with OFDI into EU countries) subjective degree of internationalization based on managers' perceptions (SDoI)

Factors	Statements	Factor Loadings	% of Variance Expl.	Cum. Exp. Variance	Reliability
Technological Capacity and the Global Branding Efforts	Success in having or attaining technological know-how	0.804	45.558	45.558	0.801
	Success in creating global brands	0.783			
	Success in having pioneering steps in R&D	0.761			
	Assessing company performance on internationalization as a whole	0.751			
	Success in having international patents and trademarks	0.503			
Increased Competitiveness in Local and Global Markets	International firms being successful in their local market first, competing with other MNCs	0.847	12.088	57.646	0.787
	Ability to buy or create new innovation	0.696			
	Success in global trade	0.648			
	Success in design	0.547			
Capacity in International Production and Access to New Sources of Finance	Making production in international markets	0.898	10.005	67.651	0.683
	Success in accessing new sources of finance	0.778			

Varimax rotation with Kaiser normalization was employed and repeated three times; total variance explained 67.651% (KMO: 0.779; Barlett: 0.000).

disclosing objective measures, like company financials. Therefore SDoI was preferred. The factor analysis on SDoI groups statements into three factors, explaining 68 percent of the total variance.

The most critical factor is *Increases in Technological Capacity and Global Branding Efforts (SDoI1)*. Company managers interviewed measure their companies' internationalization through the progress made in technological capacity as well as in building global brands.

In the second grouping, *Increased Competitiveness in Local and Global Markets (SDoI2)*, "international firms being successful in their local market first", "ability to buy or create new innovation," "having success in global trade" and "having success in design" are listed. Overall competitiveness is linked to innovation and design.

The last group is named *Increases in Capacity in International Production and Access to New Sources of Finance (SDoI3)*, stressing companies' ability to produce in international markets and their success in accessing new sources of finance.

Hence we can comment that Turkish managers with OFDI in the EU group into three factors: technology and branding, competitiveness, and production and finances, as their SDoI, of which nearly 46 percent of the variance is explained by technology and branding. Therefore, fixed assets are losing their charm in the eyes of Turkish managers. Instead, they start assigning more value to global brand building activities, know-how, patents and trademarks, thus giving higher priority to intangibles in their companies' internationalization efforts.

Dimensions of company performance

Furthermore for assessing Turkish MNCs' general and marketing PLs, managers' perceptions are grouped by a factor analysis, yielding four factors, explaining 65 percent of the total variance.

The first factor, *Added value to brand asset (PL1)* includes statements like "increase in sales," "increase of brand awareness in global markets," "having positive impact in global competition" and "improving market share," which all point towards having an added brand value.

The second factor is *Added value to expertise and internationalization experience (PL2)*. Turkish MNCs investing in the EU consider "gaining expertise in many different areas," "improved managerial skills," "new international business contacts" and "wide experience in different projects" as important company performance criteria. Furthermore, respondents mention increased profitability as another valid performance criterion. This factor exhibits that companies internationalize through OFDI, acquiring new managerial know-how, gaining expertise and in general learning new skills. When all these factors come together, it becomes easier to collaborate with international partners and take part in international projects.

The third factor is coined *Added value for using technological know-how, technological adaptation and design (PL3)*. Statements such as: "added value through improvements in technological know-how" and "adaptability of new technology"

Table 7.3 Turkish companies' (with OFDI into EU countries) general and marketing-related company performance levels (PLs) as perceived by their managers

Factors	Statements	Factor Loadings	% of Variance Expl.	Cum. Exp. Variance	Reliability
Added value to brand asset	Having a positive impact on sales	0.805	19.628	19.628	0.855
	Increase of brand awareness in global markets	0.749			
	Increase of branding in global markets	0.730			
	Having a positive impact in global competition	0.721			
	Improvement in market share	0.565			
Added value to expertise and internationalization experience	Gained expertise in different areas	0.790	15.482	35.110	0.727
	Having new international business contracts	0.733			
	Acquiring new managerial know-how in international markets	0.605			
	Positive impact on profitability	0.506			
	Making improvements in production process	0.479			
Added value for using technological know-how, technological adaptation and design	Improving technological know-how	0.778	15.298	50.408	0.807
	Increasing adaptability of the newly transferred technology	0.747			
	Increasing product quality and product portfolio	0.483			
	Improving on design	0.475			
Added value to cost effective managerial skills	Easing the application of elastic price strategies	0.868	14.688	65.096	0.742
	Making use of economies of scale	0.734			
	Making use of expertise in marketing management	0.540			

Varimax rotation with Kaiser normalization was employed and repeated seven times; total variance explained 65.096% (KMO: 0.839; Barlett: 0.000).

are mentioned. Furthermore, technology-based added value speeds up a companies' advancement by expanding the product portfolio and leading to competitive design. Turkish managers consider technological know-how and available technology as an important company performance indicator.

Lastly, the fourth factor, *Added value to cost effective managerial skills (PL4)*, indicates that Turkish companies with EU investments try to achieve effective cost management techniques by making use of economies of scale.

In summary, this analysis based on manager perceptions indicates that Turkish managers group MNCs' performance levels into four categories, namely: brand, expertise, technology and cost effectiveness. Here we observe the brand value as the first factor, helping to explain nearly 20 percent of the variance.

Analyzing Turkish MNCs' OFDI motives and managers' perceptions of becoming an international firm and reviewing managers' performance criteria for their own companies, we can state that the highest impact for Turkish MNCs with FDI in the EU are technological advances and branding efforts for their internationalization efforts while assessing company performance.

Interrelationships among motives, internationalization levels and company performance levels

Following factor analysis results, in the next section, the interrelationships among OFDI, SDoI and PL will be investigated by running regression analyses for investigating the causality among these variables.

The relation between factors affecting FDI motives and Turkish MNCs' company performance levels

In the first regression analysis, where OFDI motives taken as the independent variable and the PL factors as dependent variables, a notable relationship is observed. Firstly, the change in the *Added value to brand asset* is explained by 33 percent with the help of OFDI motives. "Having an effective international value chain" (β: .239, p: 2.095) and "increasing the company value" (β: .530, p: 4.510) both have a positive impact on the *Added value to the brand asset*; whereas an increase in "making use of feasible investment opportunities" (β: –.291, p: –2.690) decreases the chance of *Added value to brand asset*.

These results indicate that as Turkish MNCs' assigned levels of importance for having international value chain and increasing company value go up, they also perceive increases in company performance through added value in brand assets. However, creating brands and having added value to brand assets mean increased brand investments. Therefore, further research shows that managers can overlook the *Added value to the brand asset* factor, in favor of other financial investment opportunities when it comes to assessing company performance.

The change in *Added value to expertise and internationalization experience* is explained by 19.6 percent with OFDIM. As importance assigned to "increasing the company value" (β: 0.349, p: 3.366) and "having financial and cost advantage"

Table 7.4 Regression analysis measuring the relation between factors affecting foreign direct investments (OFDIM) and company performance levels (PLs)

MODEL		Turkish EMNCs' General and Marketing Performance Levels (PL1–4) DEPENDENT							
		PL1		PL2		PL3		PL4	
		Standardized beta coef. (sbc)	t	sbc	t	sbc	t	sbc	t
Factors	OFDIM1								
Affecting	OFDIM2								
Outward	OFDIM3	0.239	2.095*			0.276	2.804*	0.473	4.998**
Foreign	OFDIM4					0.302	3.454**		
Direct	OFDIM5	0.530	4.510**	0.349	3.366**	0.534	5.112**		
Investments	OFDIM6			0.265	2.551*			0.298	3.150*
(OFDIM1–8)	OFDIM7	−0.291	−2.690*			−0.444	−4.690**		
	OFDIM8								
	Adjusted R^2	33.20%		19.60%		52.40%		33.20%	
	F	13.738		10.254		21.648		19.895	
	Sign. Level	0.000		0.000		0.000		0.000	

* Significant at 95% confidence level ($p<0.05$)
** Significant at 99% confidence level ($p<0.01$)

(β: 0.265, p: 2.551) increases, managers' perception on *Added value to expertise and internationalization experience* also go up. These results may indicate that as companies get financially stronger, they feel that companies' general and marketing performance levels also increase.

Thirdly, the change in *Added value for using technological know-how, technological adaptation and design* is explained by 52 percent of OFDIM. There is a direct relationship with "having an effective international value chain" (β: 0.276, p: 2.804), "making use of less risky markets" (β: 0.302, p: 3.454), "increasing the company value" (β: 0.534, p: 5.112) and the *Added value for using technological know-how, technological adaptation and design*. However, as importance assigned to "making use of feasible investment opportunities" increases, the perceived performance level on technological know-how and design drops (β: –0.444, p: –4.690). It is worth noting that "Technological know-how" has the highest value in explaining Turkish companies' OFDI motives. Although this finding gives support that EMNCs have OFDI mainly to have access to technology-driven assets to accelerate their internationalization efforts, it also stresses a contradiction. Turkish MNCs which are more likely to make use of technological know-how and design assign more importance to international value chains, making use of less risky markets and hence increasing the company value. However, being a technology-driven company is at the same time a costly thing. When managers start assessing company performance, technology and branding may lose their initial importance.

Finally the change in *Added value to cost effective managerial skills* is explained by 33 percent of OFDIM. As importance assigned to "having an effective international value chain" (β: 0.473, p: 4.998) and "having financial and cost advantage" (β: 0.298, p: 3.150) goes up, the perceived value of cost effective managerial skills also increases.

Our findings indicate that Turkish managers that assign higher importance levels to having effective international value chain in the EU, increasing company value and making use of feasible investments exhibit higher PLs in international markets.

The relation between factors affecting FDI motives and Turkish MNCs' subjective degree of internationalization

Similarly OFDIM is taken as independent and SDoI as a dependent variable for this regression. The change in the first (SDoI) factor – *technological capacity and global branding efforts* – is explained by 20.0 percent with the help of OFDIM. As importance assigned to "increasing company value" (β: 0.352, p: 3.731) and "making use of less risky markets" (β: 0.214, p: 2.269) increases, the subjective internationalization measure of *technological capacity and global branding efforts* also goes up. In other words, managers consider technological capacity and global branding efforts as major internationalization dimensions. In their view, as the company value goes up and they operate in less risky markets, the technological capacity of a company also expands.

Table 7.5 Regression analysis measuring the relation between factors affecting foreign direct investments (OFDI) and subjective degree of internationalization (SDoI)

MODEL	Turkish EMNCs' Subjective Degree of Internationalization Perception (SDoI1–3) DEPENDENT					
		SDoI1		SDoI2		SDoI3
		Standardized beta coef. (sbc)	t	sbc	t	sbc	t
	OFIMF3			0.445	4.924*		
(OFDIM)	OFDIM5	0.352	3.731*				
	OFDIM4	0.214	2.269**			0.253	2.586**
	Adjusted R^2	20.00%		19.00%		25.30%	
	F	13.53		24.24		6.69	
	Sign. Level	0.000		0.000		0.011	

* Significant at 95% confidence level ($p<0.05$)
** Significant at 99% confidence level ($p<0.01$)

The change in *increased competitiveness in local and global markets* is explained by 19 percent with the help of only "having an effective international value chain" (β: 0.445, p: 4.924). Managers single out having an effective international value chain as the most critical factor for being more competitive both in local and global markets.

Finally the change in *capacity in international production and access to new sources of finance* is explained by 25 percent with "making use of less risky markets" (β: 0.253, p: 2.586) as an OFDI motive. Managers probably consider international production capacity and having access to new sources of finance as important dimensions of internationalization and that their internationalization perception increases if they operate in less risky markets.

The relation between subjective degree of internationalization and Turkish MNCs' perceived company performance levels

Lastly we analyze the relationship between the SDoI as the independent and the perceived company PL as the dependent variable. The change in *added value to brand asset* as a performance criterion is explained by 13 percent with SDoI, by "increased competitiveness in local and global markets" (β: 0.374, p: 3.974). Managers believe that as their company's competitiveness increases in both local and global markets, their brand asset value also increases.

The change in *Added value to expertise and internationalization experience* is explained by 20 percent with SDoI, by "increased competitiveness in local and global markets" (β: 0.200, p: 2.02) and "capacity in international production and

Table 7.6 Regression analysis measuring the relation between subjective degree of internationalization (SDoI) and company performance levels (PLs)

MODEL		Turkish EMNCs' General and Marketing Performance Levels (PL1–4) DEPENDENT							
		PL1		PL2		PL3		PL4	
		Standardized beta coef. (sbc)	t	sbc	t	sbc	t	sbc	t
Turkish EMNCs' Subjective Degree of Internationalization Perception (SDoI1–3)	SDoI1								
	SDoI2	0.374	3.974*	0.200	2.02**	0.237	2.214**		
	SDoI3			0.346	3.501*	0.321	3.002*	0.369	3.905*
	Adjusted R^2	13.10%		20.00%		24.30%		12.70%	
	F	15.80		13.22		15.27		15.45	
	Sign. Level	0.000		0.000		0.000		0.000	

* Significant at 95% confidence level ($p<0.05$)
** Significant at 99% confidence level ($p<0.01$)

access to new sources of finance" (β: 0.346, p: 3.501). Managers think, as importance assigned to global competitiveness and access to new production capacity and finances increases, the company performs better.

Furthermore, the change in *Added value for using technological know-how, technological adaptation and design* is explained by 24.30 percent with "technological capacity and the global branding efforts" (β: 0.237, p: 2.214) and "increased competitiveness in markets" (β: 0.321, p: 3.002). Once again we observe technological capacity, global branding and competitiveness having a positive effect on the companies' technology and design advancement levels.

Finally, the change in *Added value to cost effective managerial skills* is explained by 12.70 percent by SDoI factor of "capacity in international production and access to new sources of finance" (β: 0.369, p: 3.905). Overall we can say that Turkish managers assess their MNCs' general and marketing PLs mainly with the help of increased global competitiveness. As their companies' competitiveness becomes more pronounced, they perceive their MNCs to be performing better in all aspects of the discipline.

Conclusion and discussion

Our research identifies marketing and branding reasons as the most imperative motives that lead Turkish MNCS to engage in FDI in the EU, leaving financial reasons lower on the list. Similarly, when Turkish managers' perception of internationalization and general company and marketing performance criteria are questioned, once again technological capacity and global branding efforts surface as valid measures. In other words technological advancement and added brand value are considered imperative for Turkish MNCs' internationalization efforts as well as exhibiting a better company performance. Pananond (2013), studying international expansion of a Taiwanese MNE, supports our findings by indicating that international investments help firms in gaining competitive positions globally, via improving technological knowledge and having higher value added positions within the global chain. Similarly, Lau et al. (2010) stress that MNCs focusing only on OFDI may have competencies in finance and management capability in operations and can access technology-based resources from developed markets. These could be early signs that fixed assets are losing their charm in the eyes of Turkish managers; instead they start prioritizing intangible assets such as branding, know-how, patents and trademarks as important tools for their companies' degree of internationalization. Results indicate that Turkish MNCs investing in the EU mainly employ an asset-seeking approach. As Wang and Suh (2009) put it, firms using an asset-seeking approach try to maximize the value-creation opportunities by gaining new resources and building new knowledge to enhance firms' current resource base. Although it is frequently cited that there are not enough Turkish brands that have become global, we observe higher importance levels being assigned to branding 2010 onwards by Turkish MNCs, employing an asset-seeking approach while investing in the EU. This could be considered a good sign for Turkish brands aspiring to become global.

However, when OFDI motives, subjective internationalization and company measures are investigated further with the help of a series of regression analyses, we note a shift from marketing towards financial criteria. For instance, Turkish managers think that having an international value chain in the EU, increasing company value and making use of feasible investments generate higher performance levels in international markets.

Furthermore, Turkish MNCs' internationalization perception increases if they operate in less risky markets. Other researchers report different sector and country EMNCs yielding different results. For instance De Beule and Duanmu (2012), analyzing Chinese and Indian M&As from mining and high tech, conclude that Chinese and Indian corporations invest more for natural resources in high-risk countries, eliminating competition from developed countries. Similarly Maponga and Maxwell (2000), studying the Australian mineral industry, group "junior" companies as greater risk takers seeking higher returns and making them more competitive internationally.

Overall we can say that Turkish managers asesss their MNCs' general and marketing performance levels mainly with the help of increased global competitiveness. Managers consider international production capacity and having access to new sources of finance as important measures of internationalization, once again highlighting financials over branding. Therefore, when OFDI motives are questioned solely, intangible assets are cited by managers as their reason for OFDI. However, when companies' performance levels and internationalization degrees are questioned, managers convert to financial measures. As Deng (2012) points out, EMNCs enter developed countries to have new resources and capabilities. This dual international expansion strategy is said to make EMNCs compete more effectively against global rivals. Deng (2012), mentioning Turkish Sabancı Holding, expanding both organically and through acquisitions in developed and emerging economies, calls it "investing everywhere simultaneously." Hence, we can suggest that the next step for Turkish managers could be building a possible bridge between intangibles and tangibles while evaluating company performance levels and internationalization degrees and follow a different route, as Wang and Suh (2009) point out for East Asian MNEs. As one final word, it's worth quoting Parente et al. (2013): "emerging market internationalization appears to occur as a reaction to unique opportunities."

Notes

1   This chapter uses data, collected for the research project, funded by the Turkish Scientific and Technological Research Council as part of COST Action IS0905 (TUBITAK Project No:110K018; Uray, N., Vardar, N., Nacar, R., Kaplan, B., September 2012). Special thanks to Prof. Dr. Uray for conducting regression analyses included in this chapter.
2   Nükhet Vardar, El Izi Communications Consultancy, Istanbul, Turkey (Prof. Dr.)

References

Amighini, A., Rabellotti, R., and Sanfilippo, M. (2010) 'Outward FDI from developing country MNEs as a channel for technological catch-up', *Seoul Journal of Economics*, 23, 2: 239–261.

Bonaglia, F., Goldstein, A., and Mathews, J. (2007) 'Accelerated internationalisation by emerging multinationals: The case of the white goods sector', *Journal of World Business*, 42, 4: 369–383.

Cyrino, A. B., Barcellos, E. P., and Tanure, B. (2010) 'International trajectories of Brazilian companies: Empirical contribution to the debate on the importance of distance', *International Journal of Emerging Markets*, 5, 3/4: 358–376.

De Beule, F., and Duanmu, J.-L. (2012) 'Locational determinants of internationalization: A firm-level analysis of Chinese and Indian acquisitions', *European Management Journal*, 30: 264–277.

Demirbag, M., and Tatoglu, E. (2008) 'Competitive strategy choices of Turkish manufacturing firms in European Union', *Journal of Management Development*, 27, 7: 727–743.

Deng, P. (2003) 'Foreign investment by multinationals from emerging countries: The case of China', *Journal of Leadership and Organizational Studies*, 10, 2: 113–124.

–––– (2007) 'Investing for strategic resources and its rationale: The case of outward FDI from Chinese companies', *Business Horizons*, 50: 71–81.

–––– (2012) 'Accelerated internationalization of MNCs from emerging economies: Determinants and implications', *Organizational Dynamics*, 41, 4: 318–326.

Dunning, J. H. (1981) 'Explaining the international direct investment position of countries: Towards a dynamic or developmental approach', *Review of World Economics*, 117, 1: 30–64.

––––––– (1988) 'The eclectic paradigm of international production: A restatement and some possible extensions', *Journal of International Business Studies*, 26, 3: 461–491.

Erdal, F., and Tatoglu, E. (2002) 'Locational determinants of FDI in an emerging market economy: Evidence from Turkey', *Multinational Business Review*, 10, 1: 7–21.

Erdilek, A. (2003) 'A comparative analysis of inward and outward FDI in Turkey', *Transnational Corporations*, December, 12, 3: 79–105.

––––––– (2005) 'Historical background of foreign direct investment in Turkey', paper presented at the YASED Conference on the New Favorite Destination for Foreign Direct Investments: Turkey Where the Opportunities Abound, Istanbul, Turkey, November 8–9, 2005.

Eren-Erdogmus, I.,Cobanoglu, E., Yalcin, M., and Ghauri, P. N. (2010) 'Internationalization of emerging market firms: The case of Turkish retailers', *International Marketing Review*, 27, 3: 316–337.

Gammeltoft, P., Pradhan, J. P., and Goldstein, A. (2010) 'Emerging multinationals: Home and host country determinants and outcomes', *International Journal of Emerging Markets*, 5, 3/4: 254–265.

Goldstein, A., and Pusterla, F. (2010) 'Emerging economies' multinationals: General features and specificities of the Brazilian and Chinese cases', *International Journal of Emerging Markets*, 5, 3/4: 289–306.

Kalotay, K., and Sulstarova, A. (2010) 'Modelling Russian outward FDI', *Journal of International Management*, 16, 2: 131–42.

Kaya, H., and Erden, D. (2008) 'Firm-specific capabilities and FDI activities of Turkish manufacturing firms', *Journal of Management Development*, 27, 7: 761–777.

Khavul, S., Pérez-Nordtvedt, L., and Wood, L. (2010) 'Organizational entrainment and international new ventures from emerging markets', *Journal of Business Venturing*, 25: 104–119.

Kwon, Y.-C. (2010) 'Market orientation of Korean MNC subsidiaries and their performance in the Chinese and Indian markets', *International Marketing Review*, 27, 2: 179–199.

Lau, C.-M., Ngo, H.-Y., and Yiu, D. W. (2010) 'Internationalization and organizational resources of Chinese firms', *Chinese Management Studies*, 4, 3: 258–272.

Maponga, O., and Maxwell, P. (2000) 'The internationalization of the Australian mineral industry in the 1990s', *Resources Policy*, 26, 4: 199–210.

Pananond, P. (2013) 'Where do we go from here?: Globalizing subsidiaries moving up the value chain', *Journal of International Management*, 19: 207–219.

Parente, R. C., Alvaro, B.C., Nicole S., and Flavio, C. V. (2013) 'Lessons learned from Brazilian multinationals' internationalization strategies', *Business Horizons*, 56, 4: 453–463.

Rasiah, R., Gammeltoft, P., and Jiang, Y. (2010) 'Home government policies for outward FDI from emerging economies: Lessons from Asia', *International Journal of Emerging Markets*, 5, 3/4: 333–357.

Rios-Morales, R., and Brennan, L. (2010),'The emergence of Chinese investment in Europe', *Euromed Journal of Business*, 5, 2: 215–231.

Schüler-Zhou, Y., and Schüller, M. (2009)''The internationalization of Chinese companies what do official statistics tell us about Chinese OFDI?', *Chinese Management Studies*, 3, 1: 25–42.

Uray, N., Vardar, N., and Nacar, R. (2012) 'International marketing related outward FDI motives: Turkish MNCs' experience in the EU', in R. V. Tulder, A. Verbeke and L. Voinea (eds) *Progress in international business research: New policy challenges for European multinationals (7),* Bingley, UK: Emerald Group Publishing Limited, pp. 305–338.

Vardar, N., Uray, N., Nacar, R., and Aktan, C. (2011) 'Turkish companies with OFDI in the EU: An international business and marketing view', paper presented at the COST IS0905 Project, Working Group Meeting, Koc University, Istanbul, Turkey, May, 24–25, 2011.

Wang, Y., and Suh, C.-S. (2009) 'Towards a re-conceptualization of firm internationalization: Heterogeneous process, subsidiary roles and knowledge flow', *Journal of International Management,* 15: 447–459.

Part IV

Country-specific EMCs in Europe

8 Chinese investors in Europe

Some idiosyncrasies

Françoise Hay[1]

Introduction

Chinese investments in Europe became significant at the beginning of the millennium,[2] attracted by its top technologies, mature market, and relative openness. Chinese investors often bypassed the classical steps of internationalization while carrying out their first investments abroad in remote countries, far from the "Uppsala model" supposing FDI managed progressively and cautiously, first in neighbouring countries with low psychic distance. Their expansion in Europe has still been reinforced in the wake of the global financial crisis of 2008 and the eurozone debt crisis of 2011.

This paper, intentionally empirical, aims to put forward the idiosyncrasies of Chinese investors and strategies.

It relies on a proprietary database compiling qualitative and quantitative information on Chinese investors (mainland and Hong Kong) in Europe (Russia excluded) coming from various sources (Thomson Reuters, FdI Market, the economics press, and face-to-face interviews): 1,683 Chinese investments (greenfield, mergers and acquisitions, joint ventures, and extensions) have been listed during the period 2000–2012.

Who are Chinese investors in Europe?

The ownership structure of Hong Kong and of mainland investors is very different for historical reasons: while the former are all private, the latter are often under the control of the central government or local authorities to various degrees. However, their logics of investment abroad tend to converge gradually.

Hong Kong firms were the first to cross the stage of overseas investments in the 1990s, due to their more advanced development. They started to invest in mainland China[3] before going into Europe and the United States. They are all private companies, often of family origin and created in the time of the British empire. Their operation modes are very close to those of the multinationals from the industrialized countries.[4]

Chinese investors from the mainland are much more diversified, with an ownership not always disclosed and often combining a mix of public and private capital and management, this with different variants.

SOEs (state owned enterprises), public enterprises, and their subsidiaries are the main investors in Europe. They are run by SASAC,[5] by financial institutions, by ministries, by provincial or municipal governments, or collectively (such as township and village enterprises in rural areas). Some of them are publicly listed and include private funds.

Their FDI is generally in line with the national and sectorial priorities and with the comparative advantages of China and of the host countries. With the passing years, their capacity to invest abroad has been boosted, all together, by technical capacities acquired through inward FDI, by the fact that they often operated in protected sectors (telecommunications, finance, energy), by low taxations, and by substantial financial resources and supports of the Chinese state.

Private Chinese investors abroad are more and more numerous. They include start-ups as well as large conglomerates. Some of them have public stakes in their capital or include a "red-cap" (township enterprises) and benefit from tax relief or political protection.

Generally speaking, the symbiosis between politics and business is very important in China due to the proximity of managers with "official" *guanxi* (local authorities, administrative, financial, and political institutions) and to the presence of members of the Communist party on the Boards of Directors. In addition, their investments abroad have to meet national priorities and regulations and get financing from the state banks and the policy banks.

Breakdown of host European countries for Chinese investment

Chinese investments in Europe focus mainly on the most industrialized countries and those with the most important populations. Western European countries welcome more than 80 percent of them.

Three countries are, by far, the largest destinations of Chinese investors in Europe: France, United Kingdom, and Germany; they include 57 percent of the investments. Although the destination countries became more diversified after the global financial crisis, the attractiveness of this top trio has increased, due to the importance of their domestic markets, and to new opportunities for acquisition of local firms encountering difficulties and cash-flow problems.

From 2002 to 2012, France was the first destination of Chinese investors attracted by its relative advantages in technology (telecommunications, engineering), equipment, fashion industry, services, agriculture, as well as by its geographical position, its culture, and its "way of life". Recently, also, many purchases in agribusiness (vineyards) were observed. Around 39 percent of these investments concern production and R&D activities.

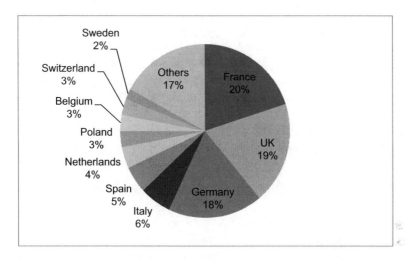

Figure 8.1 Main destinations, 2000–2012 (number of investments)
Source: Author's calculations

The United Kingdom was traditionally the most attractive European country for Chinese investors, given its historical links with Hong Kong, its openness, and the strength of its financial sector. However, since the crisis, Chinese investments have increased less quickly than in other European countries, but they often include transactions implying large amounts. Chinese activities in the United Kingdom are much diversified, with, since 2009, a new place held by the investments in public utilities, property and infrastructure, finance, and ICT.

The attractiveness of Germany for the Chinese firms has regularly increased since 2000, with a new impetus since the global crisis and the euro debt crisis. This is in line with its large industrial sector, the strength of its economy, its central position in the EU, and good diplomatic relations with China. The equipment sector is the most concerned with many purchases in the machinery sector. Investments in the automotive industry and ICT are also important and on the rise. Manufacturing and R&D are important activities (around 38 percent of the investments).

Central and eastern Europe is the destination of around 9.5 percent of Chinese investments in Europe while it combines high growth rates, low production costs, a direct access to the EU market, and many bilateral cooperation agreements. Poland comes first as host country, followed by Romania, Hungary, the Czech Republic, and Bulgaria. These investments offer a safe route for Chinese exports when located on a coastline.

Chinese investments in eastern Europe have increased and diversified since the crisis. Apart from the investments in the transport activities (generally made before

2009), they principally concern equipment, the automobile and telecom sectors, home appliances, and chemistry. For example, Haier has a factory (refrigerator) in Poland since 2003, another one with Fagor (2013), and a TV sets factory with Wistron (2013).

Manufacturing activities are prominent (60 percent of Chinese investments since 2009) and include the largest share observed in the considered European areas. That is explained by attractive labor costs, less strict regulations than in western Europe (visas), and the opportunity to use the label "made in Europe", which is important to European customers and to weaken protectionist resentments.

Breakdown of the modes of entry and of the functions

Modes of entry

Since the beginning of the millennium, Chinese investors in Europe rather favored greenfield activities (58 percent of the cases), whereas investors from Hong Kong rather focused on acquisitions and joint ventures. Indeed, up to 2005–2006, many firms from the mainland were newcomers in the field of FDI and favored the less risky forms of entry and those requiring lower amounts of investment. However, the whole picture could change in the coming years with an expected rise of Chinese acquisitions in Europe.

Since the financial crisis and the euro debt crisis, Chinese purchases are on the rise, in line with more mature and experienced investors and new opportunities for acquisitions. Also, Chinese investors increasingly aspire to be "kind" or patient shareholders, in that they do not necessarily want to win the control of the companies they buy out.

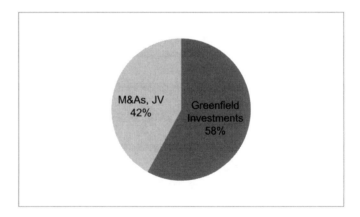

Figure 8.2 Modes of entry of Chinese investors in Europe, 2000–2012 (number of investments)

Source: Author's calculations

Box 1   Largest Chinese purchases in Europe characterized by large committed amounts

- Wanhua Industrial → BorsodChem, Hungary, $1.7bn
- ChemChina/BlueStar → Orkla Elkem, Norway, $2.2bn
- Sinopec → Talisman Energy UK, $1.5bn
- Sany Heavy → Putzmeister, Germany, €500mn
- Lenovo → 60% Medion, Germany, $800mn
- Hutchison Telecom → Orang, Austria, $1.3bn
- Brighfood → 60% Weetabix, United Kingdom, $1.1bn
- Lenovo → Medion, Germany, consumer electronics, $671mn

Source: Author's calculations

Box 2   Some Chinese purchases in Europe in utilities

- China Three Gorge → 21% EDP Energias (Portugal, $3.5bn)
- State grid → 40% REN (Portugal, $775mn)
- CIC → 30% GDF Suez (France, $3.2bn)
  - → 8.7% Thames Water (United Kingdom)
- Cheung Kong Infrastructure
  - → 40% Northumbian Water, United Kingdom, $3.5bn
  - → 40% UK Power Networks – EDF energy
  - → 47% Northern Gas Networks Limited
- CIC → Heathrow Airport (United Kingdom, $700mn)

Source: Author's calculations

Functions

The functions performed by Chinese investors in Europe are rather well balanced between the activities of production/R&D, services, and sales.

Investments in production and research activities are the most numerous. They largely increased since the crisis, in the wake of new purchases in western Europe, and of new greenfield investments in eastern Europe. Local production can help to ensure an investor's acceptance.

These investments are mainly related to activities of equipment (18 percent), automobile and other transport equipment (18 percent), agribusiness (9 percent), and textile-fashion (7 percent).

In eastern Europe, the share of production activities is particularly important and mostly includes greenfield investments.

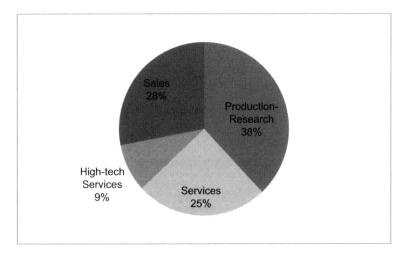

Figure 8.3 Functions performed by Chinese investors in Europe, 2000–2012 (number of
investments)

Source: Author's calculations

Investments in Services mainly concern activities of transport-logistic (35.5 percent) generally made before the crisis and activities of telecommunications,
finance, and new technologies made after 2008.

Investments in Sales activities are on the rise. They are intended to serve the
European market and specially concern equipment (47.6 percent, with many
greenfield investments in renewable energies since 2008) and textile-fashion
(21 percent).

Breakdown of activities

The sectors targeted by Chinese firms in Europe have evolved over time, with
some changes of nature and content (quality, technology, expertise) since the
global crisis of 2008.

Equipment investments are, by far, the most numerous, in line with the Chinese
priorities of growth since the beginning of the millennium, and the imperative to
develop domestic competencies. Germany, France, United Kingdom, and Italy
are the main destinations. They include significant purchases, such as those by
TCL (Thomson TV, Schneider T, Alcatel Telephone), by Dalian (Zimmerman,
Rema), by Hisun (Grosse Textile), and by Shenyang Machines (Schiess), as well
as some emblematic greenfield investments in production activities (Hisense,
Haitian). Since the crisis, new sectors of activities have emerged, such as medical
equipment (Mindray), precision equipment (Chongqing Machinery, Chunghong
Electronics), and new energies equipment (Suntech, LDK, Trina Solar, Yingli,
Sinovel Goldwind).

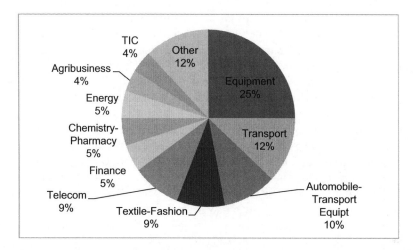

Figure 8.4 Breakdown of Chinese activities, 2002–2012 (number of investments)
Source: Author's calculations

Chinese investments in transport-logistics have been mainly made between 2000 and 2008 to accompany exports and to assert the Chinese presence in Europe. They mostly concerned shipping activities and ports by firms from the mainland and Hong Kong (COSC, China Shipping, China International Marine Container, Hutchison Port, OOCL).

The activities of fashion-textiles have been quite significant between 2000 and 2008, in phase with the top spot of Chinese textile production. Purchases of famous European brands have been made such as Guy Laroche, Marionnaud, Kruidvat, and Ici Paris, by AS Watson, Sorotex, and Aquascutum by YGM, while Esprit created many stores in the largest cities of Europe.

The decline of this activity since 2008 has been in some respects offset by new investments intended for making high-end products.

France is the first host country of these investments (40 percent), followed by the United Kingdom (17 percent), Germany (13 percent), and Italy (7 percent).

We can mention the case of Li & Fung, traditionally known as a textile subcontractor, which has made a lot of purchases of famous firms and upmarket textile brands since 2008 (Hardy Amies, Kent & Curven, Visage, Cerruti, Sonia Rykel in France) and created several stores with its own brands in Europe (LF Beauty).

Most of Chinese investments in telecom in Europe have been made by Huawei and ZTE since 2002, mainly through greenfield operations. Since 2009, new telephony actors are also present such as China Unicom, China Telecom, China Mobile, and Hutchison Telecom.

These investments include several creations of R&D centers intended to get new competencies and a privileged position in the European market (United Kingdom, France, and Germany).

Chinese investments in the automotive industry became significant in Europe from 2004; they were principally made in United Kingdom, France, Italy, and Germany. They often implied purchases such as Saia Burgess, Roegelheim, Gate, by Johnson Electric, MG Rover by Nanjing Automobile, Fuyao Glass by Wanxiang. Deutz, Kion, Beaudoin and Ferretti by Weichai, Volvo by Geely, etc.

Some firms also started to create production activities in Europe (Greatwall and BYD in Bulgaria, BAIC in Italy, and Beiqi Foton in Germany).

Chinese investments in finance gained a new dimension after the crisis (Bank of China, ICBC, Eximbank) with new subsidiaries and offices to support investments already made or to be made in Europe. The United Kingdom received 23 percent of these investments, France and Germany 11 percent each.

Chinese investments in public utilities, energy, and infrastructure appeared in the 2010s, boosted by the debt crisis in Europe and the following problems (weak and cash-strapped states). Although they generally included minority shares, they often implied large amounts of money. They have mainly been made in the United Kingdom, Greece, Portugal, Spain, and CEE.

Breakdown of the motives of Chinese firms when they invest in Europe

The motives of Chinese firms investing in Europe since 2000 are many, depending on their growth process, on their advantages, on their activity, and on the considered period.

Theoretical background on the specific advantages of Chinese investors

Chinese firms have taken advantage of the support of their state and of the globalization process to parlay their country-specific advantages and transform them into firm-specific advantages; that allowed them to become a potent force in global competition with surprising speed, despite being latecomers (Zeng and Williamson 2009).

Since the OLI eclectic paradigm (Dunning 1979), it is proved that the possession of a specific Ownership advantage is one of the three conditions needed to be met by a firm before it invests abroad (together with a Location advantage of the recipient country, and an Internalization advantage). Most of the earliest theories related to the emerging investors validate this approach but complement it as the very nature of their specific advantages are often different from those of investors from industrialized countries. While the latter generally possess endogenous advantages (mainly coming from the possession of proper technologies or brands) before investing abroad and extend their specific assets, most of the emerging multinationals invested in industrialized countries precisely to acquire or augment their own assets.

Indeed, many Chinese investors abroad have gained and shaped their specific advantages in an "exogenous" way, while learning from FDI and outsourcing and benefiting from the enabling environment of globalization, with, among others, to cite Zeng and Williamson (2009): an increasing "modularization of products and services", the advent of the "global knowledge" economy, "a more fluid international market for talent and professional services", and "a more open market for corporate control". In addition, many emerging investors – such as those from China – have taken advantage of the very specificities of their home countries: low production costs, rapid growth, large domestic market, and the capacity of their states to stimulate growth and technology transfers through FDI from 1990 and, finally, to create, at the macro level, competitive advantages their firms could capitalize at the micro level (Porter 1990).

The "Linkage, Leverage, and Learning" (LLL) framework stressed by Matthews (2006), which is especially relevant to explain Chinese FDI, emphasizes the potential advantage of a country or a firm arriving late on the industrial scene, insofar as it is able to directly access advanced technologies and use them faster and at lower cost than the very firms that created them. Linkage with foreign firms (partnerships) gives to latecomers the opportunity to acquire knowledge and market access, and hence to compensate for their own limited resources (Leverage); repeated over and over again, these sequences of linkage and leverage really enhanced their capabilities (Learning). Such an evolution, combined with a strong support of the Chinese state to optimize the advantages of its firms (infrastructures) and facilitate their internationalization (Go abroad Policy, access to WTO) and, on the other hand, with the great ability of the latter to innovate and to move up from imitation to innovation (Zeng and Williamson 2007; Hay and Milelli 2013)[6] and build a new business model (cost innovations) really allowed Chinese firms to rapidly catch up with the advanced firms. Then, they could rapidly afford to go further and invest abroad and even, sometimes, to acquire former partners or outsourcers.

Motives that accompany Chinese investments in Europe are not static; they have largely evolved since the beginning of the millennium as to their very contents and targets, in line with the rapid evolution of Chinese, European, and international contexts. Anyway, the global crisis was a turning point in the observed strategies, so, we have highlighted two major periods to analyze: before and after 2009.

Main motives before 2009

Before 2009, Chinese investments in Europe were mainly stimulated by two motives: market seeking and strategic asset seeking. Back then, investors wanted to assert themselves at the international level, to gain recognition, and to serve new and demanding consumers. Most importantly, they wanted to strengthen their position in the long term, to gain competitive advantage (Deng 2009), to close their technology gap with Western companies, and to get basic technologies they didn't have in China. Certainly, they had previously benefited from many technology transfers through FDI, but they wanted more. They more especially researched know-how, expertise, and quality standards they did not have, as well as proprietary technologies, brands, patents, and niches, principally in activities highly promising in China.

Main motives since 2009

The global financial crisis of 2009 profoundly changed the context of Chinese investments with weakened European countries and companies (sluggish markets, shortages of capital), and, on the other hand, China and Chinese firms strengthened (increasing share in global GDP, mature companies taking advantage of new opportunities of purchases).

In 2009–2010, the quest for strategic assets (advanced technologies and technologically complex segments) was, by far, the first motive of Chinese investors in Europe (Hay and Milelli 2013). Their goal was no more a technological catch-up, but an imperious need to change their brand image and to do away with the traditionally poor-quality picture of their products and their "world factory" status. They aspired to go up in range, to produce high-quality products, and, more and more, to compete with the incumbent multinationals on their domestic market in high-growth sectors, and to obtain more added values.

Investments in equipment and automobiles remained prominent, in line with their boom in China, while new activities appeared such as IT, renewable energy, and finance (first investments of the Chinese sovereign fund).

Since 2011, a relative normalization of Chinese investments in Europe has been observed, inasmuch as they become an "everyday phenomenon". They are boosted by domestic demand, by powerful firms, by the yuan's appreciation, by rising wage costs, and by some domestic overcapacities as well as by new opportunities for takeovers in Europe.

In parallel, the investment patterns of Chinese investors evolve: they are purposeful and combine all the classical FDI motives, with strategies converging towards those of incumbent multinationals. They always research in Europe new markets and strategic assets, but they look also for a new notoriety of their brands at the world level. Indeed, many of them hold valuable technologies and even start to bring into Europe effective technologies improving the productive processes (with lower production costs, for example).

Some investors research industrial resources (purchases of Talisman Energy by Sinopec and of Ineos by Petrochina) and agricultural resources (dairies and vineyards).

Also, what is new and mirrors the normalization of Chinese investors is, henceforth, their quest for efficiency (high margins, profits, scale economies) when they invest abroad. This is finally a logic evolution in line with the two-stages theory implying an "experience phase" before a "get the profits stage" often observed for newcomer investors (Bin and Tao 1997).

The fate of Chinese investments made in Europe

What have become of the investments made by the Chinese investors in Europe with the passing years? The decade's hindsight we now have allows us to identify some trends and to establish an indicative assessment of their fate.

Nevertheless, the success or not of any investment is quite difficult to assess. Indeed, it is likely to be valued differently according to the viewpoint of the analysts (Chinese or European) and the period.

By way of example, at first, we looked at some cases implying research activities which include in most of the cases highly qualified workers and strategic assets. We observed that all the R&D centers created in Europe by Chinese firms since 2002 have generally been successful and developed over the years. This is the case, for instance, for the R&D centers of Huawei (United Kingdom, France, Germany, Italy, Netherlands, Sweden), of ZTE (France, Sweden, Germany), of Haier (Italy, Netherlands, Germany, Denmark), of Hisun (Germany), of Sany Heavy (Germany), of China Dragon and State Grid (Sweden), of Changan (United Kingdom), of Chinamex (United Kingdom), of Beijing Automotive (Italy), and of Jac Anhui (Italy).

Such successes are often explained by relevant location choices made by Chinese investors in order to optimize the use of competencies (very qualified workers) in specific and specialized areas. So, in Sweden, Huawei and ZTE invested close to Ericsson headquarters, Jac Anhui and Changan invested in Italy in a Fiat stronghold, Beijing ROSE invested in Germany in the Höchst pharmaceutical industrial park, Chinamex invested in United Kingdom in an illustrious heart for the traditional textile industry, etc.

Second, if we analyze the fate of Chinese acquisitions implying production and R&D activities, several scenarios can be observed, from total success to complete failure. However, many acquisitions are successful in mid-term due to support from the Chinese public authorities and large national banks, to their large domestic market (scale economies), and to relocations of low-end items. Here are some scenarios (not exhaustive).

The activity of the purchased firm is maintained and possibly extended

This frequent case generally prevails when the purchased firms have brands and niches with great potential.

Box 3 Chinese successful purchases in Europe (extensions, new factories)

- Rhodia Silicone-Bluestar by China Bluestar
- Adisseo and Fibers Worldwide (United Kingdom) by China Bluestar
- Most of the purchases made in Germany in machinery such as Schiess (by Shenyang Machine), or Lutz (by Zhongqiang)
- Dynex by Zhuzhou CSR
- Volvo (Sweden) and LTC (London Taxi Company), bought by Geely; MG Rover by SAIC
- Port of Piraeus by COSCO

Source: Database of the author

Some interviewed Chinese investors noticed that although the fact of maintaining production in Europe generally implies higher costs for them, this also involves, in return, higher value added and higher margins.

In general, at the beginning, success is not a given because the purchased firms are weakened, while Chinese managers have to deal with a new environment, a new language, others' policies and regulations and have to honor previous debts and preserve jobs. However, their activity in China is generally boosted thanks to their appropriation of new technologies and niches. Their investments are particularly optimized when the European production activities are "copied and pasted" in China, i.e. same equipment, same technologies, and same organization.

Variants between activities maintained as such in Europe and activities that are given up

High-end production and R&D activities are maintained in Europe and low-end production is relocated in China on grounds of lower costs (consolidation-restructuration). This variant can be combined with the previous scenario along with new spatial specializations. It has often been observed in equipment activities.

The production activities are relocated in China but the R&D is maintained in Europe. This scenario can seem strange inasmuch as production and R&D activities often support each other. However, it mirrors the imperative need, for Chinese investors, to pick up strategic assets in Europe (high-level skills, quality). This option is combined with the use of low production costs in China.

Such an attitude mainly occurred at the beginning of the millennium (purchases of Grosse Textile by Hisun or of Terraillon by Fook Tin).

Some activities are abandoned in Europe as part of restructuring and streamlining inside Europe or between Europe and China. So, Johnson Electric has closed some factories following the restructuring of units following its purchases of Saia Burgess, Gate, Roegelheim, and Cetronic.

The purchased activities disappear in Europe for a while before restarting some years later. The idea is to reassure consumers and for notoriety. For instance, following the purchase of MG Rover (UK) by Nanjing automotive in 2005, production was first relocated to China before resuming one year later in Longbridge. Another example relates to the resumption of the construction of Saab automobiles in Sweden to make electric cars.

The purchased activities disappear in Europe

In this case, the purchased activities are generally relocated to China, while the European factories are closed. Chinese investors only pick up licenses, technologies, and brands, and then use the comparative advantages of China with regard to production (failure of the purchase of Goss international by Shanghai Electric).

However, the scenario is sometimes more subtle. Indeed, the factory of Thomson TV was closed two years after its acquisition by TCL and was considered as an absolute failure. However, today (ten years after), TCL uses the recognizable brand Thomson to sell mid-range TV sets in Europe and to gain a footing in this highly competitive market. The scenario is similar for Alcatel Mobile, which was also acquired by TCL.

Variant: Sometimes, a minor presence is maintained in the country of purchase for commercial purposes (Ritmuller pianos purchased by Pearl River).

The purchased companies are resold to other investors

The resale by Chinese firms of their European activities generally concerns firms encountering greater difficulties than expected and/or investors lacking skills, funding, or the will to refocus their activities. The new investors can be Chinese or not.

For instance, Milus (watches, Switzerland), bought by Peace Mark in 2002, was resold five years later to another Chinese company, Chow Tai Fook; Two Cast Foundry (France), bought by Heibei Hongye in 2008, was sold to a French enterprise (Leroy) one year later.

Conclusion

The motives and strategies of Chinese investors in Europe – and in the world – are becoming closer to those of the other multinationals, insofar as they are now seasoned, hold standard technologies, and, very importantly, are currently able to make real innovations, especially "cost innovations". At the same time, they seek to increase their market positions at the international level and to operate in high added-value activities.

Europe remains a popular M&A destination for Chinese investors because its manufacturing and services sectors are relatively strong (European companies own good technology and products) and public authorities welcome foreign investment. However, some investments made by SOEs or other public groups remain "sensitive" and are sometimes viewed with suspicion or give rise to Sinophobia or protectionist behaviors. So, to meet this challenge and facilitate their integration, many Chinese investors start to intensify their production activities in Europe: doing so, they create jobs and can use the label "made in Europe"; in this perspective, the investments in eastern Europe are often privileged. In the same direction, they also start to make the choice to acquire minority stakes in the coveted European firms, in order to build up confidence and not to alarm the other shareholders and consumers.

Chinese investors contribute to shape the global competitor landscape and require relevant adaptations from European economies and its firms.

Notes

1 Associate Researcher at CREM, University of Rennes 1, France, hay35@free.fr
2 *World Investment Reports* (UNCTAD) various years.
3 That is, before the British handover in 1997.

4 For instance, it is the case of Hutchison Whampoa, Esprit, Johnson Electric, Li & Fung, etc.
5 State-Owned Assets Supervision and Administration Commission.
6 Chinese firms started to make copying and imitations and reverse engineering, before making indigenous innovations and setting up a new business model combining low prices, mass consumption, and reduced margins (Lall and Albaladejo 2003).

Bibliography

Bin, W. and Tao, H. (1997) 'Two stage theory: Analysis modes of foreign direct investment', *Economic Research*, 7: 1–25.

Deng, P. (2009) 'Why do Chinese firms tend to acquire strategic assets in international expansion?' *Journal of World Business,* 44, 1: 74–84.

Dunning, J. H. (1979) 'Explaining changing patterns of international production: In defence of the eclectic theory', *Oxford Bulletin of Economics and Statistics,* 41: 269–96.

Hay, F. and Milelli, C. (2013) 'The endless quest to strategic assets by Chinese firms through FDI: From inward to outward flows', *Document de Travail EconomiX,* 2013, 16: 1–20.

Lall, S. and Albaladejo, M. (2003) 'China's manufactured export surge: A threat to East Asian manufactured exports?' *World Development*, 3, 9: 1441–66.

Matthews, S. A. (2006) 'Dragon multinationals: New players in the 21st century globalization', *Asia Pacific Journal of Management*, 23, 1: 5–27.

Zeng, M. and Williamson, P. J. (2007) 'Dragons at Our Door: How Chinese Cost Innovation is Disrupting Global Competition', Boston: Harvard Business School Press.

Zeng, M. and Williamson, P. J. (2009) Chinese multinationals: Emerging through new global gateways, in 'Emerging Multinationals in Emerging Markets', Ramamurti, R. and Singh, J. V., Cambridge: Cambridge University Press: 81–109.

9 Greenfield investments and acquisitions of Turkish multinationals

Trends, motivations and strategies

Caner Bakir and Nuran Acur[1]

Introduction

Emerging market multinational corporations (EMNCs) have started to play an increasingly important role in economic globalisation processes. One of the most recent trends in EMNC internationalisation is their investments in developed markets (UNCTAD 2006). For example, Ernst and Young (2015: 5) notes that foreign direct investment (FDI) from BRIC countries (Brazil, Russia, India, and China) in Europe "reached an all-time high – with 313 projects creating a total of 16,900 jobs. The majority of these investments were concentrated in the UK and Germany". Unsurprisingly, explaining the rather sudden rise of EMNC investments in developed markets has become a major concern among policymakers and scholars over the last few years (Khanna and Palepu 2006; Aulakh 2007; Goldstein 2007; Luo and Tung 2007; Ramamurti 2009; Ramamurti and Singh 2009; Brennan 2011; Cuervo-Cazurra and Ramamurti 2014).

Accelerated internationalisation of Turkish multinational corporations (TMNCs) is part of this most recent trend in FDI. According to UNCTAD (2015: 52), TMNC outward investments reached 6.7 billion US dollars in 2014, or increased by 89 percent compared with the previous year. In 10 years, from 2004 to 2013, TMNC greenfield investments increased over threefold – from 2.2 billion US dollars to 6.9 billion US dollars (fDi intelligence database). During the same period, the top 62 TMNC acquisitions, whose value exceeded 10 million US dollars, increased over 17 times – from 108 million US dollars to 1.8 billion US dollars (Thomson Reuters Mergers and Acquisitions database and *Deloitte Turkish Outbound M&A Review 2012–2013*). More significantly, over 95 percent of these investments are new investments rather than expansions of existing investments.

Thus, it is legitimate to investigate this new spectacular increase in TMNC investment activities. Further, several Turkish firms have internationalised in aggressive and innovative ways, whilst competing with established players. For example, some of the non-financial TMNCs are now among the world's global players in several industries, ranging from food (Yıldız Holding) to ferrochrome (Yildirim Group) to tiles (Eczacibasi Yapi).

One area that has not received much attention in the past literature on EMNCs, however, is the recent geographical and sectoral spread, motivations, and competitive advantages of TMNCs: whether these investments represent theoretical and empirical challenges to existing knowledge, or whether they can be explained within the existing theoretical frameworks that have been used to explain developed country MNCs (see Bakir 2016).

This chapter offers answers to questions such as: Where do TMNCs go? Do the majority of their investments concentrate in developing or developed countries? What are their firm specific advantages (FSAs) and country specific advantages (CSAs)? Why do they internationalise? Are widely used frameworks in international business (IB) theory relevant to explain TMNC behaviour? Are TMNC acquisitions in the EU motivated by the global consolidator strategy? How do *structural complementarities* inform the outcome of TMNC acquisitions?

This chapter finds that the largest TMNCs employ multiple strategies in developed and developing country markets. Seventy-five percent of TMNC greenfield FDI (or about 35 billion US dollars) is directed towards transition and developing economies. TMNCs mainly exploit FSAs (dynamic capabilities) obtained at home, such as managerial and market knowledge, expertise, technology, local/regional brands and distribution channels, and expertise in operating in relatively weak institutional environments in these economies. They also exploit traditional locational advantages, or CSAs, such as economies of scale and leadership in the home market and geographical, cultural, and institutional proximity. In contrast to greenfield investments, 50 percent of the top 62 acquisitions (or 4.9 billion US dollars) are in developed countries. TMNCs not only exploit current FSAs obtained from home CSAs, but also aim to explore FSAs obtained from host CSAs through their subsidiaries. In regard to motivations, TMNCs' greenfield investments are mainly motivated by market-seeking FDI, including access to host country markets and neighbouring regions, efficiency-seeking FDI such as cost and tax advantages, and resource-seeking FDI such as access to natural resources.

TMNCs' acquisitions are mostly motivated by strategic asset-seeking FDI such as access to global brands, international experience, knowledge, distribution networks, and cutting-edge competitive technology. In doing so, they aim to increase their market share and profitability at home and abroad. This chapter also highlights the *global consolidator* strategy of some TMNCs and the significance of structural complementarities informing TMNC investment behaviour.

Data for this chapter come from the Financial Times Ltd fDi Intelligence (2003–2013) and Thomson Reuters Mergers and Acquisitions Database (from 1 January 2000 to 30 January 2011) and *Deloitte Turkish Outbound M&A Review 2012–2013*. It also benefits from secondary written sources. Acquisitions data focus on transactions over 10 million US dollars by TMNCs where at least 51 percent of ownership belongs to a Turkish owner.

The rest of this chapter is organised as follows. The next section offers a literature review. Then the chapter focuses on greenfield investment trends by TMNCs with special reference to economic development of host countries and regional, country-based, and sectoral distribution of the value of these investments.

The chapter proceeds to do the same for outbound acquisitions, then discusses the internationalisation strategies and motivations of some of the largest TMNCs and the role of structural complementarities in informing TMNC internationalisation strategy. The conclusion summarizes the main findings.

Literature review

Research and practice regarding the internationalisation of firms have been dominated by the Eclectic paradigm (Dunning 1988), and FSAs and CSAs frameworks (Rugman and Verbeke 1990). The Eclectic paradigm is based on ownership, location, and internalisation advantages (OLI framework). Ownership advantages such as technology, know-how, and brand indicate who is going to produce abroad "and for that matter, other forms of international activity" (Dunning 1993: 142). These advantages are also labelled FSAs. Locational factors refer to home country resource endowments, such as natural resources, labour, market size, and institutions that "influenc[e] where to produce" (Dunning 1993: 143). These advantages are also known as CSAs that "can be based on natural resource endowments (minerals, energy, forests), market, labour force, and/or associated cultural factors" (Rugman 2009: 50). Internalisation advantage "addresses the question of why firms engage in FDI rather than license foreign firms to use their proprietary assets" (Dunning 1993: 145). Here, ownership advantages are exploited internally where such advantages are not sold to third parties through contracts such as licensing and the establishment of joint ventures (i.e., MNCs do not sell their FSAs to their rivals). OLI advantages are regarded as the necessary and sufficient conditions for the internationalisation of MNCs (Hennart 2012: 169). It is widely held that developed country multinationals mostly rely on the exploitation of their FSAs, such as technology, know-how, and brand, whilst developing country MNCs do not have strong FSAs, and they rely heavily on CSAs, such as cheap labour, natural resources, and access to state funds (Rugman 2009). It is widely recognised that MNCs from developing countries have home CSAs, such as cheap and skilled labour and scale advantages arising from strong demand in growing domestic markets (Luo and Tung 2007), and they enjoy monopolistic power in home markets (Klein and Wocke 2007). Several studies argued that EMNCs internationalise to gain FSAs in host countries, rather than exploiting their existing FSAs obtained in home countries (Mathews 2002; Luo and Tung 2007; Ramamurti and Singh 2009; Williamson et al. 2013).

Recently, it has been argued that EMNCs have several FSAs obtained in home markets, which are different than standard FSAs or ownership advantages of developed country MNCs. As Ramamurti (2012: 42) rightly notes:

> Among the ownership advantages attributed in the literature to EMNEs is their deep understanding of customer needs in emerging markets, the ability to function in difficult business environments, their ability to make products and services at ultra-low costs, their ability to develop "good enough" products with the right feature-price mix for local customers, and so on.

Some of the EMNCs are "global consolidators", who are the leaders in their home markets and consolidate the industry globally by acquiring firms in developed countries (Ramamurti and Singh 2009). For example, in his analysis of Indian MNCs, Ramamurti (2013: 251) identifies "the global consolidator strategy [that] typically arises in industries that have matured in developed countries but are booming in emerging markets – industries like cement, steel, chemicals, white goods, automobiles, beverages and processed food". These firms use a mix of FSA exploitation and FSA exploration for efficiency. Further, Ramamurti and Singh (2009: 141–142) note that

> [t]he distinguishing feature of the global consolidator . . . is that its competitive advantages can be leveraged in both emerging economies and advanced countries, resulting in the potential for up-market exports and FDI . . . [this is because of] industry-specific factors – specifically, in the degree to which products and production processes [that] can be standardized across countries, regardless of per-capita income, wages, or cultural differences.

Has there been any TMNC that adopted the global consolidator strategy? This chapter also aims to address this question with special reference to Yıldız Holding, the largest food manufacturer and marketer in Turkey, which acquired top global brands such as the Belgium chocolate maker Godiva in 2007 and the top manufacturer and marketer of biscuits in the UK, United Biscuits, in 2014.

Past research has also shown that MNCs have four main motivations in internationalisation (Dunning 1993; Narula and Dunning 2010). These are: (1) natural resource-seeking to access host country resources; (2) market-seeking to access host country markets and regions, to overcome trade-related and other restrictions, as well as to become closer to customers; (3) efficiency-seeking to decrease costs and reconfigure supply chains; and (4) strategic asset-seeking to acquire intangible assets such as know-how and brand. The first three motivations relate to the exploitation of FSAs obtained from home country CSAs, whilst the last one relates to the exploration of FSAs obtained from host country CSAs.

More recently, for Rugman and Nguyen (2014: 56–57), "[n]ew internationalization theory maintains that FSAs can be developed by both parent firms in the home countries and foreign subsidiaries in the host countries. . . . What is missing from all the extant literature on EMNCs is the interaction between foreign subsidiaries of EMNCs and the host CSAs." Accordingly this chapter considers FSAs obtained from both home and host CSAs.

More significantly, this chapter highlights some of the weaknesses in the IB theory, namely the significance of the largely ignored structural context that informs investment decisions and entry strategies of MNCs. It shows that structural complementarities (i.e., interdependence of structural influences on MNC behaviour) reinforce FSAs and/or CSAs, generating similar incentives that influence the internationalisation outcomes of MNCs (for a detailed discussion on the structural complementarities in the context of bank internationalisation, see Bakir 2013, Chapter 3; for the role of institutional complementarities on actor behaviour, see Crouch 2010 and Campbell 2011). In this context, the sociology and political economy literature may offer new analytical insights highlighting the utility of introducing structural variables. In doing so, we can further understand the timing and context of internationalisation of MNCs. Following Sewell (1992: 19), structures "are sets of mutually sustaining schemas and resources that empower and constrain social action and that tend to be reproduced by that social action". Here, *structures* refer to broader material and ideational contexts within which institutions (i.e., formal and informal rules and norms that guide the behaviour of agents) and agents (e.g., individuals and organisations) are embedded. Structures, like institutions, inform the internationalisation of MNCs. The examples include crises, wars, technical and technological innovations, macroeconomic structures, market structures, currency structures, ideational structures, etc., that guide the behaviour of corporations.

This nuanced view is important because it moves beyond conventional FSA- and CSA-based analysis of firms' internationalisation activities. For example, although MNCs' internationalisation activity is informed by FSAs and CSAs, the *realisation* of investment may require the existence of structural complementarities that reinforce a firm's motivations and strategies (if one wishes to race ahead, I summarise this point below in the section "Discussion and conclusions"). These complementarities may create structural-level enabling conditions for outward investment.

There are four main contributions of this chapter to these discussions on EMNCs. First, there is an empirical gap in the past literature which ignored internationalisation of TMNCs. This literature mostly focuses on MNCs from BRIC countries (see, for example, Ramamurti and Singh 2009; Guillén and García-Canal 2012; Cuervo-Cazurra and Ramamurti 2014; Demirbağ and Yaprak 2015). Second, it shows that TMNCs have ownership advantages or FSAs which are different than developed-country MNCs, such as market knowledge, regional brands, distribution networks, and managerial expertise in developing countries. This finding is largely ignored in the previous research on TMNCs and some of the IB perspectives on EMNCs which have focused on CSAs (see, for example, Rugman 2009). Third, it shows that TMNCs adopt multiple strategies based on exploration and exploitation of their FSAs obtained at home and host countries. Fourth, it also argues that "modern international business theory [which has been developed to analyse Western MNCs], with its distinctions between FSAs generated by home or host country recombinations" (Rugman and Nguyen 2014: 76), is highly relevant in explaining some of the TMNC investments. In addition to exploiting standard FSAs obtained from Turkey's CSAs, such as economies of scale and low labour cost, TMNCs also explore ownership advantages and strategic assets (also known as dynamic capabilities or FSAs) obtained from foreign MNCs and markets. Finally, it offers examples of largely ignored *structural complementarities* in informing the outcomes of EMNCs' internationalisation strategy.

This chapter also makes four main contributions to the previous literature on TMNCs and outward Turkish FDI (see, for example, Erdilek 2003, 2007; Akçaoğlu 2005; Kaya and Erden 2008; Kaya 2009). First, although TMNC internationalisation activities have exploded over the last ten years, our knowledge of such investments is limited. Earlier studies have mainly focused on the 1990s, when EMNCs were relatively opaque in the global business environment and the literature on EMNCs was underdeveloped. Second, the past research focuses on TMNCs' facilitating role in helping developed-country MNCs in Turkey's neighbourhood (see, for example, Yaprak and Karademir 2011). The current study recognising this perspective, however, pays special attention to the TMNC investments in advanced developed regions and countries, in particular the European Union, with special reference to some of the cutting edge discussions in the newly emerging EMNC literature. Third, one of the unique contributions of this chapter to the literature on TMNCs is its reliance on the analysis of private databases. The previous studies have used publicly available aggregated data supplied by the Central Bank of the Republic of Turkey, UNCTAD, or newspapers (Akçaoğlu 2005; Kayam and Hisarcıklılar 2009). The current chapter also uses private databases and firm-specific data which focus on the last decade rather than the 1990s. Thus this chapter offers discussions about individual TMNC advantages and motivations in their recent integration with the economic globalisation process.

Greenfield investments by Turkish MNCs

Table 9.1 presents data for greenfield activities of TMNCs, such as building factories and opening branches or stores between January 2003 and December 2013.

Table 9.1 Greenfield investments of non-financial TMNCs (2003–2013)

Year	Number of Investments	Number of Investor Companies	Total Investment Value (million US dollars)	Average Value of Capital Investment by Companies (million US dollars)	Total Employment Created	Average Employment Created by Companies
2003	109	58	7,750	133.6	30,574	527
2004	66	48	2,374	49.5	10,450	218
2005	67	41	4,074	99.4	25,836	630
2006	51	37	1,941	52.5	14,520	392
2007	37	33	2,399	72.7	15,346	465
2008	64	52	4,464	85.8	16,649	320
2009	63	59	4,068	68.9	20,811	353
2010	100	67	3,852	57.5	21,689	324
2011	66	50	4,911	98.2	6,699	134
2012	86	59	4,155	70.4	12,797	217
2013	83	65	6,864	105.6	20,643	318
Total	792	438	46,852	81.28	196,014	354

Source: fDi Intelligence from the Financial Times Ltd. Authors' calculations.

Note:* Includes real sector firms and financial firms.
** Share of foreign MNCs operating in Turkey in total is negligible.

During this period, 438 TMNCs invested over 46 billion US dollars in 792 investments. Over 95 percent of TMNCs are family-owned firms rather than state-owned firms. These investments created employment opportunities for over 196,000 people. On average, each TMNC invested 82 million US dollars and employed 354 people; 2003 witnessed a record in total capital investment with 7.7 billion US dollars. This could be connected to investments which may have been postponed due to the 2001 economic and financial crisis in Turkey. The second highest investment was realised in 2013. In 2009 and 2010, when the repercussions of the global financial crisis were felt, outward investment declined around 10 percent compared with 2008.

Regional distribution of investment flows

Figure 9.1 shows the distribution of the value of TMNC investments among host countries according to their level of economic development. Transition economies (21.4 billion US dollars or 46 percent of the total) and developing countries (13.7 billion US dollars or 29 percent) received the highest value of investments. Compared with these economies, investments to developed economies were higher in number, yet lower in value (10.6 billion US dollars or 22 percent).

What does it mean that around 75 percent of TMNC greenfield FDI is directed towards transition and developing economies? TMNCs use the competitive advantages in areas such as costs, management, marketing, logistics, and technology that they gained to reach new markets in developing and transition economies

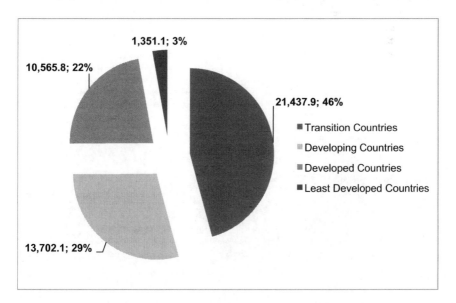

Figure 9.1 Distribution of non-financial TMNC investments by a host country's economic development (2003–2013, value of investments – million USD)

Source: fDi Intelligence from the Financial Times Ltd. Authors' calculations.

(see the section "Motivations and strategies of TMNCs' investments and structural complementarities" below). In contrast, the total value of investments by Turkish companies in developed-country economies is about 20 percent of the total. This may be due to these firms' weak FSAs in these markets. In contrast, the emerging interest of TMNCs in the least developed countries suggests that the share of LDCs (3 percent at present) might increase in time.

Geographical distribution of greenfield FDI

Figure 9.2 shows the geographical distribution of TMNC greenfield investments by value. The Commonwealth of Independent States (CIS) received the most investments, with 18.5 billion US dollars or 39 percent of the total investments. The second most attractive location for greenfield investments by TMNCs was the EU, which attracted 18 percent of the total investments – 318 investments have been made in this region by 217 TMNCs and over 41,000 people were employed by the investment worth 8 billion US dollars (fDi Intelligence database 2013).

Distribution of greenfield FDI among countries

The fDi Intelligence database (2013) shows that between 2003 and 2013, the top ten countries, ranked by the number of projects, attracted about a total of 20 billion US dollars in TMNC greenfield investments (including both financial and non-financial firms), which constituted about 50 percent of total greenfield investments.

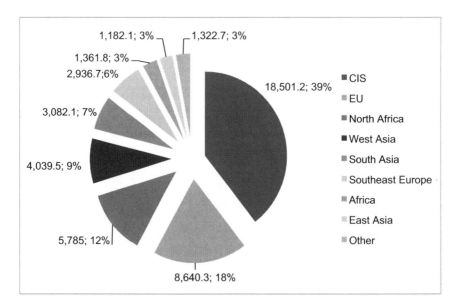

Figure 9.2 Geographical distribution of non-financial TMNC Investments (2003–2013, value of investments – million USD)

Source: fDi Intelligence from the Financial Times Ltd. Authors' calculations.

More interestingly, 96 percent of these investments were in developing and transition economies, while two developed economies, Germany and the US, each had only a 2 percent share among these top ten destinations.

Figures 9.3 and 9.4 show the number and value, respectively, of investments by TMNCs among the EU countries. The number of investments by TMNCs in Germany reached 114 (or 36 percent), which was followed by Romania (51 or 16 percent) and Bulgaria (45 or 14 percent).

In terms of the value of investments, Bulgaria, which has the largest Turkish minority population in the Balkans, and Romania together attracted over 5 billion US dollars, or about 60 percent. Germany, which hosts the largest Turkish population in Europe, attracted the third largest TMNC greenfield investments in the EU (970 million US dollars or 11 percent), and Romania received the highest employment and investment in value. Apparently, historical, cultural, and geographical proximity also informed TMNC internationalisation in these countries.

Sectoral distribution of greenfield investments by non-financial TMNCs

As Figure 9.5 shows, between 2003 and 2013, the highest value of investment was in the real estate sector (11 billion US dollars or 25 percent). It was followed by coal, petroleum, and natural resources (6.9 billion US dollars or 15 percent), textiles (4 billion US dollars, or 9 percent), hotel management and tourism (2.7 percent US dollars or 6 percent), and construction and building materials (2.2 billion US dollars or 5 percent).

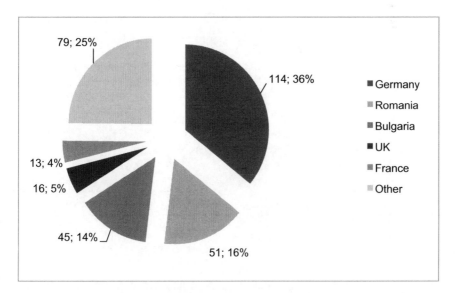

Figure 9.3 Distribution of non-financial TMNC investments in EU countries (number of investments)

Source: fDi Intelligence from the Financial Times Ltd. Authors' calculations.

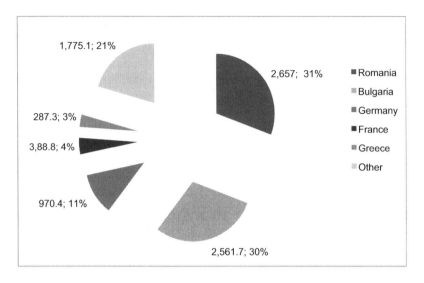

Figure 9.4 Distribution of non-financial TMNC investments in EU countries (2003–2013, value of investments – million USD)

Source: fDi Intelligence from the Financial Times Ltd. Authors' calculations.

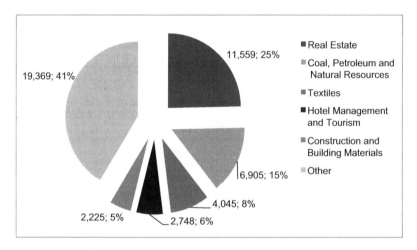

Figure 9.5 Sectoral distribution of non-financial TMNC investments (2003–2013, value of investments – million USD)

Source: fDi Intelligence from the Financial Times Ltd. Authors' calculations.

What do we know about the distribution of these top three sectoral investments of TMNCs across regions and countries? The fDi database shows that the EU is the second highest recipient of real estate investments (1.7 billion US dollars or 15 percent of the total) after CIS countries (7.2 billion US dollars or 62 percent). The EU is also the

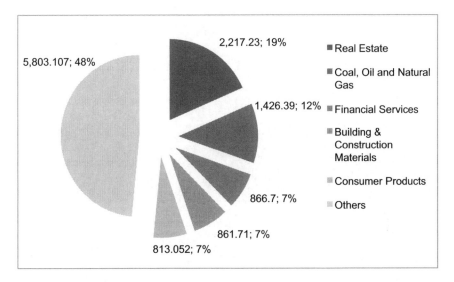

5,803.107; 48%

2,217.23; 19%

■ Real Estate

■ Coal, Oil and Natural Gas

1,426.39; 12% ■ Financial Services

■ Building & Construction Materials

■ Consumer Products

866.7; 7%

■ Others

861.71; 7%

813.052; 7%

Figure 9.6 The largest TMNC investments in EU by sector (2003–2013, value of investments – million USD)

Source: fDi Intelligence from the Financial Times Ltd. Authors' calculations.

third largest recipient of textile investments from TMNCs (443 million US dollars or 11 percent). However, the EU receives only 263 million US dollars (or 4 percent) of TMNC investments in coal, petroleum, and natural resources. Turkish investors lean towards neighbouring CIS countries and transition economies in Europe, especially countries such as Bulgaria, Romania, and Russia in the real estate, food, and mining sectors, where they have FSAs and aim to access host country CSAs.

As Figure 9.6 shows, real estate and coal, oil, and natural gas are the top two sectors in TMNC investments in the EU. It is interesting to note that financial services, building and construction materials, and consumer products each has a 7 percent share in total.

A closer look at the TMNC sectoral activities in Bulgaria and Romania shows that TMNCs invest in banking, insurance services, chemicals, home appliances, textile, logistics, parks, residential, and hotel subsectors (Bakır 2016). Specifically, Romania is a significant market for Turkish real estate investments. Bulgaria and Romania's EU membership has been a major structural event that opened a window of opportunity to Turkish construction firms to undertake some of the EU-funded infrastructure investments in these countries.

Top ten non-financial TMNCs in greenfield investments

Table 9.2 shows the top ten TMNCs that have made the highest value of greenfield investments between 2003 and 2013. These companies generate over 30 percent

Table 9.2 Top ten non-financial TNCs in terms of value of capital investments, 2003–2013 (million USD)

Investor Company	Home City	No. of Jobs Created	Value of Investment (million USD)	Sectors	Host Countries (year; number of investments)
Ramenka	Istanbul	21,826	2,452	Food and tobacco, real estate	Kazakhstan (2009, 1); Russia (2003,11; 2004, 3; 2005, 18; 2006, 4; 2013, 1)
Rixos Hotels	Antalya	3,389	2,061	Hotels & tourism, leisure & entert.	Austria (2007, 1); Azerbaijan (2012, 1); Bahrain (2010,1); UAE (2008,2; 2011,1; 2012, 1); Croatia (2007,1); Montenegro (2013, 1); Kazakhstan (2005,1; 2009,1; 2013, 1); Libya (2010,1); Egypt (2012, 1); Russia (2008, 1); Ukraine (2005,1)
Enka	Istanbul	4,625	1,847	Real estate, natural resources	Russia (2003,1; 2008;2); Tajikistan (2006, 1)
Enisa Group	Istanbul	161	1,819	Coal, oil and nat. resources	Morocco (2011, 1)
Migros	Istanbul	4,388	1,614	Real estate and entertainment	France (2004, 1); Iran (2003, 1); Macedonia (2003, 2; 2006, 1); Syria (2003,1); Ukraine (2003, 1)
Renaissance Construction	Istanbul	11,761	1,548	Real estate and entertainment	Russia (2005, 1; 2008,1; 2010, 4)
Hakkan Mining and Generation Industry and Trade	Istanbul	345	1,095	Coal, oil and nat. resources	Ruanda (2012, 2)
Opus Project & Development	Not spec.	3,000	956	Real estate	Romania (2007, 1)

Kastamonu Entegre	Wood products	Istanbul	4,241	945	Bosnia Herzegovina (2003, 1; 2007,1); Bulgaria (2006,1; 2011,1); Romania (2008,1); Russia (2009,1)
Aria	Communications	Istanbul	730	913	Germany (2003, 1); United Kingdom (2003, 1); Czech Republic (2003,1); Philippines (2003,1); Hong Kong (2003,1); Switzerland (2003,1); Italy (2003,1); Russia (2003,1); Singapore (2003,1); Taiwan (2003,1)
Total of top 10			54,466	15,250	
Total OFDI performed by Turkish MNCs			196,014	46,851	
Percentage of top 10 companies in total			28%	33%	

Source: fDi Intelligence from the Financial Times Ltd. Authors' calculations.

of the total greenfield investments. Further, these companies constitute between 20 percent and 40 percent of the total investments in a given year. They mostly originate from Istanbul and have created over 54,000 jobs, with nearly 15 billion US dollars' worth of investment in nearby transition economies and developing countries. Investments were primarily targeted towards construction projects in the real estate industry. MNCs from BRIC countries mostly have investments in developed European markets such as the UK, Germany, and France. In contrast, most of the TMNCs have such investments in transition and developing economies. As shown above, these investments are concentrated in Bulgaria and Romania.

Acquisitions by TMNCs

Figure 9.7 shows the distribution of the number and value of the top 62 TMNC acquisitions whose value exceeded 10 million US dollars between 2000 and 2013. These TMNCs had about 9.9 billion US dollars in acquisitions, which constituted 72 percent of the total investments. During this period, TMNC acquisitions increased 44 times, from about 41 million US dollars to 1.8 billion US dollars. In 2001, 2003, and 2009, no such investments were made. The 2001 Turkish economic crisis and the effects of the global financial crisis in 2009 were the main reasons for the absence of investments in these years. The highest investments in value were made in 2011, at 2.6 billion US dollars.

Here the focus is on the acquisitions of TMNCs whose majority shareholders are Turkish citizens. During the acquisition deals, TMNCs in general prefer 100 percent ownership or majority ownership. Some firms initially acquire 100 percent ownership of their investees, while others make subsequent investments to increase their shares to 100 percent or a majority position. Most of these firms are family-owned companies, which have a tendency to have 100 percent ownership of the acquired firm. However, some of the TMNCs prefer to be cautious in new markets and engage in partnerships with local firms rather than outright

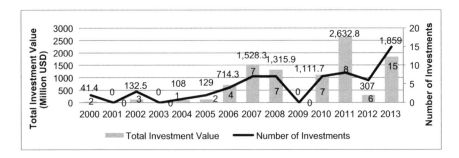

Figure 9.7 Yearly distribution of value and number of TMNC acquisitions (2000–2013)

Sources: Thomson Reuters Mergers and Acquisitions Database and Deloitte Turkish Outbound M&A Review 2012–2013.

ownership. There are two main reasons: (1) less costly partnership options in case the company needs to exit the market; (2) to overcome the liability of foreignness (i.e., additional costs experienced abroad arising from, for example, limited local knowledge). Some TMNCs that enter the new markets through partnerships make further investments for full ownership in following years. Finally, it should be noted that most of these TMNCs are holding companies; conglomerates operating in a wide range of sectors in Turkey. A holding company structure enables TMNCs to reduce transaction costs by creating internal markets inside the firm.

Geographical distribution of acquisitions by TMNCs

Figure 9.8 shows the distribution of value of investments among countries with different levels of economic development. Accordingly, unlike greenfield investments, developed countries host half of the TMNC acquisitions (4.9 billion US dollars or 50 percent). They are followed by developing countries (3.7 billion US dollars or 37 percent) and transition economies (1.2 billion US dollars or 13 percent).

Figure 9.9 shows the geographical distribution of the value of acquisitions by TMNCs. The EU, with 3.6 billion US dollars or 37 percent, is the most popular location in terms of value of acquisitions. TMNCs prefer operation in developed EU countries to improve their skills in branding, technology, R&D, design, and management. The EU is followed by North America, South Asia, CIS, and Southeast Europe. CIS countries are not a very attractive destination for TMNC acquisition activities, as opposed to their popularity in greenfield investments. Acquisitions in these regions are mainly motivated by TMNCs' desire to reach

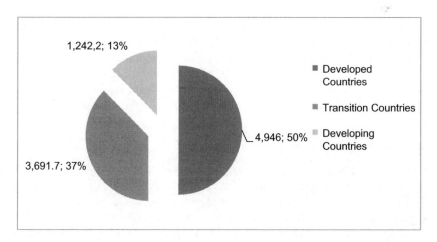

Figure 9.8 Distribution of the value of the mergers and acquisitions among economic regions (2000–2013, value of investments – million USD)

Source: Thomson Reuters Mergers and Acquisitions Database and Deloitte Turkish Outbound M&A Review 2012–2013.

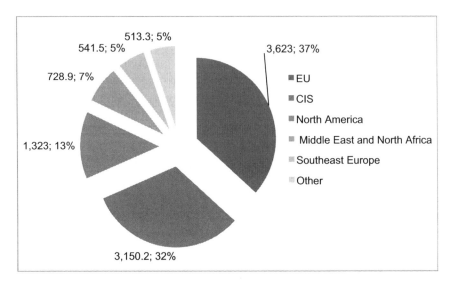

Figure 9.9 Geographical distribution of the value of the TMNC acquisitions (2000–2013, value of investments – million USD)

Sources: Thomson Reuters Mergers and Acquisitions Database and Deloitte Turkish Outbound M&A Review 2012–2013.

local markets and raw materials, by using their firm-specific advantages such as managerial experience and technology.

Figure 9.10 shows the distribution of the top 62 TMNC acquisitions, with special reference to target countries. It is interesting to note that like greenfield investments, Russia attracts the highest value of investments at 2.6 billion US dollars or 26 percent of the total (for detailed discussion on TMNCs in Russia, see Bakir and Acur 2016). Russia is followed by Holland (i.e., the Kingdom of the Netherlands) and the US (each with 1.3 billion US dollars or 13 percent).

Sectoral distribution of acquisitions by TMNCs

Figure 9.11 shows the sectoral distribution of the acquisitions of TMNCs. The highest investments in value were in food and beverages (3.4 billion US dollars or 34 percent), telecommunications (931 million US dollars or 9 percent), and banking and finance (827 million US dollars or 8 percent). How do these top three sectors score in the EU? The EU is the top destination for TMNC acquisitions in banking (750 million US dollars or 91 percent). The EU's share in telecommunications acquisitions is 270 million US dollars (29 percent). This is followed by acquisitions in the food and beverages sector, which attracts 200 million US dollars in investments (6 percent of the total in this sector).

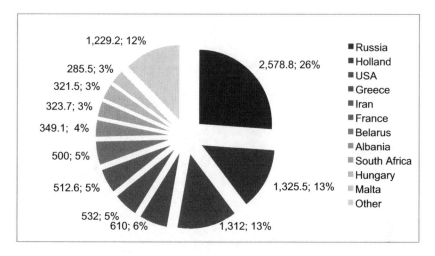

Figure 9.10 Distribution of the value of TMNC acquisitions among target countries (2000–2013, value of investments – million USD)

Source: Thomson Reuters Mergers and Acquisitions Database and Deloitte Turkish Outbound M&A Review 2012–2013.

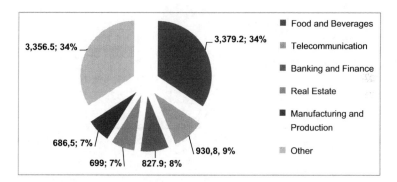

Figure 9.11 Sectoral distribution of the TMNC acquisitions (2000–2013, value of investments – million USD)

Source: Thomson Reuters Mergers and Acquisitions Database and Deloitte Turkish Outbound M&A Review 2012–2013.

Table 9.3 shows the top ten TMNCs which had the highest value of acquisitions between 2003 and 2013. The acquisitions of these firms totalled 7.6 billion US dollars, which constituted 77 percent of the sum of the largest sixty-two TMNC acquisitions worldwide. In other words, there is relative concentration of such investments in a relatively small number of firms. It should be noted that these firms operate oligopolistic markets in Turkey, exploiting CSAs such as economies of scale and scope and benefiting from non-price competition. There were 43 deals (or 58 percent of the total) completed between 2010 and 2013. Arguably, the 2008

Table 9.3 Top 10 Turkish acquirers, 2000–2013

Rank	Acquisition value (million USD)	Target Company	Sector	Target Country	Acquirer Company	Purchased Share (%)
1	2,130	Russia and Ukraine Businesses of SABMiller (2011); Efes Breweries International (2010); CJSC Efes Brewery (2013)	Beverages	Russia and Ukraine (2011); Holland (2010); Russia (2013)	Anadolu Efes	100.00 (2011); 26.00 (2010); 9.00 (2013)
2	1,211.4	CMA CGM SA (2010); Chrome Division of Mechel (2013); Malta Freeport Terminals (2011)	Transportation, mining and infrastructure	France (2010); Russia and Kazakhstan (2013); Malta (2011)	Yıldırım Holding Inc.	20.00 (2010); 100.00 (2013); 50.00 (2011)
3	1,071	Godiva Chocolatier Inc (2007); DeMet's Candy Company (2013)	Food-beverages	US	Yıldız Holding Inc.	100.00
4	598	Astir Palace (2013)	Real estate	Greece	Doğuş Holding	n/a
5	580	Finans Intl Holding NV (2006)	Banking- finance	Holland	Fiba Holding Inc.	100.00
6	532	Razi Petrochemical (2008)	Petrochemical industry	Iran	Gübretaş; Tabosan; Asia Gas Energy	83.70
7	500	Belarusian Telecom (2008)	Telecommunications	Belarus	Turkcell	80.00
8	361.2	Defy Appliances Limited (2011); Arctic (2002)	Manufacturing and household electronics, durable goods	South Africa (2011); Romania (2002)	Arçelik Inc.	100.00 (2011); 57.29 (2002); 33.85 (2002)
9	336.5	Trader Media East Ltd	Media- advertising	Holland	Hürriyet Invest B.V.	67.30
10	304.2	Al Waha (2012, 2013); Coca Cola Beverages Pakistan (2008); Coca Cola Beverages Iraq Limited (2011); Coca Cola Almaty Bottlers LLP (2007)	Food-beverages	Iraq (2011, 2012, 2013); Pakistan (2008); Kazakhstan (2007)	Coca Cola Beverage Manufacturing Inc.	n/a (2012); 49.00 (2008); 70.00 (2011); 12.04 (2007); 15.00 (2013)

Sources: Thomson Reuters Mergers and Acquisitions Database and Deloitte Turkish Outbound M&A Review 2012–2013.

global financial crisis and the eurozone crisis posed acquisition opportunities for TMNCs. Half of these deals were in the food processing, banking and finance, and telecommunications sectors.

Anadolu Efes is the top company that dominates TMNC acquisitions in the beverages sector. It has a strong concentration in the CIS region and Russia in particular (for a detailed discussion on Anadolu Efes, see Bakır and Acur 2016). The remaining top two TMNCs were Yildirim Holding and Yıldız Holding, which will be discussed below.

Motivations and strategies of TMNC investments and structural complementarities

Competitive advantages and motivations of TMNCs

Yıldız Holding is the biggest diversified food group by revenue in central and eastern Europe, Africa, and the Middle East, with about 7 billion US dollars in total sales in 2013. Its two high profile acquisitions can be considered as an example of an effort towards a global consolidation strategy of EMNCs. Yıldız Holding acquired the Belgian chocolate maker Godiva from American Campbell Soup Co. in 2007 for 850 million US dollars. This acquisition was the biggest single acquisition deal executed by a TMNC at the time.

Godiva's revenues increased by 10 percent each year following the acquisition, reaching 765 million US dollars (*Forbes* March 2014: 64). The company significantly increased its marketing, infrastructure, and staff investments by 40 percent. It increased its sales in US and Japan. Building on the Yıldız group's knowledge, networks, and expertise, Godiva identified China, the Middle East, North Africa, and Turkey as new markets. Indeed, it entered new markets including Australia, China, Saudi Arabia, Korea, Macau, and Turkey. Its international sales increased from 43 percent in 2008 to 52 percent in 2013.

Following the acquisition, Yıldız Holding entered ten new countries, increased its branches from 480 to over 600, and the number of points of sale increased from 10,000 to over 32,000. Its sales also increased from 450 million US dollars in 2007 to 765 million US dollars.

The success of the acquisition was due to "partnering" – "keeping an acquisition structurally separate and maintaining its own identity and organization" – rather than traditional post-acquisition integration:

> Instead of rushing to integrate businesses they've bought overseas, they've allowed their acquisitions to continue operating independently, almost as if there had been no change of ownership. Each organization focuses on what it does best even as it learns to use the resources and capabilities of the other to achieve its goals.
>
> (Kale, Digh, and Anand 2009)

"Partnering" has been a key step for Yıldız Holding towards a 'global consolidator' strategy, which "is characterized by FSAs in operational excellence combined with restructuring/turnaround capabilities" (Ramamurti and Singh 2009: 140; Williamson and Zeng 2009: 87). Here, Yıldız Holding and Godiva have developed effective organisational mechanisms that transferred their unique resources and capabilities into FSAs of one another.

The success of this acquisition lies in the transfer of Yıldız Holding's FSAs obtained in developing markets to Godiva, and Godiva's transfer of FSAs obtained in advanced developed markets to Yıldız Holding. In the words of Yıldız Holding's deputy chairman, Ali Ülker, "we learnt how to do a global business. We had great benefits in the context of learning [following the acquisition of Godiva]" (*Harvard Business Review* November 2012). Then-president and chief executive officer (CEO) of Godiva, Jim Goldman, referred to the transformation that Godiva had undergone since it was acquired by Yıldız Holding in 2007. He highlighted investments made in innovation and noted that

> I am certainly sure of the fact that Godiva reached success with the right partner. We came across the strongest and newest marketing programs during the restructuring of the business and we expanded our business to new destinations, such as China, which helped to increase the bulk of our sales as well as gain experience.
>
> (Cited in *Today's Zaman* 20 December 2011)

This point adds a new dimension to the so-called new internationalisation theory that FSAs of the parent company obtained at home can further FSAs of a subsidiary to operate in new markets.

On the one hand, Yıldız Holding acquired unique resources and dynamic capabilities from Godiva, such as a global brand, managerial and marketing skills, and knowledge and experience. On the other hand, Godiva also acquired FSAs from Yıldız Holding, such as consumer insights, operating in weak institutional environments, and access to cash. This argument – a mature MNC (i.e., Godiva) acquires FSAs from an EMNC (i.e., Yıldız Holding) – moves beyond the conventional wisdom that EMNCs

> use international expansion as a springboard to acquire strategic resources and reduce their institutional and market constraints at home. In so doing, they overcome their latecomer disadvantage in the global stage via a series of aggressive, risk-taking measures by aggressively acquiring or buying critical assets from mature MNEs to compensate for their competitive weaknesses.
>
> (Luo and Tung 2007: 481)

In fact, developed-country MNCs as subsidiaries of EMNCs can acquire FSAs from their parents.

Yıldız Holding took another major step towards its generic global consolidator strategy when it bought United Biscuits in November 2014 from private equity owners the Blackstone Group and PAI Partners for about 2 billion pounds

(3.2 billion US dollars). This was the highest figure in the history of TMNC acquisitions. This made Yıldız the world's third-biggest biscuit maker. In the words of the CEO of Yıldız Holding, Murat Ulker: "We want to grow United Biscuits to be *a global player* as part of Yıldız. This will include enhancing its position in the UK, where Yıldız currently has minimal presence, so we will continue to invest in the UK and Europe" (cited in *Financial Times* 3 November 2014, my italics).

TMNCs also explore FSAs in developed markets. For example, Turk Telekom acquired 100 percent ownership of Invitel International in 2010 and therefore owned "one of Central and South eastern Europe's leading independent wholesale data and capacity service providers that operates in 16 European countries with its 27 thousand kilometres long optical fibre network" (Anadolu News Agency 18 May 2010). A statement by Turk Telekom asserted that the investment in Austria aims at reaching the target company's FSAs and increasing Turk Telekom's international competitiveness to allow it to enter new markets:

> It was stated that Turk Telekom, which has an important position in terms of geographical connections, aims at improving this position by providing the access within Central and Eastern Europe and the access to the Middle Eastern and Asian markets and the Western European and American markets with this acquisition. Moreover, the statement also underscored that the acquisition will create synergy opportunities between Invitel International and Turk Telekom.
>
> (Anadolu News Agency 18 May 2010)

Similarly, Sabancı Holding, the second largest conglomerate in Turkey, sought access to DuPont's FSAs through acquisitions. DuPont SA, the largest polyester manufacturer in Europe, jointly established by Sabancı Holding and DuPont in 1996, is the leading producer of its sector in Europe. The CEO, Celal Metin from Sabancı Holding, which acquired the full ownership of DuPont SA by an investment in 2005 in the US, stresses that they want to expand their market share by obtaining technology and brands: "We foresee that DuPont SA will grow profitably thanks to its high technology, world-renowned brands and [3,500] skilled employees and the entire industry will benefit from its quality goods and services" (*Star Gazetesi* 9 October 2004).

TMNCs also acquire firms with strong market penetration and exploit FSAs in emerging European and CIS countries. For example, Hurriyet AS, a Turkish publishing company, purchased Trader Media East Ltd. (TME) in Holland in 2007. Hurriyet is owned by Dogan Sirketler Grubu Holding AS, which is one of the largest conglomerates in Turkey, with investments in media, energy, manufacturing, and tourism. TME was one of the most important advertising agencies in Russia, CIS, and eastern Europe. TME employs approximately 1,900 people in eight countries, namely Russia, Poland, Hungary, Croatia, Ukraine, Kazakhstan, Belarus, and Lithuania. Hurriyet Invest BV, Hurriyet's subsidiary located in the Netherlands, initiated this investment, which was motivated by Hurriyet's desire to enter new markets in the online advertisement business sector through incorporating TME's knowledge, experience, and specialisation in high-growth markets in Russia and CIS countries. Hurriyet's CEO, Vuslat Dogan Sabancı, noted that:

> We believe that the merger between Hurriyet and TME will create the biggest online advertisement platform in the region. The acquisition will give Hurriyet better access to high-margin online advertising and strengthen its presence in fast growing central and eastern European markets.
>
> (Anadolu Ajansi-English News 4 January 2007)

Indeed, a year later, it was noted that Hurriyet increased its operating income by 90 percent, where 45 percent was derived from TME's activities (Referans 14 November 2008).

Structural complementarities

Complex and interdependent interactions among context-dependent structural and institutional complementarities and agency-level enabling conditions affect firm behaviour (Bakir 2013). This section offers a brief assessment of interactions among structures and agents informing the realisation of investments. This nuanced view offers a new insight into FSA- and CSA-based analysis of firms' internationalisation activities. Specifically, although firms may be guided by FSAs and CSAs, the realisation of investment requires the existence of structural, institutional, and agency-level complementarities that reinforce a firm's motivations and strategies.

The acquisition of Godiva by Yıldız Holding, owner of the diversified food company Ulker Group, in 2007 is an example demonstrating such interactions. A conventional IB explanation would consider this acquisition as a reflection of both inward and outward internationalisation strategy, which requires new brands, further management skills, technical know-how, and access to new markets.

However, the investment deal would not have taken place without two main structural complementarities: the US sub-prime mortgage crisis and appreciation of the Turkish lira against the US dollar. These two structural complementarities reinforced Yıldız Holding's acquisition of Godiva. In the words of Yıldız Holding's CEO at the time:

> Our biggest competitors were the financial investors and world's giants in the chocolate sector which acquire valuable brands when they see it. . . . In those days [before the auction day], the deal price was expected to be around 1.2–1.5 billion USD. There were two things that changed the fate of this [acquisition] agreement. First, financial investors withdrew from the scene due to the credit crisis originating in the US financial markets. This was our biggest *conjectural* chance. [Second], depreciation of the US dollar against the Turkish lira has offered an advantage to us.
>
> (Anka 28 December 2007, emphasis added)

In other words, the motivations and strategies of Yıldız Holding were not sufficient to deliver an investment deal unless they were backed by structural conditions.

Thus, appreciation for the effect of such structural variables on outward investment helps us to understand when and why structural contexts complement FSAs and CSAs. One of the key agency-level enabling conditions behind the acquisition was, in the words of Ulker Group's head of the board of directors, Murat Ulker, "we had enough money" (Anka 28 December 2007).

TMNCs also benefit from structural factors such as the economic recession in Europe following the global financial crisis and euro crisis. These external shocks hit global trade, and thus firms operating in the shipping business. For example, Yildirim Group, the world's second largest chrome producer and operator in coal and metal, production and sale of fertilizer, mining and ferroalloys, shipping and ship buildings, and port management, bailed out heavily indebted shipping giant CMA CGM by acquiring 20 percent of the French firm for 500 million US dollars (380 million euros) in 2010. This was Yildirim's largest investment in Europe. CMA CGM was the world's third largest container operator and this acquisition contributed to Yildirim Group's horizontal integration strategy and profit. Yildirim has FSAs arising from its diverse activities ranging from energy trading and port operations to ferroalloy production, mining, and shipbuilding. Thus it was well positioned to control its supply chain. Therefore, the key FSA related to the acquisition included market information and knowledge of trends in the steel industry. In the words of Robert Yildirim, one of the owners and the chairman of Yildirim,

> We supply the steel industry with raw materials so we know whether they are doing well or not, we see their order books so when they are slowing down or going up, we are talking to them so then that affects the shipping. . . . If we sign a deal, we know what the market will be looking like two months ahead. So when orders are cut, that also affects shipping two months later, so we share this market information with CMA CGM. So we are saying we see the market this way and how it affects shipping, we tell them [CMA CGM] when to move their empty boxes – this is happening in the market, be careful, put your empty container in position, the market is going up.
>
> (cited in Port Finance International 25 April 2012)

Yildirim Holding also explored FSAs from the acquisition. In the words of the chairman, "We can use the CMA CGM network to use the right people to reach the right people in other businesses. . . . We can use CMA CGM as a logistics partner, it is a win-win investment for both parties, a perfect match" (ibid).

Further, the prospect of EU membership also contributed to the internationalisation of TMNCs along with institutional complementarities and agency-level enabling conditions such as FSAs. Gübretaş acquired Razi Petrochemical Co. through Iran's first privatisation opportunity activity. This investment was a reflection of the vision of becoming a "globally branded pioneer in Turkey". Since 2006, the firm has followed the strategy of investing in countries with rich raw material resources. Gübretaş general manager Osman Balta says the company plans to rehabilitate the inactive parts of Razi Petrochemical and increase the capacity utilization rate (Hazarworld February 2013). In subsequent years, Gubretas had further expansion of existing investments. Similarly, Sise Cam also acquired two state-owned glass factories during the privatisation process in Bulgaria. For example, Sise Cam had undertaken a joint acquisition with a Belgian company, Solvay Group, in 1997 to acquire one of the largest glass producers, Sodi-Devnya, with a 35 million US dollar investment. Like Gübretas, this was followed by Sise Cam's greenfield investments for the expansion of glass production in the subsequent years. Similarly, Turk Telekomikasyon AS's and Calik Grubu's investments in privatisation processes in Azerbaijan and Albania are examples of investments based on such FSAs. Turk Telekominikasyon AS entered the Azeri market by acquiring a mobile network operator with around 3 million subscribers. The company's partnerships in Georgia, Kazakhstan, and Moldova operate as the largest global system for mobiles (GSM) companies in their respective countries. These examples show that TMNCs exploit their firm-specific managerial and technological advantages obtained in Turkey in less developed markets.

In sum, acquisitions by TMNCs in developed countries are motivated by inward internationalisation strategies of reaching new markets through obtaining technology, market information, and brands. Acquisitions in developing countries aim at accessing new markets and lowering costs by using their firm-specific technological and managerial advantages.

Discussion and conclusions

This chapter offered an analysis of the current trends, competitive advantages, and motivations of TMNC investments in Europe with special reference to greenfield investments and acquisitions. It focused on geographical and sectoral distribution of these investments with particular emphasis on FSAs, CSAs, and structural complementarities. It examined the extent to which key theoretical perspectives on the MNC internationalisation can explain outbound investments from a developing economy like Turkey's.

TMNCs have their greenfield investments in neighbouring geographies, especially in transition economies and developing countries. Only 22 percent of greenfield investments are located in developed economies. There has been sectoral concentration in the construction subsector of the real estate sector. Most of these investments are in Turkmenistan and Russia. Such investments are mostly related to infrastructure investments (e.g., roads, tunnels, bridges), premises, airports, and hotels. TMNCs also have similar infrastructure investments in Bulgaria and Romania. TMNCs' greenfield investments are motivated by market-seeking (access to domestic markets as well as access to EU markets via exports) and cost-seeking FDI (e.g., tax advantages, access to raw materials and cheap labour) where these firms exploit their FSAs, such as managerial and market knowledge, expertise, and technology. Key CSAs include operating in oligopolistic industries, economies of scale and leadership in home market, geographical, cultural, and institutional proximity.

In contrast to greenfield investments, most TMNCs' acquisitions are in developed countries (72 percent of total investments). The EU is the most preferred region for these firms. Holland attracts the highest amount of investments in the

EU. This is because it offers tax advantages and has extensive bilateral invest‐
ment treaties, therefore Turkish firms incorporated in Holland (or subsidiaries of
TMNCs) for fiscal considerations tend to use it as a home country for investing in
other countries. Half of the acquisitions in the Netherlands are concentrated in the
manufacturing, banking, and telecommunications sectors.

Although the main current theoretical lenses available in IB literature such as
FSAs and CSAs are widely used for developed-country MNC internationalisation,
they are also useful in explaining the internationalisation behaviour of EMNCs,
in particular TMNCs. Thus, this chapter focuses on the FSAs of TMNCs obtained
from both home CSAs and host CSAs in understanding the motivations behind
TMNC investments in Europe. It showed that some of the largest TMNCs are
guided by various complementary motivations, including the exploitation and
exploration of FSAs and CSAs in different times and contexts. They are also suc‐
cessful in relying on both FSAs obtained in home markets and FSAs obtained from
host markets in their internationalisation activities.

TMNCs have inward and outward internationalisation strategies. In regard to
inward internationalisation, their key motivation has been to access brand, technol‐
ogy, market knowledge, and managerial knowledge/expertise in developed markets.
In doing so, TMNCs aim to build or strengthen their competitive advantages. The
acquisition of FSAs helps these firms to access new markets. Thus, one of the main
motivations has been to internalise proprietary firm-specific assets. When TMNCs
acquire firms in transition and developing countries, they benefit from outward
internationalisation to exploit their FSAs, such as relatively advanced managerial
knowledge and technology. However, it should be noted that some of the TMNCs,
such as Yıldız Holding and Yildirim Holding, have stakes in developed-country
MNCs and they exploit their FSAs and home country CSAs. These family-owned
diversified firms also utilise global consolidator strategies in their business activities.

It should be noted that complementarities arising from structural contexts, such
as the appreciation of the Turkish lira against major currencies during the global
financial crisis and euro crisis, and financial difficulties of target companies in
a crisis environment, have also contributed to TMNCs' acquisition activities.
Finally, it would be interesting to investigate in detail whether these deals make
respective TMNCs formidable global competitors.

Note

1 Bakir gratefully acknowledges the support of the Scientific & Technological Research
Council of Turkey (TÜBİTAK, 110K346 and Postdoctoral Fellowship for Research
Abroad, TÜBİTAK 2219). This paper is related to COST Action IS0905, 'The Emer‐
gence of Southern Multinationals and Their Impact on Europe'. Authors also thank Pinar
Donmez, Mustafa Yagci, and Mina Kozluca for their assistance.

Bibliography

Akçaoğlu, E. (2005). *Türk Şirketlerinin Dış Yatırımları: Saikler ve Stratejiler.* Ankara:
Türkiye Bankalar Birliği.

Anadolu Ajansı. (2010). 'Türk Telekom, Uluslararası Telekom Devini Satın Aldı', May 18.
Anadolu Ajansi-English News. (2007). 'Hurriyet to purchase trader media east', January 2.
Anka Haber Ajansı. (2007). 'Godiva'yı almamızda kredi krizi ve değerli YTL önemli rol oynadı', December 28.
Aulakh, P. S. (2007). 'Emerging multinationals from developing economies: Motivations, paths and performance', *Journal of International Management*, 13(3): 235–240.
Bakır, C. (2013). *Bank Behaviour and Resilience: The Effect of Structures, Institutions and Agents*. London: Palgrave Macmillan.
Bakır, C. (2016). *Turk Cok Uluslulari*. Istanbul: Koc University Press. (forthcoming)
Bakır, C. and Acur, N. (2016). 'Turkish multinationals in Russia', in Liuhto, K., Sutyrin, S. and Blanchard, J. (eds), *Foreign Direct Investment to and from Russia: Recent Trends and International Investment Cooperation*. London: Routledge (forthcoming).
Brennan, L. ed. (2011). *The Emergence of Southern Multinationals: Their Impact on Europe*. London/New York: Palgrave Macmillan.
Campbell, J. L. (2011). 'The U.S. financial crisis: Lessons for theories of institutional complementarity', *Socioeconomic Review*, 9: 211–234.
Crouch, C. (2010). 'Complementarity', in Morgan, G., Campbell, J. L., Crouch, C., Pedersen, O. K. and Whitley, R. (eds), *The Oxford Handbook of Comparative Institutional Analysis*. New York: Oxford University Press, 117–137.
Cuervo-Cazurra, A. and Ramamurti, R. (2014). *Understanding Multinationals from Emerging Markets*. Cambridge: Cambridge University Press.
Demirbağ, M. and Yaprak, A. (eds). (2015). *Handbook of Emerging Market Multinational Corporations*. Cheltenham: Edward Elgar.
Dunning, J. H. (1988). *Explaining International Production*. London: Unwin Hyman.
Dunning, J. H. (1993). *Multinational Enterprises and the Global Economy*. New York: Addison Wesley.
Erdilek, A. (2003). 'A comparative analysis of inward and outward FDI in Turkey', *Transnational Corporations*, 12(3): 79–105.
Erdilek, A. (2007). 'Outward Foreign Direct Investment by Enterprises from Turkey', *Global Players from Emerging Markets: Strengthening Enterprise Competitiveness through Outward Investment*. New York/Geneva: UNCTAD, 147–162.
Ernst and Young. (2014). *EY's Attractiveness Survey Europe 2014: Back in the Game*. Available at www.ey.com/Publication/vwLUAssets/EY-2014-European-attractiveness-survey/$FILE/EY-2014-European-attractiveness-survey.pdf
Financial Times. (2014). 'Blackstone and PAI seal sale of United Biscuits to Turkish group Yıldız', November 3.
Forbes. (2014). 'En Zenginler Listesi', s.64.
Goldstein, A. (2007). *Multinational Companies from Emerging Economies*. London/New York: Palgrave Macmillan.
Guillén, M. and García-Canal, E. (2012). *Emerging Markets Rule: Growth Strategies of the New Global Giants*. New York: McGraw-Hill.
Harvard Business Review (Turkey). (2012). 'Lokalden Globale' [From Local to Global]. Istanbul, November, 66-69.
Hazarworld. (2013). *Bölgenin Güçlü Oyuncusu Gübretaş*. Available at www.hazarworld.com/201302/roportaj/bolgenin-guclu-oyuncusu-gubretas
Hennart, J. F. (2012). 'Emerging market multinationals and the theory of the multinational enterprise', *Global Strategy Journal*, 2: 168–187.
Kale, P., Singh, H. and Raman, P. A. (2009). 'Don't integrate your acquisitions, partner with them', *Harvard Business Review*, 87: 109–115.

Kaya, H. (2009). 'Unfavorable business environment and foreign direct investment activities of Turkish manufacturing firm', *BDDK Bankacılık ve Finansal Piyasalar*, 3(1): 101–118.

Kaya, H. and Erden, D. (2008). 'Firm-specific capabilities and foreign direct investment activities of Turkish manufacturing firms: An empirical study', *Journal of Management Development*, 27(7): 761–777.

Kayam, S. and Hisarcıklılar, M. (2009). 'Türkiye'den Çıkan Doğrudan Yatırımları Belirleyen Etmenler: 1992–2005', *İşletme, İktisat ve Finans*, 24(280): 47–70.

Khanna, T. and Palepu, K. (2006). 'Emerging giants: Building world class companies in developing countries', *Harvard Business Review*, 84(10): 60–69.

Klein, S. and Wocke, A. (2007). 'Emerging global contenders: The South African experience', *Journal of International Management*, 13(3): 319–337.

Luo, Y. and Tung, R. L. (2007). 'International expansion of emerging market enterprises: A springboard perspective', *Journal of International Business Studies*, 38(4): 481–498.

Mathews, J. A. (2002). *Dragon Multinational: A New Model for Global Growth*. New York: Oxford University Press.

Narula, R. and Dunning, J. H., (2010). 'Multinational enterprises, development and globalization: Some clarifications and a research agenda', *Oxford Development Studies*, 38(3): 263–287.

Port Finance International. (2012). 'Black Sea 2012 special | Exclusive interview with Robert Yuksel Yildirim', April 25. Available at http://portfinanceinternational.com/features/item/ 157-pfi-black-sea-2012-special exclusive-interview-with-robert-yuksel-yildirim

Ramamurti, R. (2009). 'What have we learned about emerging market MNEs?', in Ramamurti, R. & Singh, J. V. (eds), *Emerging Multinationals from Emerging Markets*. Cambridge: Cambridge University Press.

Ramamurti, R. (2012). 'What is really different about emerging market multinationals?', *Global Strategy Journal*, 2: 41–47.

Ramamurti, R. (2013). 'Cross-border M&A and competitive advantage of Indian EMNEs', in Williamson, P., Ramamurti, R., Fleury, A. and Fleury, M.T.T. (eds), *The Competitive Advantage of Emerging Market Multinationals*. Cambridge: Cambridge University Press, 239–259.

Ramamurti, R. and Singh, J. V. (2009) *Emerging Multinationals in Emerging Markets*. Cambridge: Cambridge University Press.

Rugman, A. M. (2009). 'Theoretical aspects of MNEs from emerging economies', in Ramamurti, R. and Singh, J. V. (eds), *Emerging Multinationals in Emerging Markets*. Cambridge: Cambridge University Press, 42–63.

Rugman, A. M. and Nguyen, Q.T.K. (2014). 'Modern international business theory and emerging economy MNCs', in Cuervo-Cazurra, A. and Ramamurti, R. (eds), *Understanding Multinationals from Emerging Markets*. Cambridge: Cambridge University Press, 53–80.

Rugman, A. M., & Verbeke, A. (1990). *Global Corporate Strategy and Trade Policy*. London: Croom Helm.

Sewell, W. H. (1992). 'A theory of structure: Duality, agency and transformation', *American Journal of Sociology*, 98: 1–29.

Star Gazetesi. (2004). 'DuPont SA Sabancı'nın', October 9.

Today's Zaman. (2011). 'Godiva CEO says company needed a Turkish partner to grow', December 20.

UNCTAD. (2006). *World Investment Report 2006: FDI from Developing and Transition Economies: Implications for Development*. New York/Geneva: United Nations.

UNCTAD. (2015). *World Investment Report 2015: Reforming International Investment Governance*. New York/Geneva: United Nations.

Williamson, P. and Zeng, M. (2009). 'Chinese multinationals: Emerging through new gateways', in Ramamurti, R. and Singh, J. V. (eds), *Emerging Multinationals in Emerging Markets.* Cambridge: Cambridge University Press, 81–109.

Williamson, P., Ramamurti, R., Fleury, A. and Fleury, M.T.T. (2013). *The Competitive Advantage of Emerging Market Multinationals.* Cambridge: Cambridge University Press.

Yaprak, A. and Karademir, B. (2011), 'Emerging market multinationals' role in developed country multinationals' regional expansion: A critical review of the literature and Turkish company examples', *Journal of World Business*, 46: 438–446.

10 Indian firms in Europe

Main characteristics, competitive advantages and strategies

Christian Milelli

Introduction

Economic relations between India and the EU have increased since the new millennium in a general context where transnational investment flows are an important pillar of the integration of national economies within the global economy. While India–EU trade (imports + exports) modestly grew – compared with China–EU trade, for example – from €507 million in 2003 to €1.1 billion in 2012, Indian investment in the EU increased from €615 million in 2003 to €2.2 billion in 2011, whereas EU investment in India rose sharply in the same time frame from €759 million to €13.8 billion.[1, 2]

Mutual engagement between India and the EU was primarily based on trade cooperation which was converted into a strategic partnership in 2014. Negotiations for a comprehensive and ambitious free trade agreement, officially dubbed the 'Broad-based Trade and Investment Agreement' – to reduce tariffs significantly on goods, to liberalize services and to make investment provisions – started in June 2007. Discussions are still ongoing, with several gaps still remaining between both parties. Experts believe that the agreement, once in place, would help Indian companies to expand their presence across Europe.

The current contribution emphasizes two aspects. First, it intends to provide a better understanding of the arrival and expansion of Indian affiliates in Europe, with a particular focus devoted to potential specificities of Indian companies. Second, the impact of the financial crises on the strategies of those companies is assessed in a global context of 'shifting wealth' (Pezzini 2013).

Indian companies have internationalized in two sequential periods (Ramamurti and Singh 2009): the first wave lasted during the 1970s and 1980s, and the second one began after the adoption of economic reforms in 1991. The most striking difference between both periods lies in the fact that a great majority of investments during the second wave were directed to advanced countries, whereas it was the reverse in the previous wave (Lall 1983).

Indian investment in Europe really emerged in 2002 when the presence of Indian companies attained a critical amount, either in number of companies or in investment outlays. It was also more visible due to the acquisitions made by Indian companies of iconic European companies.

A look at the data shows that India outward direct investment (ODI) stock in the EU remains tiny compared with the stock of EU direct investments made by extra EU-27 – 0.2 percent at the end of 2012 – and compared with other BRICs. For the same year, Brazil accounted for 2.5 percent, China plus Hong Kong and Russia 2 percent each. However, the figure changed recently. Indeed, Indian ODI flows peaked just shy of 2 percent in 2008 when compared with EU direct investment flows from extra EU-27 before receding to 0.8 percent in 2011 due to the eurozone crisis.[3]

To conduct our analysis we constructed a firm-level dataset given the limits and inconsistency of official data (balance of payments) with many round tripping investments and the use of special purpose entities to channel financial resources across borders. The resulting database compiles secondary sources of information such as Thomson Reuters for M&A deals or fDi Markets for greenfield; additional information was gleaned from systematic gathering of professional newspapers, including *Financial Times* and *The Economist*, or company websites. It provides a better understanding of the presence of Indian companies across Europe, particularly useful in a crisis period.[4]

Our dataset contains 585 Indian companies which have conducted 1,112 operations of investment in Europe for the period 2002–2012. Because of the deficit of systematic information in terms of value, we focus on the number of operations. It is frustrating in a particular way but by doing so we bypass the bias resulting from one huge amount of investment made in a particular year (De Beule and Van Den Bulcke 2012).

Indian companies that have invested are from different sectors and capital origins: the Tata group, which is a private conglomerate, outstrips any other Indian company, with 85 operations across Europe in numerous activities (e.g. agribusiness, automobile, steel, software). Coming up behind are Wipro Technologies with 29 investments, Infosys Technologies (18) and Satyam Computer Services (15),[5] which are specialized companies focused on information processing. The State Bank of India (13 operations), which is a public entity, and Reliance group (10), a family-owned conglomerate (Ambani), follow. The previous heterogeneity both between different companies and between companies of the same group concerns also internationalization strategies as much as internationalization process and geographical orientation. To date, the share of European sales compared with global sales is still low on average except for some SMEs in technology-intensive sectors.

When looking at the number of investments made in Europe by Indian companies during the period 2002 to 2012 (Figure 10.1), one can clearly identify the effect of both crises (subprimes and eurozone): a steep fall in 2009 and afterwards a steady lessening from a sharp rebound in 2010. This trend is well correlated, for the same period, with the number of M&As carried out by Indian firms in Europe and in the US (Milelli and Le Goff 2012). When comparing with other BRICs members the results are mixed: on one side, the acquisitions made by Brazilian companies in Europe display the same profile, with, however, fewer operations (Alonso 2014), whereas, on the other side, Chinese and Russian investors display a quite opposite figure. In particular, during the crises period, Russian investors have heavily invested in Europe, particularly in CEE, through acquisitions (Panibratov 2014).

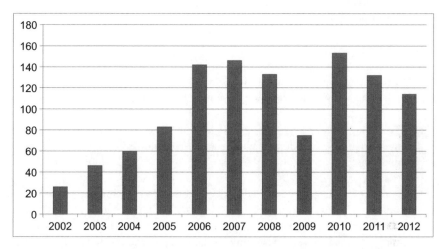

Figure 10.1 Investments made in Europe by Indian firms, 2002–2012 (in number)
Source: Computed from the database set up by the author, 2013

Breakdown by capital origin

The major share of Indian companies located in Europe is held by private entities; only a tiny amount, around 3 percent, are of public origin. Besides the oil and gas sector, state ownership is well represented within the banking sector, with the State Bank of India, Punjab National Bank, Union Bank of India and the Exim bank of India.

Besides large companies, Indian corporate presence in Europe is also driven by SMEs, particularly in technology-intensive sectors such as pharmacy and ICT.

One peculiar characteristic of Indian companies in Europe, which mirrors the situation of the home country, is the family nature of the ownership and control, be they large groups such as Tata or Reliance, or others. One exception to this idiosyncratic feature is the software-and-data processing sector in which companies managed by professional appointed staff had a more international commitment at the early stage of their development. Indeed, the rise and the development of this sector was entirely driven by foreign markets – essentially the US, resulting from the specialization and outsourcing revolution that occurred there in the 1980s.

Breakdown by motives

Evidence of motives behind investments made by Indian firms in Europe is drawn from the proprietary dataset and the reading of corporate websites. It appears that the main difference lies between greenfield investment and M&As.

Indeed, as far as greenfield investments are concerned, two main motives can be put forward.

(1) Access to markets, i.e. proximity to markets or customers and domestic market growth potential.

For example, Dimexon Diamonds (Antwerp, Belgium) decided in 2005 to set up a unit to conduct sales activities for diamonds. Antwerp has been well known since the Middle Ages as a center for cutting and trading diamonds. Actually, it has surpassed the long-established Jewish community in activities related to diamonds.

(2) Skilled professional availability. This motive is essentially driven by the importance of professional services and it determines in large part the locational choice.

This point can be illustrated by the decision taken in 2004 by the Indian biological company Aventha to locate in the life science cluster, 'Medicon Valley', which spans from eastern Denmark to southern Sweden.

Actually, Indian firms are increasingly combining the above motives when they invest in Europe.

Efficiency reasons, particularly economies of scope, which are on the rise due to the need to differentiate goods or services, have to be taken into consideration. For example, the acquisition of a German polyester producer, Trevira, in 2004, by Reliance supported a differentiated product portfolio by the latter.

For M&As, two underlying motives are at play.

(1) Access to new markets or increased access to existing ones.

For example, the acquisition of Alti by Tata Consultancy Services in 2013 to corner a market share in France, a market viewed by Indian software companies as closed.

(2) Access to strategic assets, particularly intangible assets such as R&D, brands or distribution networks. Actually, mergers and acquisition operations allow the embedded transfer of knowledge such as intellectual property rights or other knowledge-based capital, through the hand-over of company ownership.

Increasingly, the access to new markets is associated with the access to strategic assets when Indian companies acquire local companies in Europe. The strategy followed by Bharat Forge since 2004 with the acquisition of two German mid-sized enterprises is emblematic: indeed, the Indian company aims to become the largest manufacturer of forgings globally and, at the same time, to use its European acquisitions to displace its core business from auto parts towards new high-growth sectors.

Breakdown by host countries

For their location choices, Indian companies mainly focus on countries with large market size; this feature underlines the importance of market-seeking motivations. The positive relationships between host countries' GDP and ODI has been shown

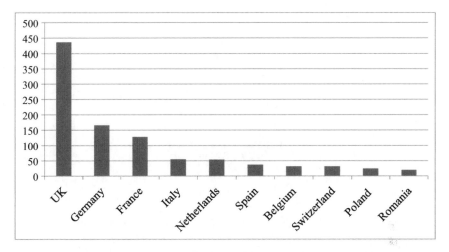

Figure 10.2 Main European host countries for Indian investment, 2002–2012 (in number)
Source: Computed from the database set up by the author, 2013

by scholars (Buckley et al. 2007; Cheng and Ma 2007; Kolstad and Wiig 2010); but other aspects may also be of importance (history, language, culture or ethnic community).

Ten European countries receive the major share of the number of investments carried out in Europe by Indian companies for the period 2002–2012 (Figure 10.2). The three largest countries – Germany, France and UK – capture some 70 percent of the whole number, whereas their cumulative GDP reached 50 percent of the total EU GDP in 2012.

CEE, particularly Poland and Romania (Figure 10.2), are emerging as an alternate destination for manufacturing or professional services in a 'near-shoring approach'.[6] Western Europe is still attractive. In particular, it is the main destination for the setup of R&D units.

Breakdown by modes of entry

Greenfield investments and M&As are quite similar in terms of number of operations (Figure 10.3), whereas based on anecdotal evidence there is a substantial difference in terms of value, with M&As largely ahead.

M&A activity picked up during 2006–2008 (pre-crisis period), particularly in 2007, with several high-profile operations, such as the Tata acquisition of Corus in the UK and the Netherlands, the Suzlon takeover of REpower in Germany, and the United Spirits buy-out of Whyte & Mackay in the UK. In some cases, where the turnover of the target companies was several times larger than that of the acquiring firm, the acquisition could be problematic due to debt burden, to say nothing of other aspects, such as cultural gap and difference in governance schemes.

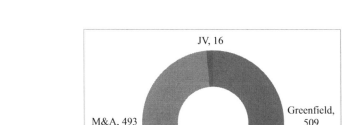

Figure 10.3 Different modalities of entry or presence in Europe for Indian companies, 2002–2012 (in number)

Source: Computed from the database set up by the author, 2013

Greenfield investment and extensions were the preferred modes of entry of Indian investors for the years 2010–2012. As a matter of fact, extensions increased six times from 2009 to 2010 to recede the following year; they were related quite exclusively to previous greenfield investments except in some cases, such as the iconic acquisition made by the Tata group of the automotive firms Jaguar and Land Rover.

Last, there is no evidence of large divestments conducted by Indian companies during the crises period.

The above result showing that greenfield is the preferred mode of entry suggests that the low valuation of local companies with even fire-sale prices, as a consequence of the European debt crisis, was not seen as a genuine opportunity by Indian firms. On the contrary, greenfield investments were seen to expand or shore up their sales bases and to ramp up their manufacturing support and their delivery hubs for services across Europe. A more constrained access to financial resources in Europe due to the protracted crisis was the main cause advanced.

Figure 10.4 confirms this point by showing that Indian firms had a preference after the financial crisis erupted for extensions over M&As in order to consolidate their sales bases, development centers or plants.

When looking at the distribution of the Indian modes of entry according to the three main host European countries (UK, Germany and France), we find a similar profile between greenfield investment and M&As, with, however, greenfield being always ahead.

The spatial concentration is higher for extensions and lower for M&As. This last result is quite unexpected but revealed that the acquisition dynamic is rather driven by manufacturing functions and sectors which are scattered across Europe. On the contrary, the polarization on extensions, particularly since the crisis, reveals the willingness of Indian affiliates to consolidate a presence in main European markets.

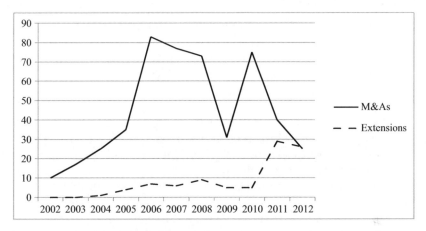

Figure 10.4 Contrasted trends of M&As and extensions related to Indian companies in Europe, 2002–2012 (in number)

Source: Computed from the database set up by the author, 2013

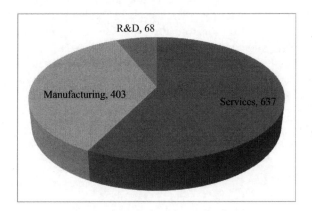

Figure 10.5 Distribution of functions targeted by Indian companies when they invest in Europe, 2002–2012 (in number)

Source: Computed from the database set up by the author, 2013

Breakdown by functions

Services before manufacturing are the main function operated by Indian companies when they invest in Europe (Figure 10.5). Services consist either of a large array of professional services (software, consulting, financial or marketing) or of sales (delivery, logistics and after-sales). Manufacturing receded during the last years, whereas R&D was not viewed as an option during the crisis period, to climb the technological ladder or diversify towards new products or services. When considered in detail, it appears that pharmacy has limited its investment in R&D, whereas ICT has kept investing.

Breakdown by sectors

Three sectoral clusters can be identified: IT services in general, pharmaceuticals and related products and engineered goods and metals. Actually, ICT is the main sector of Indian investment in Europe, thanks to the presence of numerous software development and information processing companies – be they the three largest (Tata Consultancy Service, Infosys Tech and Wipro Tech) or smaller ones (Figure 10.6).

Pharmacy, particularly generics, is well represented since early 2000s, with a wave of acquisitions of European companies or subunits, or even North American affiliates in the generics (Milelli et al. 2010). More recently, the equipment and automobile combined sectors have surpassed it and taken the second rank, with sizeable investments made by firms such as Tata Motors, Avantha Group and Ruia Group. The main motive was to get deeper linkages in the host economy, particularly Germany, through inherited business relationships.

Interestingly, Indian banks are not targeting domestic banking markets in Europe but rather Indian communities. Indeed, as India is the largest remittance recipient country in the world, with $69 billion in 2012,[7] Indian banks are keen to serve this lucrative segment by locating in countries such as the United Kingdom[8] and places where 'non-resident Indians' are concentrated (London or Antwerp in Belgium, for example). Some Indian banks are also supporting Indian corporate activities in Europe, notably by facilitating the acquisition of local companies.

Further, it's interesting to discriminate between high technology versus low technology according to OECD typology (OECD 2011), for two main reasons. First, for M&As, as a prominent explanation advanced for these operations is the access to new technology and know-how. And when one looks at the data, one can find support for this assumption. Indeed, the more technology-intensive the sectors are, the more numerous the number of M&As: ICT, pharmacy, equipment, automobiles and chemistry added together constitute 65.5 percent of all Indian M&As realized during the period 2002 to 2012.

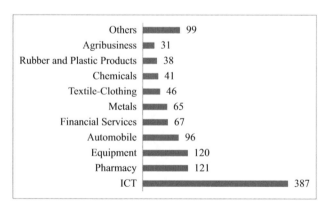

Figure 10.6 Sectoral distribution of Indian investment in Europe, 2002–2012 (in number)
Source: Computed from the database set up by the author, 2013

Second, it allows for better identification of the different impacts on recipient countries, particularly in terms of innovation or skills. The case of India, among BRIC, is specific, as services, particularly high value-added ones, are the prominent sector in Europe (Figure 10.6). As a result, when considering only manufacturing, one finds medium-low or medium-high technology industries, whereas when adding services, the resulting new distribution is closer to a high technological intensity level.

What about their specific advantages?

The quest for ownership advantages by Indian firms as part of the OLI paradigm is consistent with the resource-based view which stresses existing resources and capabilities on one side, and the evolutionary view which rather focuses asset accumulation and learning capabilities on the other. Actually, ownership advantages stems from two sub-advantages: one is FSA and the other is CSA.

So far, ownership advantages of Indian firms in Europe are basically of CSA nature, and the explanation put forward by Ramamurti and Singh (2009) to explain CSA is verified in Europe. Let's recall the underlying factors: first, the continental size of the Indian economy; second, the substantial resources in technical and managerial capabilities; third, market-friendly institutions (rule of law) that are rather uncommon in countries with the same level of development; fourth, a well-established entrepreneurial tradition. As a result, when FSAs can be identified, they are derived from CSAs.

However, in some sectors, Indian firms are erecting FSAs, particularly in IT-enabled services through very sophisticated project management expertise. In addition, they can reap advantages from their latecomer status, which could be used as leverage in some European manufacturing sectors such as auto parts or metals with many European enterprises with huge fixed costs and legacy issues.

Strategies of internationalization

Two main strategies of internationalization followed by Indian companies in Europe arise. As ideal types, they fit well the general scheme advanced by Rugman (2009): first, a low-cost partnering strategy that chiefly concerns IT-enabled services. Flagship companies such as TCS, Infosys and Wipro and mid-cap or SMEs are following this strategy. Thanks to the Internet revolution and the low cost of cross-border telecommunications, Indian companies have developed a very innovative business model combining outsourcing and offshoring. These firms are advancing in system integration and internal managerial coordination that can be viewed as an indication of FSAs of their own. Indeed, Indian firms have the highest rating worldwide for process capability.[9]

The second one is deftly denominated a global or regional consolidator strategy. Amtek Auto is a particularly illustrative case of this strategy in Europe which is gaining momentum for two reasons. First, a growing number of firms in engineered goods or metals are embarking on this strategy. Second, it allows for the restructuring or consolidation of assembly industries in a more efficient way. For example, by acquiring the German forging and integrated machining company Neumayer Tekfor, in 2013, Amtek Auto integrated a wide range of products (e.g. high precision camshafts, valves, train components) to its existing portfolio. In addition, due to scattered localizations, Amtek Auto can better supply its global customers.[10] As a result, the impacts at the industry level are more important than in the previous strategy.

The last strategy, called the global first-mover is rather limited and somehow receding in Europe. For example, Suzlon Energy, which was identified by Rugman (2009) as a perfect representative of this strategy, encountered difficulties and had to disengage from European activities.

Typology on the life cycle: what happens to the investments over the years?

Be aware that success and failure depend on the point of view. Indeed, what can be viewed from a European lens or the standard economic approach as a failure may be considered by Indian eyes as a success or at best giving mixed results.

However, there is anecdotal evidence that several Indian acquisitions that occurred before the financial crisis faced challenges from 2009 onwards. Indeed, in their move to acquire overseas assets, several Indian companies paid a premium. For example, in 2006, Tata Steel outbid Companhia Siderúrgica Nacional of Brazil to acquire the Anglo-Dutch steelmaker Corus. In the end, Tata Steel bought Corus for €9 billion and raised €4.5 billion of debt: it was then considered the most expensive steel deal when compared with the earnings of the target company. Indeed, the turnover of Corus was four times larger than the turnover of Tata Steel.

As a result, many operations were at high valuations, forcing the acquirer to raise debt by borrowing heavily on international markets. Besides financial constraints not anticipated when deals were launched or concluded, cultural issues (a strong family-oriented management) have jeopardized the post-integration process of several Indian M&As.

We tried to go further in order to have a better understanding by dividing the period of reference (2003–2012) into two equivalent sub-periods (five years long each): first, from 2003 to 2007, a pre-crisis period, and second, from 2008 to 2012, a crisis and post-crisis period. Further, we did research on company websites and through the Internet to check what happened to these operations during the crisis period, with several options in line: downsizing, divestment, closure or delocalization on one side, or extension or new acquisition(s) on the other, or, if fine, nothing in particular (same perimeter and scope of activity).

We selected the pharmacy sector, which was characterized by the highest level of acquisitions of European companies in the pre-crisis period (2003–2007): forty-six acquisitions were realized by thirty different Indian companies. During the following five years, the number of acquisitions slowed to thirty-three deals (a 30 percent decrease) with twenty-five different Indian firms involved. Furthermore, 60 percent of firms that conducted acquisitions in the pre-crisis period continued to buy

European companies in the following years. However, several companies (Dishman Pharmaceuticals, Ranbaxy, Strides Arcolab, Wockhardt) which were very active during the first period were out of the business afterwards. But there is no evidence that they faced severe problems with their previous acquisitions; rather the Indian firms needed time to integrate them. When looking in detail at the fate of all the acquisitions made in the pre-crisis period in the pharmacy sector (forty-six deals), there is no compelling evidence of downsizing, delocalization, reselling or closure.

In fact, Indian firms were very cautious in their move to acquire European companies or European affiliates from US parent companies, particularly Pfizer. Debts on average were sustainable and synergies were promoted in areas where Indian firms had a competitive advantage, be they based on economies of scale or technological-scientific expertise (e.g. generics, active pharmaceutical ingredients or contract research, manufacturing service).

However, it is obvious that the economic environment in the crisis period was less favorable for business activities. Accordingly, Sun Pharmaceutical, which already had a European base, withdrew in mid-2013 from the race to buy the Swedish firm Meda Pharmaceuticals for up to $6 billion. The reasons advanced were both a sharp fall in the rupee and a patent settlement with Pfizer in the US worth $550 million. As a consequence, the Indian company, which had no cash left, was not willing to incur a lot of debt.

In summary, pharmacy is a specific sector in which Indian companies have a truly competitive advantage: smart strategies are conducted by professional and very dedicated people.

To get a broader view of the behavior of Indian companies in Europe, one can switch and see a 'representative' actor. The Tata group is a quite natural candidate: to be sure, it is the largest Indian investor in Europe and is present and active in several activities (e.g. data and information processing with Tata Consultancy Services, automobiles with Tata Motors, steel with Tata Steel), thanks to its conglomerate nature.

Table 10.1 highlights the strategies followed in Europe by the Tata group during the period 2003–2012. It shows, as expected, that Tata made fewer acquisitions after the crisis; it is also quite natural that the decrease was significant, as Tata made numerous acquisitions before the crisis in different industries. In the crisis period, there was only one reduction of the workforce in the automotive industry, resulting from a sharp decrease in the demand for luxury cars. In parallel, the Tata group has continued to invest through acquisition or by combining acquisition and extension in industries where they had already heavily invested (i.e. automotive and steel).

Conclusion

In conclusion, Indian firms have generally followed a cautious investment behavior: either when they look for the target companies or when they took control having the patience not to push for immediate changes by imposing their way of doing business (EICC 2012). As they are quite exclusively private firms, they had

Table 10.1 Acquisitions, extensions and reduction realized by the Tata group in Europe, 2003–2013 (in number)

	Years 2003–2007	Years 2008–2012		
	Acquisition	Acquisition	Extension	Reduction
Tata Auto Components	1			
Tata Chemicals	1	1		
Tata Consultancy Services	3		1	
Tata Interactive Systems	1			
Tata Motors	2	2 (Jaguar and Land Rover, 2008)	1	1 (450 layoffs, 2009)
Tata Tea	1			
Tata Technologies	1			
Tata Steel	2 (Corus, 2006)	1	2	
Total	**12**	**4**	**4**	**1**

Source: Computed from the database set up by the author, 2013

to finance their acquisitions by internal cash or/and debts, which is a real constraint on their balance sheets. However, this constraint was somehow downplayed in conglomerate structures thanks to the possibility of cross-financing.

As a consequence, the acquisitions made in Europe by Indian companies (e.g. pharmacy sector, the Tata group) were quite immune during the crisis period. Few Indian companies encountered a lot of difficulties in Europe during the crisis except those which had followed an aggressive strategy of acquisition either overseas or at home.

Suzlon and United Breweries are two prominent examples. Wind turbine maker Suzlon Energy sold, in 2011, its remaining 26 percent stake in Belgium-based Hansen Transmissions to a German company, ZF Friedrichshafen AG; one can recall that Suzlon acquired Hansen's entire shareholding in 2006 where the motivation was to gain access to needed technology and know-how. More generally, the international development of Suzlon was triggered by acquisitions made overseas by making extensive use of debt.

United Breweries through its flagship company sold, in 2012, to Diageo, a UK drink maker, 25 percent of its shares in order to get cash for the family parent company to rescue another member group, Kingfisher Airlines, which faced huge difficulties to stay afloat.

Notes

1 This paper was presented at the workshop "Emerging Market Firms in Europe" of the COST Action IS0905, KU Leuven University, April 4, 2014.
2 Eurostat website, 2014.

3 Eurostat database, balance of payments.
4 As a matter of fact, this source does not take into consideration investments made in Europe resulting from profit made locally or access to financing.
5 Before its acquisition in 2009 by Mahindra Group, due to internal difficulties (massive accounting fraud).
6 The practice of bringing manufacturing operations or services closer to a domestic market.
7 Followed by China ($60bn), the Philippines ($24bn) and Mexico with $23bn (World Bank 2013).
8 Indeed, the UK has the largest Indian community in Europe with 1.5 million individuals.
9 Based on the Capability and Maturity Model (CMM) delivered by the Carnegie Mellon University's Software Engineering Institute.
10 Neumayer Tekfor is headquartered in Germany with nine plants and services in Brazil, India, Italy, Mexico and the US.

References

Buckley, P. J., Clegg, L. J., Cross, A. R., Liu, X., Voss, H. and Zheng, P. (2007) 'The determinants of Chinese outward foreign direct investment', *Journal of International Business Studies*, 38, 4: 499–518.
Cheng, L. K. and Ma, Z. (2010) *China's Outward FDI: Past and Future*, Working School of Economics, Working Paper Series, Beijing, Renmin University.
De Beule, F. and Van Den Bulcke, D. (2012) 'Locational determinants of outward foreign direct investment: An analysis of Chinese and Indian greenfield investments', *Transnational Corporations*, 21, 1: 1–34.
Europe India Chamber of Commerce/ EICC (2012) *Indian Companies in the European Union: Reigniting Economic Growth*, Beijing.
Kolstad, I. and Wiig, A. (2010) 'What determines Chinese OFDI?', *Journal of World Business*, 47: 26–34.
Lall, S. (1983) *The New Multinationals: The Spread of Third World Enterprises*, Chichester: John Wiley, IRM Series on Multinationals.
Milelli, C., Hay, F. and Shi, Y. (2010) 'Chinese and Indian firms in Europe', International Journal of Emerging Markets, 5, 3–4: 377–397.
Milelli, C. and Le Goff, J. (2012) *European Inroads by BRICs Firms: The M&A Avenue*, MPRA Paper, 39865, Munich, Munich University Library.
OECD (2011) Economic Analysis and Statistics Division, Technology Intensity Definition, Working Document.
Pezzini, M. (2013) *Shifting Wealth*, Paper presented at the XV World Economy Meeting and OECD, Santander, June 5.
Ramamurti, R. and Singh, J. V. (2009) 'Indian multinationals: Generic internationalization strategies', in R. Ramamurti and J. Singh (eds), Emerging multinationals in Emerging markets, Cambridge: Cambridge University Press, pp. 110–166.
Rugman, A. M. (2009) 'Theoretical aspects of MNEs from emerging economies', in R. Ramamurti and J. Singh (eds), *Emerging Multinationals in Emerging Markets*, Cambridge: Cambridge University Press, pp. 42–63.

11 Collaborative innovation within Chinese MNCs' international networks

The role of cultural and institutional distances

Stefano Elia, Lucia Piscitello and Vittoria G. Scalera

Introduction

Emerging market multinational companies (EMNCs) have achieved impressive competitive positions in the global economy in a relatively short time. A key to explaining their rapid surge can be found in their strategies to fill the technological gap that has traditionally characterized firms from emerging economies (Kumar and Russell 2002; Awate et al. 2012). In fact, innovative and technical competencies are critical for EMNCs, as long as they aim at creating a sustainable competitive advantage to effectively compete with MNCs from advanced economies in the global marketplace and to participate in the high value-added stages of the global value chain (Mudambi 2008).

To develop such competencies and skills, EMNCs may use external knowledge sourcing that occurs through different channels and at various levels, including acquisitions and alliances, as well as personal relationships, buyer-supplier relationships or spillovers (Awate et al. 2015; Perri et al. 2015; Piscitello et al. 2015). This process of international knowledge sourcing enables EMNCs to tap into local repositories of knowledge and access different typologies of skills and innovative organizational conduits. The technological upgrading process of EMNCs can be favoured by international innovative collaborations among inventors located worldwide and the use of foreign subsidiaries' networks enabling the EMNCs to access high-quality knowledge generated in more advanced locations, where the bulk of innovation has been traditionally located (Cantwell 1989). This may be particularly crucial in high-tech industries, where innovation is the prominent competitive advantage, and firms experience constantly growing competitive pressure in terms of time and cost (Powell et al. 1996).

However, the literature has highlighted that when innovative collaborations and research projects involve individuals and institutions located in different countries, an array of crucial factors need to be evaluated in order to understand how to achieve impactful results and minimize costs and frictions. We focus our attention on the role played by institutional and cultural diversity of the actors involved in the innovation process as the literature has widely shown both positive and negative impacts of diversity on innovativeness and creativity (e.g. Meirovich 2010; Stahl et al. 2010) and economic outcome in general (Guiso et al. 2006). Namely, we pose the following research question: how do institutional and cultural distances affect EMNCs' innovative performance generated through international collaborations arising from their network of subsidiaries?

In order to investigate the proposed research question, we focus on Chinese multinational companies (MNCs), as they represent one of the most successful cases of international expansion and rapid technological upgrading, even if the process is still ongoing. In particular, we analyze the innovative performance generated by international innovative collaborations of high- and medium-tech Chinese MNCs within their foreign subunits. In order to measure this specific type of innovation output, we use patent data provided by the United States Patent and Trademark Office (USPTO) and granted to Chinese MNCs or their subsidiaries between 1975 and 2012. We consider a patent to be the result of an international collaborative innovation either when it is assigned to the foreign subsidiary of the Chinese MNCs, having at least a Chinese inventor, or when it is assigned to the Chinese parent MNC, having at least one inventor located in an MNC foreign country. We found that both cultural and institutional distance foster, rather than decrease, the international collaborative innovation arising from the network of subunits, either through the direct patenting of the subsidiaries or through the indirect contributions of the inventors located in the countries of the subunits to the patenting activity of the parent Chinese company.

Our work provides new empirical evidence on the strategies employed by Chinese MNCs to upgrade their technical competencies, namely by putting in place external knowledge sourcing through international collaborative innovation. We also contribute to the lively debate regarding the impact of both cultural and institutional distance on MNC innovative performance, focusing on international collaborations and technological upgrading.

Conceptual framework: international innovative collaboration and distance

The role of institutional distance

Although several empirical contributions have studied the role of institutional differences between countries in shaping firm performance and global strategies, the results are not unanimous yet. On the one hand, institutional distance may create a barrier to the transfer of organizational knowledge and routines (Kostova 1999). This may happen because the differences of the institutional settings hinder the creation of trust between peers, augmenting the uncertainty perceived by cooperating in international networks with organizations and individuals coming from different foreign countries (Zhao et al. 2004). Organizations and individuals coming from distant institutions are less likely to create a common ground where they can easily exchange ideas, technical competencies, resources and managerial skills, because the risk of an opportunistic behaviour of the partners is too high (Chen and

Hennart 2004; Demirbag et al. 2007). Conversely, lower institutional distance facilitates the establishment of an effective monitoring mechanism of the partners. Conversely, collaborating actors coming from similar institutional environments feel a sense of familiarity and are more prone to transfer intra-organizational practices and exchange knowledge. So, the above risks and challenges can be significantly lessened when the institutional distance is low.

However, as highlighted by De Beule et al. (2014), traditional approaches studying the impact of institutional distance primarily consider the *magnitude* of distance, mainly from the perspective of MNCs coming from advanced economies. Here, we focus on Chinese MNCs that, leveraging their network of foreign subsidiaries, establish innovative collaborations with foreign inventors, located mainly in advanced economies. Therefore, it becomes crucial to consider also the direction of the distance (Zaheer et al. 2012). In particular, when Chinese MNCs collaborate with inventors operating in advanced countries, they face lower risks and uncertainty, as they have moved to contexts with a higher institutional quality. Thus, contrary to previous arguments, it may be possible to find a positive impact of institutional distance on collaborative innovative performance within Chinese MNCs' subunits located in advanced economies.

The role of cultural distance

In this work, we consider cultural distance as a broad concept extensively used in the international business literature (e.g. Dow and Karunaratna 2006; Baack et al. 2015) and known as *psychic distance.* Johanson and Wiedersheim-Paul (1975: 308) define psychic distance as "the sum of factors preventing or disturbing the flow of information between firm and market. Examples of such factors are differences in language, culture, political systems, level of education, level of industrial development, etc.". Cultural factors have been widely shown to influence the process of ideas' generation and the interpretation of information, but also the interaction mechanism between peers (Kroeber and Kluckhohn 1952). In particular, cultural differences play a strategic role in shaping innovative processes and performance (Milliken et al. 2003), determining how individuals collaborate, learn from each other, transfer knowledge and competencies and share information.

Traditionally, cultural distance has been identified as a barrier or a difficulty to be overcome when collaboration is in place, since it may normally generate information asymmetry among peers (Zaheer and Hernandez 2011; Shenkar 2012). Culturally distant environments can hinder the transfer of intra-organizational practices and raise communication problems, thus reducing the possibility of learning and knowledge exchange. Therefore, we can expect that cultural diversity may have a negative impact on the innovative performance arising from collaboration of individuals and organizations located worldwide, since it increases the complexity to be managed, thus hindering the beneficial effects arising from knowledge recombination of different external sources.

Nevertheless, a complementary view of cultural diversity highlights that cultural heterogeneity can also lead to the exploration of new innovation paths and original competencies or routines (West 2002). In fact, the combination of different cultures may enable and revitalize creativity processes, thus possibly re-determining the effect of cultural diversity on collaborative innovative performance (Stahl et al. 2010). Creativity and innovation also come from technologies and competencies that are widespread worldwide, and the possibility of collaborating with internationally dispersed R&D teams favours the recombination of different knowledge sources, which may be locally bounded. Thus, the literature suggests that there may also be a positive effect of cultural diversity on the collaborative innovative performance, as far as it allows for creation and exploration of new and/or complementary innovative trajectories bringing together new perspectives, ideas, competencies and preferences (Stahl et al. 2010; Berry 2014).

Empirical analysis

The data

In order to investigate how institutional and cultural distances may affect the international collaborative innovation activities of Chinese MNCs, we employed a meticulous step procedure to identify our sample. First, we collected data about all Chinese MNCs operating in high-tech and medium-high-tech industries[1] in 2012[2] (ORBIS database, Bureau van Dijk). For each MNC, we collected information about the host location (country), age (foundation or acquisition year) and establishment mode (greenfield or M&A) of its domestic and international subsidiaries, by relying also on other databases to complete the information, i.e. FDI Markets, Zephyr, SDC Platinum and Lexis Nexis. The first step ended up with an initial sample of 302 high- and medium-high-tech Chinese MNCs with their 1,213 subsidiaries. Secondly, we collected data about the patents granted to the mentioned Chinese MNCs from the USPTO[3] in the period from 1975 to 2012 by searching for patents assigned either to the parent company or to one of its subsidiaries. We found that 49 out of 302 Chinese MNCs operating in high- and medium-high-tech industries had at least one patent granted by the USPTO. In the third step, we identified the patenting Chinese MNCs engaged in international collaborative innovation. In order to identify those patents created through international collaborative innovation, we considered the following two typologies: (1) patents assigned to the Chinese MNC and with at least one inventor located in a foreign country where the MNC is present with one of its subsidiaries, (2) patents assigned to the foreign subsidiary of the Chinese MNCs and with at least a Chinese inventor. We found that 171 patents originated from international collaborative innovation associated with 11 Chinese high- and medium-high-tech MNCs. Table 11.1 shows the 11 parent companies involved in international collaborative innovation and the distribution of the patents across the host countries. It can be noticed that most of the subsidiaries are located in advanced countries, which typically lie on the knowledge frontier and offer strong intellectual property rights regimes.

The Chinese MNCs included in our analysis had subsidiaries in 59 different countries, and recorded at least one collaborative innovation in at least one of the

Table 11.1 Distribution of collaborative patents by MNE and host country

MNE Name	Host Country (no. of collaborative patents)
China Aerospace International Holdings	Hong Kong (1)
Guangdong Elecpro Electric Appliance Holding	US (1)
Guangzhou Automobile Group Co., Ltd.	Hong Kong (1)
Hanergy Holding Group	US (5)
Huawei Investment	Austria (1), Belgium (1), Switzerland (1), Germany (3), Finland (4), France (2), UK (3), Hong Kong (1), India (1), Italy (4), Japan (7), the Netherland (3), Sweden (47), US (24)
Lenovo Group	Singapore (21)
Tasly Pharmaceutical	US (1)
TCL Corporation	France (11), Italy (1), US (2)
Tsinghua Tongfang	Singapore (1)
Vtech Electronics Industrial	US (6)
ZTE Corporation	Sweden (1), US (17)

host countries where their subsidiaries were located.[4] The final database involves all of the 11 parent companies and all of the 59 host countries, for a total of 139 observations, each corresponding to a pair parent-host country, i.e. to a subunit.

The variables and the methodology

Our dependent variable is *Collaborative Innovation*, which measures, for each subunit, the number of patents granted by the USPTO to the Chinese MNC or to one of its subsidiaries and resulted from the international collaborative innovative activities of the MNC. A total amount of 171 patents have been identified as collaborative innovation and are distributed among 15 different foreign countries (all categorized as advanced economies).

The first main explicative variable is *Institutional Distance*, which has been computed by applying the Kogut and Singh (1988) formula to the ten items provided by the Heritage Foundation.[5] The same index has been employed to account for the second main explicative variable, *Cultural Distance*, by combining the five psychic distance dimensions provided by Dow (2000) (https://sites.google.com/site/ddowresearch/home/scales).[6] The two indexes have been computed as follows:

$$Institutional\ Distance_{at} = \frac{1}{10}\sum_{i=1}^{10}\frac{\left(I_{ia}-I_{it}\right)^2}{Var_i}$$

$$Cultural\ Distance_{at} = \frac{1}{5}\sum_{i=1}^{5}\frac{\left(I_{ia}-I_{it}\right)^2}{Var_i}$$

where I_{ia} and I_{it} represent the value of the item i^7 for China (a) and for the subunit (t), and Var_i is the variance of the whole sample.

We also employ the following variables as controls: *Parent Knowledge Base*, i.e. the number of accumulated patents assigned directly to the parent companies and not generated from international collaboration (not belonging to the dependent variable); *Subunit Portfolio Depth,* i.e. the number of the MNC subsidiaries in each host country); *Subunit Portfolio Breadth,* i.e. the total number of subunits (host countries in which the company has subsidiaries) of each parent company; *Subunit Age,* a variable taking a value of 1 if the oldest subsidiary in the subunit was founded or acquired after 2008, a value of 2 if between 2004 and 2008, and 3 if before 2004;[8] *Parent Size,* which is measured through the total number of employees of the parent company in the year 2012 (source: Orbis); *Geographic Distance,* i.e. the distance between China and the subunit, which is accounted for through the variables provided by CEPII[9]; *Subunit R&D Intensity*, measured as the ratio between total R&D expenditures and GDP in the year 2012 for each subunit (source: World Bank database); *Foreign Inventors Share,* i.e. the number of foreign over total inventors of the patents that have been employed to account for collaborative innovation for each subunit; *High Tech Industries*, a dummy accounting for high-tech industries according to the classification of the OECD; *Greenfield,* i.e. a dummy taking a value of 1 if at least one subsidiary of the subunit (parent–host country pair) is a greenfield investment.

Table 11.2 provides the correlation matrix and the descriptive statistics of the dependent and explicative variables.[10] Due to the presence of high correlations, we computed the Variance Inflation Factors (VIFs). The highest value, which refers to the variable *Parent Knowledge Base*, is 5.04, thus below the threshold of 10 over which multicollinearity problems may arise.

As regards the methodology, since *Collaborative Innovation* is a non-negative count variable, meaning that it arises from a Poisson-like process, we employ the negative binomial econometric model to run our regression analysis.

Results and conclusions

Table 11.3 provides the results of our negative binomial model, including coefficients and Incidence Rate Ratios (IRRs). Column 1 displays only the control variables, column 2 introduces the institutional distance, column 3 introduces the cultural distance and column 4 includes both.

As regards the controls, results show that *Parent Knowledge Base, Foreign Inventors Share, High-Tech Industries and Subunit R&D Intensity* are positively and significantly ($p<0.01$ for the first three variables, $p<0.05$ for the last variable) correlated with the dependent variable. Conversely, *Subunit Portfolio Breadth* displays a negative and significant coefficient ($p<0.01$), revealing that Chinese MNCs are more likely to engage in collaborative innovation when they focus their subsidiaries in few countries. As regards our explicative variables, results show that *Institutional Distance* and *Cultural Distance* have a positive and significant

Table 11.2 Correlation matrix

	1)	2)	3)	4)	5)	6)	7)	8)	9)	10)	11)	12)	13)
1) Collaborative Innovation	1.000												
2) Parent Knowledge Base	0.145	1.000											
3) Subunit Portfolio Depth	0.001	-0.170	1.000										
4) Subunit Portfolio Breadth	0.120	0.842	-0.075	1.000									
5) Subunit Age	-0.037	-0.114	0.211	0.021	1.000								
6) Parent Size	-0.103	-0.619	0.060	-0.692	0.048	1.000							
7) Geographical Distance	-0.001	0.078	-0.229	0.111	0.057	-0.117	1.000						
8) Subunit R&D intensity	0.247	-0.067	-0.089	-0.014	-0.169	-0.095	-0.022	1.000					
9) Foreign Inventors Share	0.474	0.171	0.259	0.273	0.017	-0.231	-0.068	0.232	1.000				
10) High-tech Industries	-0.006	0.168	-0.159	0.079	-0.056	0.170	-0.010	-0.068	-0.287	1.000			
11) Greenfield	0.021	0.554	-0.145	0.521	0.107	-0.390	0.153	-0.080	0.108	-0.098	1.000		
12) Institutional Distance	0.129	-0.183	0.485	-0.060	0.006	-0.093	-0.246	0.125	0.302	-0.210	-0.231	1.000	
13) Cultural Distance	0.226	-0.169	-0.075	-0.027	-0.250	-0.134	0.077	0.494	0.313	-0.170	-0.104	0.380	1.000
N. of observations	139	139	139	139	139	139	139	139	139	139	139	139	139
Mean	1.230	0.000	0.000	0.000	2.410	0.000	0.000	0.000	0.000	0.964	0.547	0.000	0.000
Standard deviation	5.118	1.000	1.000	1.000	0.657	1.000	1.000	1.000	1.000	0.187	0.500	1.000	1.000
Min	0.000	-0.866	-0.315	-1.210	1.000	-1.122	-1.838	-1.222	-0.436	0.000	0.000	-0.977	-1.598
Max	47.000	1.445	7.920	2.791	3.000	1.484	2.641	4.412	2.848	1.000	1.000	2.676	1.753

Table 11.3 Negative binomial analysis (dependent variable = Collaborative Innovation)

	(1) Coeff.	IRR	(2) Coeff.	IRR	(3) Coeff.	IRR	(4) Coeff.	IRR
Parent Knowledge Base	0.915*** (0.285)	2.496	0.955*** (0.259)	2.598	0.922*** (0.273)	2.513	0.969*** (0.255)	2.637
Subunit Portfolio Depth	-0.260 (0.163)	0.771	-0.411*** (0.136)	0.663	-0.253 (0.173)	0.776	-0.395** (0.156)	0.674
Subunit Portfolio Breadth	-0.909*** (0.247)	0.403	-0.703*** (0.197)	0.495	-0.981*** (0.252)	0.375	-0.768*** (0.195)	0.464
Subunit Age	-0.223 (0.504)	0.800	-0.137 (0.457)	0.872	-0.0831 (0.515)	0.920	0.00933 (0.475)	1.009
Parent Size	-0.293 (0.310)	0.746	-0.0151 (0.252)	0.985	-0.363 (0.296)	0.695	-0.0746 (0.228)	0.928
Geographical Distance	0.116 (0.181)	1.123	0.303 (0.200)	1.355	-0.161 (0.184)	0.851	-0.00500 (0.191)	0.995
Subunit R&D Intensity	0.503** (0.221)	1.654	0.576** (0.246)	1.780	0.386 (0.253)	1.471	0.465 (0.295)	1.592
Foreign Inventors Share	1.943*** (0.246)	6.979	1.782*** (0.223)	5.940	1.854*** (0.275)	6.387	1.693*** (0.231)	5.436
High-Tech Industries	1.489*** (0.526)	4.433	1.669*** (0.537)	5.308	1.652*** (0.522)	5.216	1.819*** (0.541)	6.163
Greenfield	-0.703 (0.506)	0.495	-0.0103 (0.543)	0.990	-0.769 (0.495)	0.464	-0.0943 (0.523)	0.910
Institutional Distance			0.668** (0.291)	1.950			0.656** (0.283)	1.927

(Continued)

Table 11.3 (Continued)

	(1)		(2)		(3)		(4)	
	Coeff.	IRR	Coeff.	IRR	Coeff.	IRR	Coeff.	IRR
Cultural Distance					0.492**	1.636	0.514**	1.671
					(0.250)		(0.219)	
Constant	−2.887**	0.056	−3.784***	0.023	−3.466***	0.031	−4.384***	0.012
	(1.364)		(1.440)		(1.311)		(1.436)	
Ln alpha constant	0.249	0.249	0.146	0.146	0.240	0.240	0.123	0.123
	(0.244)		(0.243)		(0.240)		(0.240)	
Obs.	139		139		139		139	
Chi-square	140.790***		134.674***		163.725***		169.586***	
Log pseudo-likelihood	−87.748		−85.622		−86.726		−84.577	

* If *p*<0.10.
** If *p*<0.05.
*** If *p*<0.01; robust standard errors in parentheses.

Note: Variables have been standardized.

effect ($p<0.05$ in Models 2, 3 and 4 for both *Institutional Distance* and *Cultural Distance*) on *Collaborative Innovation*.

Our results confirm that the relationship between collaborative innovation and institutional and cultural distance may assume a specific facet when considering MNCs from an emerging country such as China. Indeed, on the one hand, not only the magnitude but also the "direction" of the institutional distance needs to be taken into account when considering the strategic decisions undertaken by MNCs from an emerging country. As shown by De Beule et al. (2014), the shift towards less uncertain and risky institutional environments (such those of advanced countries, which host most of the investments undertaken by high-tech Chinese innovative MNCs) displays a significant effect on innovative collaboration, by increasing the intensity of this phenomenon. Indeed, Chinese MNCs take advantage of the more efficient foreign institutional frameworks, based on structured contracts and effective intellectual property regimes, to decrease the probability of opportunistic behaviours from the subsidiaries and from the inventors and to increase the effectiveness of the internal knowledge transfer process and of the external protection of collaborative innovation. On the other hand, cultural distance – which has been traditionally described as one of the main reasons underlying the failure or underperformance of foreign direct investments being responsible for misunderstandings and frictions – can become a source of creative diversity that fosters the collaborative innovation between subunits and parents and among inventors of different nationalities.

We believe that our results provide some initial interesting insights concerning knowledge sourcing strategies by MNCs from emerging countries. Indeed, we show that institutional and cultural distance tend to boost (rather than to hamper) the contribution of the network of subunits to the innovative activity of the parent companies. Chinese MNCs engaged in this phenomenon of collaborative innovation are likely to benefit from an increase in the effectiveness of the knowledge sourcing and transfer process and an accelerated catching-up. Managers of multinational firms should try to exploit their network of subunits to trigger this phenomenon, by taking advantage of the institutional and cultural distance rather than fearing it. On the other side, policymakers of the host countries should better understand to what extent the collaborative innovation undertaken by emerging countries also benefits their host economies or whether potential risks of knowledge leakages hold.

Our study represents a preliminary analysis aimed at exploring the phenomenon of collaborative innovation between parent companies and subunits. However, this phenomenon needs to be further investigated. First of all, the effect of cultural and institutional distance should be better disentangled by disaggregating the institutional items and the Dow distances, in order to assess whether the single indicators have heterogeneous effects with respect to the aggregate indexes. Secondly, future studies should better explore why collaborative innovation does not involve the majority of the Chinese patenting firms, by investigating more in depth other microeconomic (e.g. firm-level or individual-level characteristics related to the managers or the inventors teams) and macroeconomic (e.g. international governance organizations) factors underlying this phenomenon. Finally, future studies should compare internal (e.g. among parents and subunits) and external (e.g. between the parent or subunit and external partners) collaborative innovation, by exploring differences and similarities as regards the effect of cultural and institutional distances.

Notes

1 The industries have been identified by relying on the OECD 2007 classification, which defines as "High-Tech Manufacturing Industries" the following: aerospace, computers, office machinery, electronics-communications, pharmaceuticals and scientific instruments, and as "Medium-High-Tech Industries": motor vehicles, electrical machinery, chemicals, other transport equipment and non-electrical machinery.
2 We selected the year 2012 because we started to collect the data at the end of 2013, so the last available data were referred to 2012.
3 We employed the USPTO because it is considered the most reliable patent office to capture innovative dynamics, given the strength of intellectual property protection laws in the US (Phene and Almeida 2008).
4 Conversely, not all of the fifty-nine host countries considered are involved in collaborative innovation.
5 The ten items provided by the Heritage Foundation are: property rights, freedom from corruption, fiscal freedom, government spending, business freedom, labour freedom, monetary freedom, trade freedom, investment freedom and financial freedom. See www.heritage.org/index/ for more details
6 The five psychic distances provided by Dow (2000) are language, education level, industrial development, political system and religion.
7 Please note: while the Heritage Foundation provides the single items for each country, i.e. the single I_{ia} and I_{it}, Dow (2005) directly provides the distances, i.e. $(I_{ia} - I_{it})$.
8 The first threshold (2008) accounts for the subsidiaries that have been opened after the last economic crisis; the second threshold (2004) refers to the year after which the trend of outward foreign direct investments from China started to dramatically increase.
9 Centre d'Etudes Prospectives et d'Informations Internationales, the French institute for research into international economics; see www.cepii.fr/CEPII/en/welcome.asp for more details.
10 The variables *Subunit Portfolio Breadth* and *Parent Size* have been normalized to smooth their distribution.

References

Awate, S., Larsen, M. M., and Mudambi, R. (2012) 'EMNE catch-up strategies in the wind turbine industry: Is there a trade-off between output and innovation capabilities?', *Global Strategy Journal*, 2, 3: 205–223.
——— (2014) 'Accessing vs sourcing knowledge: A comparative study of R&D internationalization between emerging and advanced economy firms', *Journal of International Business Studies*, 46, 1: 63–86.
Baack, D. W., Dow, D., Parente, R., and Bacon, D. R. (2015) 'Confirmation bias in individual-level perceptions of psychic distance: An experimental investigation', Journal of International Business Studies, 46, 8: 938–959.
Berry, H. (2014) 'Global integration and innovation: Multicountry knowledge generation within MNCs', *Strategic Management Journal*, 35, 6: 869–890.

Cantwell, J. (1989) *Technological Innovation and Multinational Corporations*, London: Basil Blackwell.

Chen, S.F.S., and Hennart, J. F. (2004) 'A hostage theory of joint ventures: Why do Japanese investors choose partial over full acquisitions to enter the United States?', *Journal of Business Research*, 57, 10: 1126–1134.

Contractor, F. J., Lahiri, S., Elango, B., and Kundu, S. K. (2014) 'Institutional, cultural and industry related determinants of ownership choices in emerging market FDI acquisitions', *International Business Review*, 23, 5: 931–941.

De Beule, F., Elia, S., and Piscitello, L. (2014) 'Entry and access to competencies abroad: Emerging market firms versus advanced market firms', *Journal of International Management*, 20, 2: 137–152.

Demirbag, M., Glaister, K. W., and Tatoglu, E. (2007) 'Institutional and transaction cost influences on MNEs' ownership strategies of their affiliates: Evidence from an emerging market', *Journal of World Business*, 42, 4: 418–434.

Dow, D., and Karunaratna, A. (2006) 'Developing a multidimensional instrument to measure psychic distance stimuli', *Journal of International Business Studies*, 37, 5: 578–602.

Guiso, L., Sapienza, P., and Zingales, L. (2006) 'Does culture affect economic outcomes', *Journal of Economic Perspectives*, 20, 2: 23–48.

Johanson, J., and Wiedersheim-Paul, F. (1975) 'The internationalization of the firm – four Swedish cases', *Journal of Management Studies*, 12, 3: 305–323.

Kostova, T. (1999) 'Transnational transfer of strategic organizational practices: A contextual perspective', *Academy of Management Review*, 24, 2: 308–324.

Kroeber, A. L., and Kluckhohn, C. (1952) 'Culture: A critical review of concepts and definitions', *Peabody Museum of Archaeology and Ethnology, Harvard University*, 41, 1: 223.

Kumar, S., and Russell, R. R. (2002) 'Technological change, technological catch-up, and capital deepening: Relative contributions to growth and convergence', *American Economic Review*, 92, 3: 527–548.

Meirovich, G. (2010) 'The impact of cultural similarities and differences on performance in strategic partnerships: An integrative perspective', *Journal of Management and Organization*, 16, 1: 127–139.

Milliken, F., Bartel, B. and Kurtzberg, J. (2003) 'Diversity and creativity in work groups: A dynamic perspective on the affective and cognitive processes that link diversity and performance', in P. Paulus, and B. Nijstad (eds.) *Group Creativity: Innovation through Collaboration*, Oxford: Oxford University Press, pp. 32–62.

Mudambi, R. (2008) 'Location, control and innovation in knowledge-intensive industries', *Journal of Economic Geography*, 8, 5: 699–725.

Perri, A., Scalera, V. G., and Mudambi, R. (2015) *An analysis of the co-inventor networks associated with the Chinese pharmaceutical industry*, paper presented at the DRUID Conference 2015, Rome.

Piscitello, L., Rabellotti, R., and Scalera, V. G. (2015). 'Chinese and Indian M&As in Europe: The relationship between motive and ownership choice', in A. Risberg, D. King, and O. Meglio (eds.) *The Routledge Companion to Mergers and Acquisitions*, London: Routledge, 114–129.

Powell, W. W., Koput, K. W., and Smith-Doerr, L. (1996) 'Interorganizational collaboration and the locus of innovation: Networks of learning in biotechnology', *Administrative Science Quarterly*, 41, 1: 116–145.

Shenkar, O. (2012) 'Beyond cultural distance: Switching to a friction lens in the study of cultural differences', *Journal of International Business Studies*, 43, 1: 12–17.

Stahl, G. K., Maznevski, M. L., Voigt, A., and Jonsen, K. (2010), 'Unraveling the effects of cultural diversity in teams: A meta-analysis of research on multicultural work groups', *Journal of International Business Studies*, 41, 4: 690–709.

West, M. A. (2002) 'Sparkling fountains or stagnant ponds: An integrative model of creativity and innovation implementation in work groups', *Applied Psychology*, 51, 3: 355–387.

Zaheer, A., and Hernandez, E. (2011) 'The geographic scope of the MNC and its alliance portfolio: Resolving the paradox of distance', *Global Strategy Journal*, 1, 1–2: 109–126.

Zaheer, S., Schomaker, M. S., and Nachum, L. (2012) 'Distance without direction: Restoring credibility to a much-loved construct', *Journal of International Business Studies*, 43, 1: 18–27.

Zhao, H., Luo, Y., and Suh, T. (2004) 'Transaction cost determinants and ownership-based entry mode choice: A meta-analytical review', *Journal of International Business Studies*, 35, 6: 524–544.

Part V
Country and industry studies

12 Foreign direct investments of the BRIC countries in Norway

Per Heum and Armando J. Garcia Pires

Introduction

Traditionally FDI has flowed from advanced developed economies into developed and developing countries. More recently, a new trend has emerged in the pattern of FDI. Outward FDI from emerging economies has begun to increase significantly and has been growing at a faster pace than FDI from the advanced developed world in general. This raises some new research questions. In particular, researchers, politicians, and the media and the general public have been asking if the impact of Southern multinationals differs from that of multinationals in general, and if so, why? This knowledge is needed in order to assess existing EU-wide and national policies in relation to this phenomenon and to make policy recommendations.

In this context, the main purpose of this paper is to shed some light on the extent that multinationals from some of the major emerging economies, the so-called BRIC countries (Brazil, Russia, India, and China), are directly involved with firms in the Norwegian economy. Specific data were commissioned from Statistics Norway in order to provide relevant information.

We do, however, want to place this information on inward FDI from the BRIC countries to Norway into a broader context. Thus, we start by providing some general information on FDI and the BRIC countries. We will show the magnitude of outward and inward FDI in these countries, how FDI has developed over time, the relative magnitude of FDI involving the BRIC countries compared with the total level of FDI in the world, and the GDP share of inward and outward FDI for the BRIC countries.

The main focus is nevertheless on the operations of multinationals from the BRIC countries in Norway. This also includes considerations of FDI into these countries from multinationals registered in Norway. Our aim is to provide some basic information as to what extent Norway is directly affected by the operations of Southern multinationals originating in the BRIC countries.

General statistics on FDI in Norway do not provide information on the BRIC countries. The reason, as we will see in this paper, is obvious and simple. Inward and outward FDIs involving these countries are at a very low level in the case of Norway. Thus, in order to have some relevant data, we have asked Statistics Norway to provide us with more detailed data of FDI flows in Norway.

Our main argument to explain why Norway has not been until now a preferred destination for FDI flows from BRIC countries is that Norway stands out and differs in relation to other developed countries for a number of reasons. First, Norway is not part of the EU, and as a result, it does not apply the tariff-jumping argument. As we will see in the next section, the tariff-jumping argument states that firms with headquarters outside the EU gain in being located inside the EU market in order to not pay tariffs. Such gain is in principle also present in Norway, being part of the European Economic Area (EEA). However, for non-EU investors, this entails political risk, which is avoided by locating investments in a country that actually is a member of the EU. Second, Norway was not significantly affected by the financial crisis that began in 2008. As a result, contrary to other countries deeply affected by the financial crisis, like Greece and Portugal, where many local firms are for sale at good prices, the opposite is the case in Norway.

Finally, Norway is a high wage and a high tax country. Due to this, Norway is not an attractive location in terms of cost competitiveness relative to other countries. The fact that Norway is a high tax country can also explain the mode of entry of multinationals. In particular, we observe that multinationals from BRIC countries prefer the use of debt to equity to finance their operations in Norway. The opposite occurs for Norwegian multinationals that operate in the BRIC countries. This indicates the use of transfer pricing and other mechanisms to avoid paying taxes in Norway.

The rest of this paper is organized as follows. In the next section, we revise the literature in the field and position our paper relative to the literature. Next, we discuss the BRIC countries in terms of FDI in the world. Then we look at FDI from BRIC countries in Norway, and FDI from Norway in the BRIC countries. This is followed by an analysis of the impacts of FDI from BRIC countries in Norway. Next, we discuss some of the reasons for the low investment of BRIC countries in Norway. We conclude by discussing the main findings.

Related literature and main contributions

The literature on FDI is very extensive. However, since FDI from emerging economies in developed countries is a recent phenomenon, there are still very few papers analyzing this directly. Our paper wishes to contribute to fill this gap.

The first question that arises is what motivates FDI? Most of the answers to this question were made in the context of developed countries. There were very good reasons for this, since the large majority of FDI was among developed countries. We can then ask if the motives that apply to firms from developed countries apply to firms from developing countries. Until more knowledge of the patterns and modes of investment by firms from emerging economies is available, we have to continue to assume that many of the motivations behind FDI choices are the same for firms from developed and developing countries.

The main framework to analyze FDI is the OLI framework of Dunning (see, for instance, Dunning 2000). Several authors have revisited this paradigm repeatedly, and the paradigm is very well known amongst researchers in the field. In any case, we still summarize it briefly here. The OLI framework states that multinational firms arise because they either have some types of ownership advantages, location advantages, or internalization advantages. Ownership advantages are related, for example, to brands and patents that are worthwhile for the firm to explore directly by locating in a foreign market. Location advantages occur, for instance, when the destination market is either important and justifies the location of the firm there, or the destination market has some raw materials or cheap or qualified labour that can only be obtained by locating there. Internalization advantages arise when the firm has, so to say, advantages in keeping the production in-house instead of outsourcing to third parties.

Applying the OLI framework to Norway, we should pay special attention to the location advantages, since the ownership and internalization advantages relate to the firm itself. For Norway, three main issues arise: taxes, wages, and exchange rates. These three factors have indeed been identified in the literature as important for FDI flows (see, for instance, Hines 1996; Altshuler et al. 1998; Davies 2004; Egger et al. 2006; Razin and Sadka 2006, 2007; Davies and Kristjansdottir 2010). We can say that these three factors go against FDI in Norway, since Norway is a high tax, high wage country, and after the financial crisis, the Norwegian kroner appreciated considerably (since oil prices started to fall, the Norwegian kroner started again to depreciate but our analysis does not cover this period).

Another way to classify FDI is between horizontal FDI and vertical FDI (e.g. Helpman 1984, 2006; Markusen 1984, 1997; Markusen et al. 1996). Horizontal FDI occurs when a firm has the same stage of production at home and in the foreign country. This type of FDI is prevalent among developed countries because rich countries have by definition large markets. Vertical FDI occurs when a firm has different stages of production located in different countries – for instance, design at the headquarters and production in a foreign country. Vertical FDI is prevalent between developed and developing countries because this type of FDI is done most of the time to explore cost advantages in terms of labour costs in developing countries. In spite of the growing importance of vertical FDI (very much publicized in the case of Apple, Nike, and other multinationals), a large part of FDI in the world economy is still of the horizontal kind (for a discussion of the evidence, see, for example Markusen and Maskus 2001; Blonigen 2005; Helpman 2006; Blonigen and Piger 2011). In what concerns horizontal and vertical FDI, we should expect that in Norway, FDI is more of the horizontal kind.

Another FDI motive found in the literature that can be relevant for the case of Norway is the so-called tariff-jumping argument (e.g. Blonigen 2002; Egger and Pfaffermayr 2004; Ekholm et al. 2007). The tariff-jumping argument says that when some countries constitute a customs or economic union (like the EU), firms from third countries (outside the economic union) have incentives to locate in one of the member countries. This is so because by doing so, firms from third countries avoid paying tariffs to export to all the countries inside the economic union. There is some evidence that this has occurred in the European Union (see, for example, Ekholm et al. 2007). A related argument is found when countries establish a monetary union like the eurozone (e.g. Di Giovanni 2005; Petroulas

2007; Baldwin et al. 2008). In either case – tariff-jumping or monetary union – this looks to be to the disadvantage of Norway, since Norway is outside both the EU and the eurozone.

To our knowledge, our paper is the first to analyze FDI from developing countries in Norway. There have been obviously studies of FDI in Norway, but these studies have generally excluded FDI from developing countries (see, for instance, Balsvik and Haller 2011). As we have mentioned in the introduction, this is due to the fact that until now FDI from emerging economies has been almost nonexistent in Norway. In this sense, Norway stands out as an exception in relation to other European countries.

We use two data sources. The first is the UNCTAD FDI data and the second is the FDI data from Statistics Norway. As we have also mentioned before, FDI from emerging countries does not show up in the official statistics, since it is negligible. As a result, we have to directly ask Statistics Norway to provide us this information. We analyze these data using descriptive methods, since the scarcity of FDI from BRIC countries in Norway does not allow us to use more advanced statistical techniques.

BRIC countries and FDI

In this section, we analyze FDI to and from BRIC countries. We use data from UNCTAD.

FDI is increasing rapidly

Table 12.1 shows the stock of FDI in Brazil, Russia, India, and China (excluding Hong Kong) in 2000 and 2011. It can be observed that it is the stock of outward

Table 12.1 The stock of inward and outward FDI in BRIC countries, 2000 and 2011 (million USD and growth from 2000 to 2011)

	FDI Inward Stock			FDI Outward Stock		
	2000	*2011*	*2011/2000*	*2000*	*2011*	*2011/2000*
Brazil	122,250	669,670	5.5	51,946	202,586	3.9
Russia	32,204	457,474	14.2	20,141	362,101	18.0
India	16,339	201,724	12.3	1,733	111,257	64.2
China	193,348	711,802	3.7	27,768	365,981	13.2
Sum BRIC countries	364,141	2,040,670	5.6	101,588	1,041,925	10.3

Source: Annex table I.2 FDI stock by region in *World Investment Report 2012 – Towards a New Generation of Investment Policies*, UNCTAD 2012

Note: There are separate figures for Hong Kong, China. These are for the stocks of inward FDI: 455 469 in 2000 and 1 138 365 in 2011. For the stock of outward FDI, the figures are 388 380 in 2000 and 1 045 920 in 2011.

FDI that reflects the expansion of multinationals originating in these emerging economies.

The growth column, where the stock of FDI in 2011 is measured relative to the stock in 2000, shows that in nominal values the stock of outward FDI for the BRIC countries has increased ten times over just a decade. This is a much higher growth rate than for the stock of inward FDI to these countries in the same period.

We can see that the stock of outward FDI from India envisages huge growth rates. Notice, however, that this growth is from a very low level. In addition, it has been the stock of outward FDI from Russia and China that has grown most substantially in absolute terms.

For India and China, the growth of outward FDI has been much faster than that of inward FDI. The same is true for Russia, but the difference here is not substantial. The growth rate, with regard to both outward and inward FDI, is much lower when it comes to Brazil, where, in the same period, inward FDI has grown faster than outward FDI. Thus, the notion of rapidly expanding Southern multinationals does not hold true for all the BRIC countries.

The table also shows that the stock of outward FDI is smaller than the stock of inward FDI in each of the BRIC countries. This indicates that despite the emergence of Southern multinationals, emerging economies are still mainly host countries for multinational corporations.

Playing a minor role in world FDI

For multinationals from BRIC countries to gain a more important role in the world economy, the growth rate of outward FDI from emerging economies should be significantly higher than that for other countries. Table 12.2 shows the stock of inward and outward FDI and their growth over the period 2000–2011 for the world, for developed economies and for Norway.

Comparing the growth rates in Tables 12.1 and 12.2, it is evident that both outward and inward FDI have grown at a rate well above the world average for

Table 12.2 The stock of inward and outward FDI in Norway, developed economies and the world, 2000 and 2011
Million USD and growth from 2000 to 2011

	FDI Inward Stock			FDI Outward stock		
	2000	2011	2011/2000	2000	2011	2011/2000
Norway	30,265	171,524	4.7	34,026	207,469	6.1
Developed economies	5,653,715	13,055,903	2.3	7,074,435	17,055,964	2.4
World	7,450,022	20,438,199	2.7	7,952,878	21,168,489	2.7

Source: Annex table I.2 FDI stock by region in *World Investment Report 2012 – Towards a New Generation of Investment Policies*, UNCTAD 2012

all the BRIC countries. However, this is also the case for Norway and several other small, open economies. As for outward FDI, growth rates for Norway are at a significantly lower level than for Russia, India, and China, but still above the growth rate for Brazil.

The growth rate of FDI for all the developed economies is much lower than the world average. This means that the share of outward FDI controlled by companies investing from a country belonging to the group of developed economies is in relative decline. In 2000, the share was 89 percent; in 2011, it was 81 percent. However, as more than 80 percent of the stock value of the world's FDI is held by companies making FDI investments from a country belonging to the group of developed economies, multinational business is still mostly originating here.

It is a fact, however, that the stock value of FDI held by multinationals from BRIC countries has increased quite rapidly in the same period. Consequently, the share of the world's total FDI that is controlled by companies investing from one of the BRIC countries is on the rise. Nevertheless, it is still quite low – just below 5 percent of FDI in the world in 2011. This is, however, up from just above 1 percent in 2000.

FDI is still at relatively low levels

When considering the role of FDI in the economies of different countries, it is relevant to consider the relative magnitude of FDI to the domestic economy. One common measure is to calculate the stock of FDI in percent of GDP. In Table 12.3 this is done for the BRIC countries, as well as for Norway, for all countries that are regarded as developed economies, and for the world as a whole, for the sake of comparison.

The stock of a country's outward FDI generally reflects activities of multinationals operating from that country. It is quite evident that the share of FDI is much

Table 12.3 FDI stock in percent of GDP for the BRIC countries, Norway, developed economies and the world, 2000 and 2011

	Inward FDI		Outward FDI	
	2000	*2011*	*2000*	*2011*
Brazil	19.0	27.7	8.1	8.4
Russia	12.4	24.8	7.8	19.7
India	3.5	10.4	0.4	5.7
China	16.2	10.1	2.3	5.2
Norway	18.0	35.9	20.2	43.5
Developed economies	22.2	30.1	28.0	39.4
World	22.7	28.7	24.5	30.0

Source: Web tables 8 and 9 Inward/Outward FDI stock in percent of GDP, www.unctad.org/WIR

higher in developed economies and that the share of outward FDI to GDP in all the BRIC countries is well below the world average. The share of outward FDI to GDP has increased considerably in all the BRIC countries except Brazil. However, it is still below 10 percent in Brazil, India, and China. The relative growth of outward FDI has been particularly strong in Russia, reaching a share of outward FDI in percent of GDP up to close to 20 percent. However, this is still only half of the average for all developed economies.

It is further a fact that the relative share of inward FDI measured as the stock value relative to GDP is larger than the stock value of outward FDI in all the four BRIC countries. In India and Russia the stock of inward FDI has also grown relatively fast compared with the growth of outward FDI, and faster than outward FDI for Brazil. Only in China is the relative share of foreign multinationals in the domestic economy in decline, while the share of outward FDI has more than doubled. Thus, Southern multinationals may be on the rise, but so are the operations of multinationals in general with regard to the BRIC countries.

FDI from the BRIC countries to Norway

We now turn to FDI to and from BRIC countries in Norway. We use data from Statistics Norway. These data are not publicly available. As we see below, the reason for this is that FDI to and from BRIC countries in Norway is very small.

Magnitude

Table 12.4 shows that foreign direct investments from the BRIC countries to Norway have increased manifold from 2004 to 2011, albeit from very low levels (NOK = Norwegian kroner).

It is also clear that FDI to Norway from Russia and India is almost nonexistent. The same is more or less the case for Brazil. For Southern multinationals from

Table 12.4 The stock of FDI from BRIC countries to Norway, 2004–2011 (million NOK)

	BRIC Total	Brazil	Russia	India	China
2004	1,249	342	−34	3	938
2005	780	471	−47	1	355
2006	504	420	16	13	55
2007	518	504	2	11	1
2008	2,928	1,158	2	78	1,690
2009	20,511	1,215	7	79	19,210
2010	22,282	621	6	119	21,536
2011	19,430	1,731	27	45	17,627

Source: Special analysis from Statistics Norway

these three countries (Russia, India, and Brazil), the trend is that FDI in Norway is nearly nonexistent.

Investments from Chinese multinationals in Norway increased rapidly in 2009 and have stayed at the same level since then. This is mainly linked to two large investments. One is the takeover of the Norwegian company Elkem by China National Bluestar, and the other is the operations of Huawei Technologies Ltd in Norway.

As the stock of inward FDI from the BRIC countries is so low, it is evident that the direct impact of multinationals from BRIC countries on Norway's economy is of minor importance. Taken together, the stock of FDI held by multinationals from the BRIC countries makes up just above 1 percent of inward FDI in Norway.

The composition of inward FDI

FDI is partly registered as the value of equity invested by foreign investors and partly as the value of debt from these investors. As Figure 12.1 clearly shows, the engagement of multinationals from all the BRIC countries is made up of considerably more debt than equity when it comes to their operations in Norway.

On average the multinationals from the BRIC countries differ somewhat from other multinationals in this respect, as total inward FDI in Norway in 2011 was almost split equally between equity (593,553 million NOK) and debt (549,300 million NOK). This might indicate the use of transfer pricing from multinationals from the BRIC countries. Norway is a high tax country and as a result, multinationals from the BRIC countries may prefer to declare profits in low tax countries, rather than in Norway.

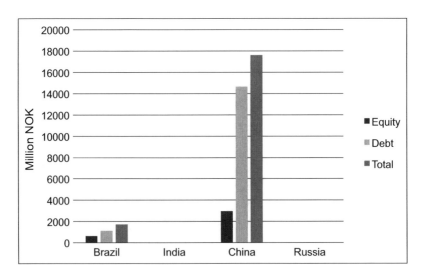

Figure 12.1 Inward FDI in Norway from Brazil, Russia, India, and China, 2011
Distribution on equity and debt. Million NOK.

FDI from Norway to the BRIC countries

Magnitude

The operations of multinationals from Norway investing in the BRIC countries started earlier than the operations from multinationals from BRIC countries in Norway. This is evident when comparing the information in Table 12.5 with that in Table 12.4. The stock of outward FDI is also slightly higher.

It is also evident that Norwegian multinationals primarily have a presence in Brazil, even though some presence is registered in the other three BRIC countries as well.

Outward FDI from Norway to Russia has been significantly reduced recently. However, this might be related to accounting registers rather than real physical investment. For example, Telenor's ownership in VimpelCom is still significant, but the ownership arrangement has been changed via a tax haven and is no longer linked directly to Russia. It is unclear whether similar rearrangements of ownership may explain the reduction in the stock of outward FDI to India as well.

However, outward FDI is in general higher than inward FDI in the case of Norway, with FDI from multinationals investing in the BRIC countries making up less than 2 percent of Norway's outward FDI. This means that the investment relations between Norway and the BRIC countries are at a very low level.

The composition of outward FDI

When considering the composition of outward FDI from Norway to the BRIC countries, it is clear that equity is far more important than debt. Figure 12.2 clearly reveals that Norwegian multinationals operating in the BRIC countries prefer to use equity rather than debt to finance their local activities.

This pattern is almost the opposite of the one observed for BRIC country multinationals investing in Norway. The explanation may be the same in both cases,

Table 12.5 The stock of FDI from Norway to the BRIC countries, 2004–2011 (million NOK)

	BRIC Total	Brazil	Russia	India	China
2004	9,681	4,543	4,038	234	866
2005	18,662	3,767	4,305	118	791
2006	15,081	8,510	4,805	170	1,596
2007	25,109	10,596	13,296	325	892
2008	30,902	9,174	14,049	6,162	1,517
2009	28,730	10,062	11,840	4,941	1,887
2010	20,768	15,547	2,592	497	2,132
2011	26,827	19,368	2,894	1,185	3,380

Source: Special analysis from Statistics Norway

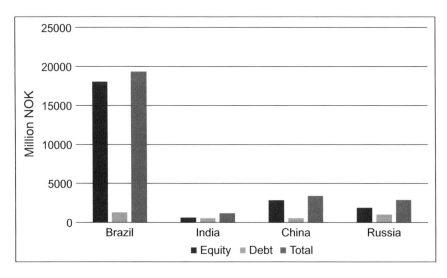

Figure 12.2 Outward FDI from Norway to Brazil, India, Russia, and China, 2011
Distribution on equity and debt. Million NOK.

however, and mirrors different contexts for Norwegian and BRIC country multi-nationals. The BRIC countries have in general lower tax levels than Norway. Therefore, Norwegian multinationals operating in the BRIC countries may be expected to prefer to report profits in the BRIC countries rather than in Norway, which explains the use of equity. On the other hand, multinationals from the BRIC countries investing in Norway apply in essence exactly the same considerations, which explain the use of debt in their FDI in Norway.

The impact of BRIC country multinationals on Norway

Inward FDI in Norway from the BRIC countries is a measure of the direct relation-ship between multinationals from BRIC countries and Norwegian interests. The larger these investments are, the more significant impact may be expected. Data clearly illustrate that FDI from the BRIC countries into the Norwegian economy is very small.

We can highlight that it is just a couple of large investments from Chinese mul-tinationals that really count. One is an acquisition of a Norwegian firm; the other is a greenfield investment. So far, there is no evidence that any of them operate differently from other multinationals in the Norwegian economy. Thus, despite the limited experience of Norway with regard to Southern multinationals, it may be worth noting that there is no indication that the impact of Southern multination-als in the Norwegian economy differs from the impact that can be expected from foreign multinationals in general.

The other way firms operating in Norway may interact directly with Southern multinationals is through outward investments in the home countries of the multinationals. However, such investments by Norwegian firms in the BRIC countries are also quite small, and just a little larger than the magnitude of inward FDI from multinationals of these countries.

Data on FDI do not establish any direct relationship from which the operations of Southern multinationals may be expected to have significant impact on the Norwegian economy or society. However, FDI is not necessarily registered as capital flows between the countries in question. Investments may be channeled through units located in other countries (such as tax havens), and may hence not be taken into account when bilateral investment flows are considered. As already mentioned, this is the major explanation for the reduction of outward FDI from Norway to Russia.

Telenor, which is the major telecom company in Norway and a large international player in mobile telecommunications, used to have a direct ownership interest in the Russian company VimpelCom. In 2009, however, VimpelCom was reorganized. This meant that the company was incorporated in Bermuda and that the headquarters was located to the Netherlands. Operations continued as before and covered Russia and several of the former Soviet Republics in addition to Italy. As Telenor owns 33 percent of VimpelCom, this is an FDI in a company which in reality is Russian but which, according to FDI statistics, is registered in a tax haven.

Through this minority interest, Telenor is exposed to business operations in countries with rather different and quite often inferior institutions regulating market-based activities. In particular, with regard to the operations in Uzbekistan, the media has focused on irregular business activities, such as corruption. This has been strongly disputed by VimpelCom and Telenor. However, in February 2016 VimpelCom agreed to pay $835m to settle the US and Dutch charges that it paid massive bribes to enter the Uzbekistan telecommunication market. This indicates that Southern multinationals may have other business traditions and standards or that conducting business in emerging economies may clearly challenge what are generally regarded as sound business practices and standards.

Reasons for the low investment of BRIC countries in Norway

The main question that arises is why BRIC countries have invested so little in Norway. One reason could be that Norway is a low FDI intensive economy relative to other developed economies. A closer look at the data does not support this hypothesis.

In fact, historically foreign investors have played an important role in developing Norwegian industry. In the first decades of the twentieth century, foreign investors in particular engaged in the development and exploitation of hydropower to establish energy intensive industries in chemical and metal production. Later, foreign investors invested in mechanical and electrical engineering. In the 1970s, the petroleum sector attracted foreign firms, which increasingly engaged in trade and service industries.

Table 12.6 Stock of inward FDI in Norway and EU15 countries, percent of GDP, 1990–2013

	1990	2000	2010	2013
Austria	6.7	16.2	42.6	44.1
Belgium	28.8	83.9	185.1	182.4
Denmark	6.7	45.9	46.0	48.1
Finland	3.7	19.9	36.6	39.4
France	7.8	29.4	38.5	39.4
Germany	6.4	14.4	21.6	23.4
Greece	6.0	11.2	11.9	11.4
Ireland	78.7	130.5	136.3	172.3
Italy	5.2	11.1	15.9	19.5
Netherlands	24.3	63.3	75.4	83.9
Norway	10.5	17.9	41.1	37.7
Portugal	13.6	27.3	48.7	58.4
Spain	12.6	26.9	45.3	52.7
Sweden	5.0	37.9	74.9	67.6
United Kingdom	20.0	31.0	49.4	63.3

Source: *Inward Foreign Direct Investment Stock, Annual 1980–2013*, UNCTADstat

In addition, Norway has been historically more open to foreign investors than the neighbouring countries in the Nordic region. As Table 12.6 shows, as late as 1990, the share of inward FDI in percent of GDP was higher in Norway than in Denmark, Finland, and Sweden. In 1994, Finland and Sweden became members of the EU, as Denmark had become in 1972, while Norway continued to be an EFTA country.

The figures in Table 12.6, then, do not suggest that Norway is less open to FDI than other developed countries in Europe. A more likely explanation is that when non-European investors want to invest in industrial activities to serve the European market, they choose to invest in a member country of the EU. Thus, Norway, as a non-EU country, can expect only non-European investors to engage in industrial activities, which serve global markets or the domestic Norwegian market.

We can get some more clues on the reasons for the low investment in Norway from BRIC countries by analyzing the two largest foreign investments from these countries. As mentioned above, two investments stand out: the Elkem acquisition by the China National Bluestar Co. and the greenfield investment by Huawei Technologies.

- Elkem was acquired by the China National Bluestar Co. for 2 billion USD in 2011. Elkem produces silicon, special alloys for the foundry industry, carbon, and microsilica and has factories in Europe, South America, South Africa and Asia. Elkem as of 2015 had 3,600 employees around the world. Thus, Elkem serves markets globally as part of the China National Bluestar (Group) Corporation.

• Huawei Technologies Norway was established in 2007 as a greenfield investment by Huawei Technologies Co. Ltd. Huawei supplies telecommunications
equipment, as of 2015 had 170,000 employees worldwide, and is represented
in 140 countries around the world. Huawei Norway serves the Norwegian
telecom market and contributes to Telenor's and NetCom's new networks for
mobile telecommunications. In 2010, Huawei became the largest telecom supplier in Norway. The number of employees are, however, no more than 140.

These two major Chinese investments in Norway seem to be in line with the reasoning above. In fact, nothing is particularly specific to these investments relative
to other foreign investments from, let us say, Europe.

Another factor that can be relevant to explain the low investment of BRIC
countries in Norway is the presence of active policies to attract foreign direct
investment. In this respect, we can say that Norway is less active than other European countries, and in particular other Scandinavian countries (see, for example,
Benito and Grünfeld 2011). In the 1990s Norway established an agency to promote
foreign investment, the "Invest in Norway" agency. This agency was part of the
Norwegian Industrial and Regional Development Fund (SND), which is now part
of Innovation Norway. However, "Invest in Norway" operations were always very
modest, and a few years ago this agency was discontinued. In this sense, Norway
has a less active policy to attract FDI. For instance, in other Scandinavian countries
transitory tax relief schemes have been implemented to attract foreign capital and
human skills. Such is not the case in Norway.

In addition, while many countries in the last two decades have entered into
bilateral investment treaties (BITs), Norway has not done so since 1998 (see, for
instance, Benito and Grünfeld 2011). The main reasons for this are legal issues,
since the Norwegian constitution forbids the transfer of sovereignty to foreign
courts. Again, this is also in deep contrast to other Scandinavian countries, as well
as other European countries, which have established several BITs in the last two
decades.

Nevertheless, the limited role of Norway in promoting FDI cannot be the main
culprit of the low investment from BRIC countries. In fact, this policy inactivity
affects symmetrically FDI from BRIC countries and FDI from other countries.
In this sense, it cannot explain the low level of investment by BRIC countries in
Norway relative to other regions and countries (in particular, Europe and the US).

In our view, the main reasons are that Norway is not part of the EU, Norway is
not "for sale," since it was not very affected by the financial crisis, and Norway is a
high wage, high cost country in which to invest. In this respect, other countries are
more attractive locations for FDI.

Conclusions

Southern multinationals are gaining increased attention. In fact, as we have
shown, multinationals from the BRIC countries have become more prominent
in the world economy in the last decade. This is in particular the case for
Chinese and Russian multinationals. However, these multinationals from

China and Russia still represent a small share of the world's multinational investments.

In Norway, the trend with regard to BRIC multinationals is somewhat different from the trend in the rest of the world. Not only do investments of BRIC country multinationals in Norway represent a small share of total foreign investment in Norway, but also, with the exception of two large investments of Chinese multinationals, they have not gained importance in the last decade.

The difference between Norway and the rest of the developed world is, we believe, mainly due to the fact that Norway is not a member of the European Union. Thus, Southern multinationals that want to approach the European market are more likely to choose a location within a member country of the EU rather than locate their European investments in an "outsider" country such as Norway.

Another explanation may be differences in macroeconomic conditions between Norway and most other developed economies. Norway was one of the few developed countries that were not deeply affected by the world financial crisis. As a result, contrary to other countries, the price of firm acquisitions in Norway is still high. Banks and firms in Norway have so far not experienced problems with cash flows and financing of their activities, and therefore have not needed to recur to selling off assets.

A third set of explanations come from the fact that Norway is an expensive country in which to operate, since wages and taxes are both high. The fact that Norway is a high tax country might also explain the favored mode of entry observed by multinationals from BRIC countries. In particular, we have observed two opposite patterns. Multinationals from the BRIC countries prefer the use of debt rather than equity to finance their activities in Norway, while Norwegian multinationals operating in the BRIC countries prefer the use of equity. Both patterns are consistent with the use of transfer pricing to manipulate profits obtained by subsidiaries in the host countries, since Norway is a high tax country.

References

Altshuler, R., Grubert, H., and Newlon, T. (1998) 'Has US Investment Abroad Become More Sensitive to Tax Rates?', NBER Working Paper No. 6383, National Bureau of Economic Research.

Baldwin, R., Di Nino, V., Fontagné, L., De Santis, R., and Taglioni, D. (2008) 'Study on the Impact of the Euro on Trade and Foreign Direct Investment', *European Economy Economics Paper*, 321. European Commission.

Balsvik, R. and Haller, S. (2011) 'Foreign Firms and Host-Country Productivity: Does the Mode of Entry Matter?', *Oxford Economic Papers*, 63, 158–186.

Benito, G. and Grünfeld, L. (2011) 'Inward FDI in Norway and Its Policy Context', Columbia FDI Profiles. Columbia Center on Sustainable Investment.

Blonigen, B. (2002) 'Tariff-Jumping Antidumping Duties', *Journal of International Economics*, 57, 31–50.

Blonigen, B. (2005) 'A Review of the Empirical Literature on FDI Determinants', *Atlantic Economic Journal*, 33, 383–403.

Blonigen, B. and Piger, J. (2011) 'Determinants of Foreign Direct Investment', NBER Working Paper No. 16704. National Bureau of Economic Research.

Davies, R. (2004) 'Tax Treaties and Foreign Direct Investment: Potential Versus Performance', *International Tax and Public Finance*, 11, 775–802.

Davies, R. and Kristjansdottir, H. (2010) 'Fixed Costs, Foreign Direct Investment, and Gravity with Zeros', *Review of International Economics*, 18, 47–62.

Di Giovanni, J. (2005) 'What Drives Capital Flows? The Case of Cross-Border M&A Activity and Financial Deepening', *Journal of International Economics*, 65, 127–149.

Dunning, J. (2000) 'The Eclectic Paradigm as an Envelope for Economic and Business Theories of MNE Activity', *International Business Review*, 9, 163–190.

Egger, P., Larch, M., Pfaffermayr, M., and Winner, H. (2006) 'The Impact of Endogenous Tax Treaties on Foreign Direct Investment: Theory and Evidence', *Canadian Journal of Economics*, 39, 901–931.

Egger, P. and Pfaffermayr, M. (2004) 'Foreign Direct Investment and European Integration in the 1990s', *The World Economy*, 27, 99–110.

Ekholm, K., Forslid, R. and Markusen, J. (2007) 'Export-Platform Foreign Direct Investment', *Journal of European Economic Association*, 5, 776–795.

Helpman, E. (1984) 'A Simple Theory of International Trade with Multinational Corporations', *Journal of Political Economy*, 92, 451–471.

Helpman, E. (2006) 'Trade, FDI, and the Organization of Firms', *Journal of Economic Literature*, 44, 589–630.

Hines, J. (1996) 'Altered States: Taxes and the Location of Foreign Direct Investment in America', *American Economic Review* 86, 1076–1094.

Markusen, J. (1984) 'Multinationals, Multi-Plant Economies, and the Gains from Trade', *Journal of International Economics*, 16, 205–226.

Markusen, J. (1997) 'Trade Versus Investment Liberalization', NBER Working Paper Working Paper No. 6231. National Bureau of Economic Research.

Markusen, J. and Maskus, K. (2001) 'Multinational Firms: Reconciling Theory and Evidence', in: Blomström, M. and Goldeberg, L. (eds.) *Topics in Empirical International Economics: A Festscrift in Honor of Robert E. Lipsey*. University of Chicago Press, Chicago, pp. 71–98.

Markusen, J., Venables, A., Eby-Konan, D., and Zhang, K. (1996) 'A Unified Treatment of Horizontal Direct Investment, Vertical Direct Investment, and the Pattern of Trade in Goods and Services', NBER Working Paper No. 5696. National Bureau of Economic Research.

Petroulas, P. (2007) 'The Effect of the Euro on Foreign Direct Investment', *European Economic Review* 51, 1468–1491.

Razin, A. and Sadka, E. (2006) 'Vying for Foreign Direct Investment: A EU-Type Model of Tax Competition', NBER Working Paper No. 11991. National Bureau of Economic Research.

Razin, A. and Sadka, E. (2007) 'Productivity and Taxes as Drivers of FDI', NBER Working Paper No. 13094. National Bureau of Economic Research.

13 Network configurations in the white goods global value chain

Michał Zdziarski, Jagjit Singh Srai and Rasha Rezk

Introduction: networks, markets and hierarchies

Markets, hierarchies and networks are alternative mechanisms of resource allocation in the economy. Of these three fundamental mechanisms that help explain how the economy really works, networks have been the least studied and understood. Recently, however, we have been able to observe an exponential growth of network studies in organisational and management research (Borgatti and Foster 2003). The central argument of network theory is that economic processes are embedded in the structure of social relationships (Granovetter 1985). Due to embeddedness, firms vary in their opportunities and constraints, depending on their position in the network of interfirm relationships (Dyer and Singh 1998; Borgatti and Halgin 2011; Greve, Shipilov and Rowley 2014).

The concept of embeddedness (Granovetter 1985) was formulated long after the hierarchy had been proposed as an alternative mechanism to the market allocation of resources (Coase 1937). The phenomenon of hierarchies explains why firms exist in the economy, as well as explaining the logic of the fundamental choice between "to make" and "to buy", based on transaction cost analysis. Network exchange occurs in enduring relationships that often take the form of complex, evolving and incomplete transactions, but cannot be described usefully through the market metaphor. The coordination of networks is not assured by a hierarchy based on ownership.

In the IB literature, proponents of the network approach to internationalisation are becoming influential. The authors of the article "Markets as Networks: Implications for Strategy Making" contrast the artificial, theoretical construct of a market with how internationalisation really happens in an enduring network of relationships of interconnected firms (Johanson and Vahlne 2011). The central components in the network view are relations that constrain or create opportunities for firms participating in the broader industry ecosystem in which multiple firms are interconnected. Relations and networks rather than isolated firms are becoming the central level of analysis in international business. In their formulation of the relational view, other authors have pointed out that a firm's critical resources often lie outside the firm's boundary, as "55% of the value of each product an average manufacturing firm produces in the US, and 69% in Japan, are purchased from outside" (Dyer and Singh 1998: 660). With the evolution of communication, globalisation and interconnectivity of business, this proportion is even higher in the current economy. This is supported by evidence from UNCTAD, which reports that over 60 percent of global trade, amounting to over \$20 trillion, consists of trade in intermediate goods and services at various stages of global value chains (UNCTAD 2013).

The network approach to internationalisation

The resources and capabilities to which any one firm has access can extend well beyond that firm's boundaries (Dyer and Singh 1998). Competitive advantage does not reside in a single firm's capabilities and resources, but in interfirm networks that compete with other networks (Gulati 1998; Gulati and Gargiulo 1999). Networks with reciprocal patterns of exchange are alternatives to hierarchical or market-based governance structures. Network models better represent companies involved in collaborative exchanges and continuing transactions with other firms over extended periods of time (Podolny and Page 1998). Extending their original process model of internationalisation, authors from the Uppsala Scandinavian School of IB focused on the interplay between experimental learning and commitment facilitated in business relationships that serve as the main learning opportunity in interfirm networks (Johanson and Vahlne 2011). Knowledge about internationalisation can be acquired from other members in a firm's network, and thus the firm's network activities become a strong antecedent of foreign investment decisions (Coviello 2006; Elango and Pattnaik 2007).

In the network approach to internationalisation, firms are considered as entities embedded in a web of relationships, rather than autonomous units within which decisions are taken in isolation from external pressures and opportunities. Linking resources of interdependent organisations and units, in both domestic and foreign markets, shifts the level of analysis from that of the firm and FDI to that of networks and relationships in the global value chain (Forsgren, Holm and Johanson 2005; Sydow et al. 2010). Interactions and the combination of capabilities and resources facilitate internationalisation, moderate the perception of risks of entry to foreign markets, reduce the cost of investment and time of process integration and improve internationalisation performance (Hosseini and Dadfar 2012).

The network perspective is particularly relevant to explain the internationalisation of firms lacking ownership advantage, capabilities and accumulated resources. The network approach has been used in research on the internationalisation of SMEs (Zhou, Wu and Luo 2007), international new ventures (Coviello 2006) and companies in emerging economies (Elango and Pattnaik 2007; Yiu, Lau and Bruton 2007). Embeddedness in the network of relationships moderates the effects of a firm's competitive advantage and directly influences the results of firms that enter new markets (Zhou, Wu and Luo 2007). Two types of relationships have been of particular interest in studies of the internationalisation of firms from emerging markets: business relationships and governmental relationships (Peng and Luo 2000; Li, Zhou and Shao 2008).

Networks consist of nodes (actors), which may be persons, animals, firms, organisations, groups or nations, and are connected by one or more ties (relations, links, arcs) that form distinct, analysable patterns (Wellman 1988). In the case of white goods global value chains, the nodes in the network will be companies, including producers, their suppliers and distributors, these being connected by transactions or links which will form network patterns.

Global value chains

Global rivalry is evolving from firm-versus-firm competition into supply chains and interconnected sets of firms competing against other interfirm networks and value chains (Craighead, Hult and Ketchen 2009). As international manufacturing firms increasingly operate based on fragmented supply networks, the configuration of the network becomes a critical area of study (Srai and Gregory 2008). Yet "the amount of research devoted to the global dimensions of supply chain management has been small relative to its practical significance" (Conelly, Ketchen and Hult 2013: 228). This can be partially explained by the complexity of such research and data constraints. In defining the configuration of the supply chain, authors demand that it should encompass "network shape and structure, ownership, levels of vertical and horizontal integration, relationships and inter-dependencies between network partners, unit operations (manufacturing processes, optimum sequence, platforms, sub-assembly, modularity, complexity, flexibility, etc.), product offering (product, spares, through-life support and services)" (Srai and Gregory 2008: 393–394). While all of these aspects are indeed important in understanding the complexities of the configuration problem, its operationalisation and lack of data availability limit the accumulation of knowledge in the domain of supply chain configuration reseach.

The global value chain (GVC) concept was developed to acknowledge opportunities and constraints that depend on different configurations of supplier and buyer networks. The value chain denotes "the process by which technology is combined with material and labor inputs, and then processed inputs are assembled, marketed, and distributed. A single firm may consist of only one link in this process, or it may be extensively vertically integrated, such as steel firms that carry out operations that range from mining ore to fabricating final goods" (Kogut 1985: 15). Dispersion of the value chain in global markets, variation in configurations of the value chain, differences in functional activities that firms internalise, and embeddedness of competing companies are all becoming increasingly important in IB research. Of particular importance is the relationship between GVC configuration and the creation and distribution of value. GVCs impact opportunities and constrain developing-economy firms in their efforts to enhance their position in the global economy (Gereffi, Humphrey and Sturgeon 2005). Value creation in GVCs can occur in both upstream and downstream activities, which are often globally dispersed and modular. Through the value chain, firms internationalise in webs of relationships with their suppliers and buyers, and the market-as-network perspective on internationalisation seems appropriate for the study of GVCs (Johanson and Vahlne 2011). Related to GVCs is the concept of global factories – interfirm structures through which multinational enterprises integrate globalisation strategies combining production, distribution and innovation (Buckley 2009). Firms from different sectors and industries may contribute to value created in the same value chain, which requires a perspective beyond the traditional firm and sector levels used by IB researchers (Giuliani, Pietrobeli and Rabellotti 2005).

The theory of value chain governance was developed based on three factors: the complexity of information and knowledge transfer required to sustain a particular transaction, the extent to which information and knowledge can be codified, and the capabilities of actual and potential suppliers related to the transaction. Based on a combination of these factors, five types of governance have been proposed: markets, modular value chains, relational value chains, captive value chains and hierarchy (Gereffi, Humphrey and Sturgeon 2005).

Emerging market multinationals

The internationalisation of companies from emerging markets is becoming an area of primary interest for IB and entrepreneurship scholars (Peng and Luo 2000; Meyer and Peng 2005; Mathews 2006; Buckley et al. 2007; Luo and Tung 2007; Brutton, Ahlstrom and Obloj 2008; Brennan 2011; De Beule and Van Den Bulcke 2012; Contractor 2013; Nolke 2014). There are good reasons explaining the growing interest in studying companies from developing economies. We can observe increasing levels of investment flows in a direction opposite to the well-explored internationalisation of established firms from developed to emerging economies. Moreover, developing countries' share in global FDI flows is increasing, and investments from one developing country to another are also becoming more common. Yet there is relatively little published research presenting the strategies, models and patterns of internationalisation of firms based in emerging economies (Mathews 2006).

Firms from emerging markets are latecomers to the globalisation game, and lack the OLI (ownership, location and internalisation) advantages that were useful in explaining globalisation from developed to developing countries. The ownership advantage is derived from extending proprietary assets abroad, such as brands or proprietary technologies. The location advantage comes from the ability to integrate and dislocate activities in the value chain around global economies so that the firm can benefit from different factor and resource costs. The internalisation advantage refers to the ability to enjoy economies of scale and scope that would not be possible should firms' operations be disintegrated into country units (Dunning 1981).

Mathews (2006) proposed the LLL model of internationalisation, which is more useful for describing the phenomenon of latecomers in the globalisation game. His theoretical proposal was supported by an empirical study of dragon multinationals – Asian firms which were latecomers to globalisation and expanded rapidly. Dragon multinationals were assumed to rely on links to other firms in the global web of the interconnected economy to gain access to resources from the network. They were able to leverage these resources quickly through accelerated internationalisation, and learn from repeated links and leverages in internationalisation projects. These firms executed a rapid "gestalt switch" from domestic to global players, which paradoxically enabled them to enjoy a latecomer advantage rather than liabilities. This is due to the dragon multinationals' rapid leapfrogging into advanced technologies and management systems, which they combine with low labour costs and demand in local markets.

Another theoretical attempt to explain internationalisation from emerging to developed countries was made by the originators of the springboard perspective, who proposed that emerging market multinationals will aim to overcome latecomer disadvantages by a set of aggressive, proactive tactics such as acquisition of critical assets, know-how and brands from mature MNEs (Luo and Tung 2007). Related to this is the problem of upgrading and innovating to increase value added, achieved by entering higher-value market niches, implementing more efficient processes through superior technologies and reorganisation of production, introducing more sophisticated value-added products and services and acquiring new, superior functions in the chain such as marketing, branding and design (Giuliani, Pietrobeli and Rabellotti 2005).

The white goods sector

Many emerging market multinationals operate in mid-tech industries that were often in decline in developed markets, but growing in catching-up countries. This fact offered a more favourable business field in which latecomers to the globalisation game had fewer technological entry barriers and enjoyed enough demand in their home markets to generate the resources needed to begin internationalisation (Ramamurti 2009). A prominent example of such a sector in which latecoming contenders compete against established multinational companies is the white goods industry.

The white goods industry has been used as an empirical field for the development of IB theory (Baden-Fuller and Stopford 1991; Bonaglia, Goldstein and Mathews 2007). Studies in the development of the white goods sector in Europe have proved that national strategies are often superior to global strategies in market conditions in which complexity due to development cycles and variety of demand make the economy of scale irrelevant as a source of competitive advantage. The early success of Italian manufacturers such as Zanussi, Zoppas, Indcsit, Ignis (IRE) and Candy in the 1970s, which gained a European market share of almost 40 percent based on standardisation, economies of scale, falling transport costs and declining institutional barriers, seemed to prove the superiority of the international strategy over a domestic one. Although some national companies were effectively put out of business as a consequence of the "Italian recipe", the remaining ones proved to be more profitable than global players. This observation has led to the concept of frustrated globalisation, in which exogenous factors not controlled by a firm are usually of greater importance than those being at the discretion of managers when pursuing a global strategy. One such factor on the supply side was the increasing modularity of production, driven by technological developments that reduce the minimum efficient scale of production (Baden-Fuller and Stopford 1991). In this type of environment, modular value chains emerge in which technical standards simplify interaction by reducing the range of components and the specificity of modules that can be delivered by suppliers. Another factor explaining frustrated globalisation is the nature of the product itself, which in the case of white goods is of relatively low value and large weight, increasing the relative importance of distribution costs that depend on the distance from production facilities to retail distribution points (Capgemini Consulting 2012).

The sector, somewhat uniquely, remained composed of global, regional and local firms with relatively low concentration levels, no firm having a market share of more than 10 percent (Bonaglia, Goldstein and Mathews 2007). The white goods industry is characterised by the use of mostly mature technologies, strong demand in developing countries, and low levels of growth in developed economies. The demand in developing economies opened a window of opportunity for new multinationals to emerge, such as Haier and Midea from China, Arcelik from Turkey, Mabe from Mexico and Mahindra and Mahindra from India. Somewhat uniquely, we can find in this sector old multinationals (Whirlpool, Electrolux, GE), firms that internationalised in the so-called first wave of globalisation (LG and Samsung from South Korea) and latecomer contenders who have joined the globalisation game recently. This setting motivated a study of the internationalisation of three latecomers: Haier, Arcelik and Mabe (Bonaglia, Goldstein and Mathews 2007). It was shown that while the globalisation strategies of those firms differed, they had some important similarities. Two of the most important were:

1   high speed of internationalisation, differentiating these firms from traditional multinationals that globalised in a rather slow, incremental process
2   use of strategic linkages that enabled these multinationals to transform from low-cost service providers, through OEMs for the industry, to the position of contenders which market products in international markets under their own brands (Bonaglia, Goldstein and Mathews 2007).

The white goods industry remains regionally differentiated and globally frustrated. For example, Capgemini presented a European ranking of white goods companies for 2010. According to their data, the market leader in the region was BSH (with the main brands Bosh, Siemens, Gagenaum and Neff) with white goods turnover estimated at €6.7 bn, followed by Electrolux (with the brands Electrolux, AEG and Zanussi) at €4.8 bn, Indesit at €2.7 bn, Whirlpool (the global market leader in 2010) with €2.2 bn EMEA turnover, Samsung, LG, Miele, Haier, Amica and Fagor (Capgemini Consulting 2012).

There are also notable differences among countries and major regions in distribution channels for white goods. For example, in the American market, the three most important retail channels for white goods and electronics were found to be hypermarkets, home and garden retailers and mass merchandisers, while in China the largest category of retailers was electronics and appliance specialists, followed by department stores and hypermarkets (Branston 2010). The major differences in retail systems fit different business models of producers, which is likely another factor explaining the frustrated globalisation in the white goods industry.

Emerging versus established multinationals' embeddedness in the global value chain of the white goods industry

Our empirical illustration of a global value chain involving the white goods industry is exploratory and presents only a partial picture of the entire industry and its value contributors. In June 2014 we gathered data on suppliers and distributors for several firms operating in that industry, including the following seven: Haier, Electrolux, Whirlpool, LG, Samsung, GE and Arcelik. These firms include three multinationals that have been present in the industry for many decades (Electrolux, Whirlpool and GE), two Korean firms that are examples of the "first wave" of internationalisation from emerging to developed economies (LG and Samsung) and two current contenders (Haier and Arcelik). The selection of value-creating partners was based on information provided by Thomson Reuters. We chose those suppliers that accounted for more than 0.2 percent of annual turnover. This threshold selection based on transaction size enabled us to focus on only those transactions that are likely to be of an enduring and strategic nature. Included in the dataset were first-tier (direct) suppliers, second-tier suppliers, and vendors distributing white goods. Based on these selection criteria, there emerge 325 companies, which we treat as nodes in the network of the global value chain, and 520 transactions that create the network linkages. The global value chain network that we present in Figure 13.1 is by no means complete and should thus be treated only as a proxy for the assessment of embeddedness.

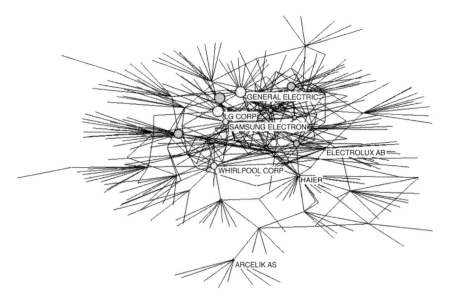

Figure 13.1 Global value chain in the white goods industry

Source: Author's own work created with Pajek software (Batagelj, Mrvar 1998)

The sizes of the vertices are proportional to betweenness centrality in the graph. Vertices are coloured as follows: white for white goods companies, grey for their partners in the global value chain. Based on the observed network of the 325 companies included in our dataset, and the registered transactions among them listed in the Thomson Reuters database, we can see that the most central positions are occupied by General Electric, LG, Samsung and Whirlpool, followed by the less central positions of Haier, Electrolux and Arcelik. Betweenness centrality is equal to the number of times the shortest paths between any two vertices in a network pass through a node. High betweenness centrality signals boundary spanning opportunities such as quick access to information, knowledge and resource combination from the network (Borgatti and Halgin 2011). Treating this observation as a proxy, we can suggest that indeed emergent multinationals like Haier and Arcelik have less chance to enjoy boundary spanning opportunities than their established competitors, with the exception of Electrolux. Since this analysis was performed, Electrolux has bought GE Appliances, enabling it to take advantage of the latter firm's more central position in the global value chain. Haier and Arcelik have two options to compensate for the constraints resulting from their less central positions in the network. They can either internalise some activities or create new fragments of value chains which they would control. Paradoxically, this can lead to innovative strategic moves and business models. For example, lacking local distribution partners, Haier created its own retail operations in China which enabled it to dominate and effectively control the fast-growing market. In 2012 Haier, under the Goodaymart brand, operated a network of 7,000 self-owned stores across China (EUROMONITOR 2013). It is also noteworthy that LG and Samsung have very central positions in the observed network, which signals that former newcomers are able to move into key roles in the network of suppliers and distributors.

In the next step of our analysis we focused only on the value chains of three leading companies in the industry: Haier, Whirlpool and Electrolux. We included major vendors and first- and second-tier suppliers based on data from Thomson Reuters for June 2014.

As can be seen in Figure 13.2, Haier, Electrolux and Whirlpool are all present at eleven retailers. These retailers are key players in the American white goods market. Electrolux, which has the largest set of retailers in which its direct competitors do not have a presence, is more established in South America and in the small but affluent Scandinavian markets. Although all competitors are present in the US and compete head-to-head through several partner chains, their market positions differ. This cannot be seen from the network graph, which reflects retail presence but lacks information about the value of each partnership. We can estimate that for Haier, links with American retailers represent evidence only of starting relationships of relatively low value. The volume of units sold in China in 2012 was almost twenty times larger than in the US (EUROMONITOR 2013).

In Figure 13.3, we add first- and second-tier suppliers to the value chain network of Electrolux, Whirlpool and Haier.

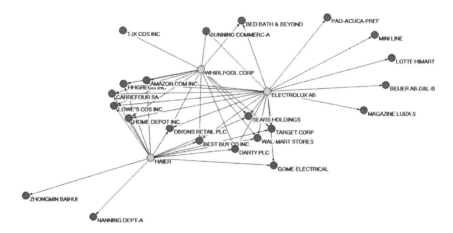

Figure 13.2 Retail distributors for Haier, Electrolux and Whirlpool

Source: Author's own work created with Pajek software (Batagelj, Mrvar 1998). Colours: grey – white goods companies; black – retailers.

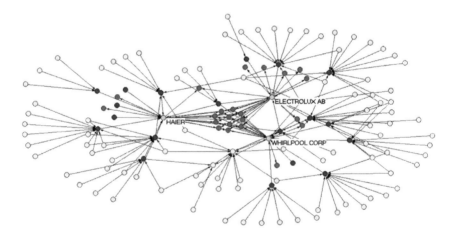

Figure 13.3 Value chain of three companies: Haier, Electrolux and Whirlpool

Source. Author's own work created with Pajek software (Batagelj, Mrvar 1998). Colours: black – white goods producers, retail distributors, and first-tier suppliers; white – second-tier suppliers.

We can observe that the three firms Haier, Whirlpool and Electrolux compete head-to-head through the eleven large retail partners present in the centre of the figure above, which were analysed previously. Each of them also has unique relationships with retailers through which white goods are sold to individual customers. According to transactional data available from Reuters, and later verified through websites, Electrolux has the largest set of unique relationships with retailers, followed by Haier and Whirlpool. Comparing first-tier suppliers, we can see that there is more overlap between Electrolux and Whirlpool than for the other pairs among the three white goods producers analysed. Another observation is that Haier's first-tier suppliers have on average fewer second-tier suppliers in our dataset than those of Electrolux and Whirlpool. There are also more registered connections among second-tier suppliers in the value chains of Electrolux and Whirlpool than in the corresponding subnetwork of Haier's suppliers. Otherwise, the observed networks of value chains for Whirlpool, Haier and Electrolux are quite similar.

Conclusions

We see our study as constituting explorative research into the problem of embeddedness of emerging market multinationals in the global value chain. The use of standard graphic displays of networks, produced using Pajek software, for social network analysis sheds some light on how position in the global value chain not only facilitates the internationalisation of emerging market multinationals, but also constrains it. We have found that GE, LG, Samsung and Whirlpool tend to be more central and have access to a wider variety of information, resources and potential combinational gains. The relative disadvantage of Electrolux, Haier and Arcelik imposes constraints on all of them. On studying additional information on companies in the white goods value chain, we can observe a range of different responses to these limitations. Haier has compensated for its disadvantage by the internalisation of distribution in China – the fastest growing white goods market in the world. In this way it secured dominance in that market and a flow of resources that enabled it to develop several innovations and become the leading producer of white goods by volume, with a market share close to 10 percent (EUROMONITOR 2013). Electrolux acquired GE in 2014, which has enabled it to move into a central position in the industry's global value chain, achieve the highest transnationality index in the sector, and take over the position of US market leader from Whirlpool. Whirlpool had earlier bought the Italian Indesit and increased its presence in Europe (Hansegard and Hagerty 2014). Arcelik has chosen to grow regionally in Europe, where it has concentrated its value chain activities.

We have been able to present only a fragment of the industry value chain, in which several regional competitors such as BSH Siemens, Mabe, Panasonic, Sharp, Mahindra and Mahindra, Amica and Gorenje were not covered due to lack of data. The data that we were able to use for our exploratory analysis of value chains only partially cover their transaction activities. We hope to investigate the issue further, combining qualitative and quantitative study of the white goods industry. The goal of qualitative study of the dynamics of the global value chain would be to investigate whether and how latecomers are able to accommodate to the established network in a mature industry.

To arrive at more assured conclusions on the interplay between embeddedness in the global value chain and internationalisation, more studies will have to be conducted concerning other industries and other cases of EMNEs. This should enable the generalisation of findings on the network properties of global value chains and the specifics of latecomer internationalisation. To enable this, it is necessary for companies to report on major transactions in a more standardised way, and for international institutions managing international statistics on globalisation, such as UNCTAD and OECD, to change their focus from firms and countries to global value chains. As the world has become a more connected, networked economy, we need to develop data sources and analytic practices that enable us to better understand the competitive dynamics of interconnected chains of firms. Networks not only create opportunities for accelerated internationalisation, but can powerfully constrain its scope and force alternative strategies to globalisation.

Bibliography

Baden-Fuller, C.W.F., and J. M. Stopford (1991) 'Globalization frustrated: The case of white goods', *Strategic Management Journal, 12(7)*: 493–507.

Batagelj, V., and A. Mrvar (1998) 'Pajek – Program for large network analysis' *Connections, 21(2)*: 47–57.

Bonaglia, F., A. Goldstein and J. Mathews (2007) 'Accelerated internationalization by emerging markets' multinationals: The case of the white goods sector', *Journal of World Business, 42(4)*: 369–383.

Borgatti, S. P., and D. S. Halgin (2011) 'On network theory', *Organizational Science, 22(5)*: 1168–1181.

Borgatti, S. P., and P. C. Foster (2003) 'The network paradigm in organizational research: A review of typology', *Journal of Management, 29(6)*: 991–1013.

Brandenburger, A. and B. Nalebuff. (1995) 'The right game: Use game theory to shape strategy', *Harvard Business Review, 73(4)*: 57–71.

Branston, A. (2010) *Retail Digest. Blowing a Fuse? Electronics and Appliance Retailers Deal with the Downturn.* London: Euromonitor International.

Brennan, L. (2011) *The Emergence of Southern Multinationals: Their Impact on Europe.* Basingstoke, Hampshire: Palgrave Macmillan.

Brutton, G., D. Ahlstrom and K. Obloj (2008) 'Entrepreneurship in emerging economies: Where are we today and where should the research go in the future?', *Entrepreneurship Theory and Practice, 32(1)*: 1–14.

Buckley, P. (2009) 'The impact of global factory on economic development', *Journal of World Business, 44(2)*: 131–143.

Buckley, P. J., L. J. Clegg, A. R. Cross, X. Liu., H. Voss, and P. Zheng (2007) 'The determinants of Chinese outward foreign direct investment', *Journal of International Business Studies, 38*: 499–518.

Capgemini Consulting. (2012) *White Goods Distribution in the Spotlight.* Utrecht: Capgemini Consulting.

Coase, R. H. (1937) 'The nature of the firm', *Economica, 4(16)*: 386–405.

Conelly, B. L., D. J. Ketchen, and T. M. Hult (2013) 'Global supply chain management: Toward a theoretically driven research agenda', *Global Strategy Journal, 3(3)*: 227–243.

Contractor, F. (2013) 'Punching above their weight: The sources of competitive advantage for emerging market multinationals', *International Journal of Emerging Markets, 8(4)*: 304–328.

Coviello, N. E. (2006) 'Network dynamics in the international new venture', *Journal of International Business Studies, 37(5)*: 713–731.

Craighead, C. W., T. M. Hult, and D. J. Ketchen (2009) 'The effects of innovation: Cost strategy, knowledge, and action in the supply chain on firm performance', *Journal of Operations Management, 27(5)*: 405–421.

De Beule, F., and D. Van Den Bulcke. (2012) 'Locational determinants of outward foreign direct investment: An analysis of Chinese and Indian greenfield investments', *Transnational Corporations*, *21(1)*: 1–34.

Dunning, J. H. (1981) *International Production and the Multinational Enterprise.* London: Allen & Unwin.

Dunning, J. H. and S. Lundan (2008) *Multinational Enterprises and the Global Economy.* Cheltenham: Edward Elgar Publishing.

Dyer, J. H., and H. Singh (1998) 'The relational view: Cooperative strategy and sources of interorganizational competitive advanatage', *Academy of Management Review*, *23(4)*: 660–679.

Elango, B., and C. Pattnaik. (2007) 'Building capabilities for international operations through networks: A study of Indian firms', *Journal of international Business Studies*, *38(4):* 541–555.

EUROMONITOR. (2013) *Haier Group in Consumer Appliences.* London: Euromonitor.

Forsgren, M., U. Holm, and J. Johanson (2005) *Managing the Embedded Multinational – A Business Network View.* Cheltenham: Edward Elgar.

Gereffi, G., J. Humphrey, and T. Sturgeon (2005) 'The governance of global value chains', *Review of International Political Economy*, *12(1)*: 78–104.

Giuliani, E., C. Pietrobeli, and R. Rabellotti (2005) 'Upgrading in global value chains: Lessons from Latin American clusters', *World Development*, *33(4)*: 549–573.

Granovetter, M. (1985) 'Economic action and social structure: The problem of embeddedness', *American Journal of Sociology*, *3:* 481–510.

Greve, H., T. Shipilov and A. Rowley (2014) *Network Advantage.* San Francisco, CA: Jossey-Bass.

Gulati, R. (1998) 'Alliances and networks', *Strategic Management Journal*, *19(4)*: 293–317.

Gulati, R., and M. Gargiulo (1999) 'Where do interorganizational networks come from?', *American Journal of Sociology*, *104(5)*: 1439–1493.

Hansegard, J., and J. R. Hagerty (2014) 'Electrolux to buy GE Appliances business for $3.3 billion.', *Wall Street Journal*, www.wsj.com approached September 8, 2014.

Hosseini, M., and H. Dadfar (2012) 'Network-based theories and internationalization of firms: Applications to empirical studies', paper presented at International Trade and Academic Research Conference (ITARC), London.

Jaklič, A., and M. Svetličič (2002) 'Outward FDI by selected transition economies; Comparative evaluation', paper presented at the Annual Meeting of EIBA – European International Business Association.

Johanson, J., and J. E. Vahlne (2011) 'Markets as networks: Implications for strategy-making', *Journal of the Academy of Marketing Science, 39(4)*: 484–491.

Kogut, B. (1985) 'Designing global strategies: Comparative and competitive value added chains', *Sloan Management Review*, *26(4):* 15–28.

Li, J. J., K. T. Zhou, and A. Shao (2008) 'Competitive position, managerial ties, and profitability of foreign firms in China: An interactive perspective', *Journal of International Business Studies, 40(2)*: 339–352.

Luo, Y., and R. Tung. (2007) 'International expansion of emerging market enterprises: A springboard perspective', *Journal of International Business Studies*, *38:* 481–498.

Mathews, J. A. (2006) 'Dragon multinationals: New players in 21 st century globalization', *Asia Pacific Journal of Management, 23(1)*: 5–27.

Meyer, K. E., and M. W. Peng (2005) 'Probing theoretically into central and eastern Europe: Transactions, resources, and institutions', *Journal of International Business Studies*, *36:* 600–621.

Nolke, A. ed. (2014) *Multinational Corporations from Emerging Markets.* Basingstoke, UK: Palgrave Macmillan.

Peng, M. W., and Y. Luo (2000) 'Managerial ties and firm performance in a transition economy: The nature of micro-macro link', *Academy of Management Journal, 43(3)*: 486–501.

Podolny, J. M., and K. L. Page (1998) 'Network forms of organization', *Annual Review of Sociology, 24*: 57–76.

Porter, M. (2001) *Porter o konkurencj* [Porter on competition]. Warszawa: PWE.

Ramamurti, R. (2009) 'What have we learned about EMNEs', in *Emerging Multinationals from Emerging Markets*, edited by Ravi Ramamurti and Jitendra Singh. Cambridge: Cambridge University Press, pp. 399–426.

Srai, J. S., and M. Gregory (2008) 'A supply network configuration perspective on international supply chain development', *International Journal of Operations & Production Management, 28(5):* 386–411.

Sydow, J., A. Windeler, C. Wirth, and U. Staber (2010) 'Foreign market entry as network entry: A relational-structuration perspective on internationalization in television content production', *Scandinavian Journal of Management, 26(1)*: 13–24.

UNCTAD. (2013) *The 2013 World Investment Report. Global Value Chains: Investment and Trade for Development.* New York and Geneva: United Nations Publishing.

Wellman, B. (1988) 'Structural analysis: From method and metaphor to theory and substance.' In *Social Structures: A Network Approach*, edited by Barry Wellman and Stephen Berkowitz. Cambridge: Cambridge University Press, pp. 19–62.

Yiu, D. W., C. Lau, and G. D. Bruton (2007) 'International venturing by emerging economy firms: The effects of firm capabilities, home country networks, and corporate entrepreneurship', *Journal of International Business Studies, 38(4)*: 519–540.

Zhou, L., W. Wu, and X. Luo. (2007) 'Internationalization and the performance of born-global SMEs: The mediating role of social networks', *Journal of International Business Studies, 38:* 673–690.

14 Central European transition economies' multinationals

Are they different from third world multinationals?[1]

Marjan Svetličič

Introduction

When discussing the transition to a market economy, outward foreign direct investments (OFDIs) have, with few exceptions (Svetličič's two ACE projects,[2] Andreff 2002, 2003; Kalotay 2003; Liuhto and Jumpponen 2003), been almost left out of consideration. Nevertheless, since 1997 firms from more advanced transition economies (TEs) have started investing abroad, even though they were not devoid of any previous experiences from the socialist period (Hamilton 1986; McMillan 1987). Such activities were more an exception than the rule. The motives were quite different from those of 'normal' internationalization. The situation has changed recently, but most attention has shifted to emerging economies' multinationals. It almost looks as if emerging economies' outward internationalization is a completely new phenomenon. Yet the origin of such multinational companies (MNCs) can be traced back nearly a century in history. Third world[3] (TW) multinational companies[4] (TWMNCs) or investing abroad by firms from developing countries (LDCs) started to attract attention back in the 1980s (Kumar and McLeod 1981; Wells 1982, 1983; Lall 1983; Dunning 1986; Khan 1986; Svetličič 1986, 1987). Moreover, such companies became part of the 'official' development strategy of developing countries in the context of enhancing their economic and technical cooperation. Such forms were also regarded as part of their strategy towards Western MNCs. Articles on South-South investments emerged (Svetličič 1987; Svetličič in cooperation with Rojec 1987; Aykut and Ratha 2004).

Initially, the literature on TWMNCs concentrated on the 'exotic' nature of such corporations. More recent literature has started to look into such internationalization in its own right (Mathews 2002). This is also the case with central European transition economies' multinational companies (CEMNCs[5]). In spite of this benign neglect, both types of firms are putting themselves on the map of MNCs. Some have already become global (e.g. Agtmael 2008), while those from CE economies (CEEs) are still lagging well behind Western and TWMNCs.[6] On this basis, we can start exploring whether there is a need for differentiated approaches, new theories due to the different internal and external conditions involved or whether such "new trends are different only by degree" (Thomsen 2010: 459).

This paper will compare the similarities and differences between CEMNCs and TWMNCs in terms of the timing of internationalization, the motivations, the type of competitive advantages and the role of the external environment. It is based on our own survey[7] of OFDI by five CEEs (Czech Republic, Estonia, Hungary, Poland and Slovenia), complemented with some of the other latest research and general data on FDI flows abroad. Secondary sources were used in the case of TWMNCs. We will mostly confine our analysis to manufacturing firms' expansion abroad.

The structure of the paper is as follows. After this introduction stating the objectives, the limitations and background of the paper, we proceed to the theoretical framework. The third section is devoted to the characteristics of OFDI by CEEs. The fourth section provides a short overview of TW firms' investments abroad to set the stage for the next section, a comparative evaluation of the two types of MNC, identifying the similarities and differences between them. The paper concludes with some theoretical generalizations.

Theoretical framework

The most general theory which can explain the internationalization of firms, apart from internalization theory, is the eclectic paradigm (Dunning 1993) predicting that a firm has to possess firm-specific advantages (FSAs) to be able to invest abroad, that the foreign location should be better than the one at home and that internalization is the best mode for maximizing such FSAs. The issue is therefore whether firms from CEEs and the TW possess strong enough FSAs to invest abroad, where they can best complement such advantages with location-specific ones, and whether they are able to internalize them.

The Dunning (1981) investment development path (IDP) paradigm postulates that before investing abroad, countries first host FDI and that investing abroad is a function of GDP per capita. The new version of the IDP model (Dunning and Narula 1998) postulates that in a globalized world, OFDI starts earlier and the amplitudes of the stages are shorter.

The Uppsala sequential internationalization process model (Johanson and Wiedersheim-Paul 1975; Johanson and Vahlne 1977) predicts a 'normal' sequential step-by-step learning process of internationalization in stages. Critics of the sequential internationalization model claim that internationalization is not necessarily sequential, that 'internationalization' knowledge can be gained from other firms (Turnbull 1987; Eriksson et al. 1997) and by networking with others (Mattsson 1985; Johanson and Mattsson 1986, 1993).

The fourth stage of the product life cycle, proposed by Balakrishnan (1975), predicts investment among countries at lower stages of development. His argument is that in the fourth, post-mature stage FDI takes place among developing countries when technology becomes adapted to local needs.

Resource-based theories (Penrose 1959; Wernerfelt 1984; Prahalad and Hamel 1990) claim that resources are the key to a superior firm performance. A firm has to possess specific tangible and intangible heterogeneous and immobile resources which can also be exploited as a specific core advantage abroad. OFDI cannot be

explained without looking into (strategic) management theories or "why management superiority of foreign investors over their domestic counterparts is more
pronounced when the corporate governance in the host country is weak and financial institutions are not so well developed" (Razin 2002: 17). This is precisely the
situation in TEs. This has two main implications – first, that managerial superiority plays a relatively more important role in the case of investing in transition
than in developed industrial countries, and second, that firms from more advanced
TEs have developed transition-management-specific advantages which they can
'cash in on' in other TEs or, perhaps, in some emerging markets still undergoing
institutional changes. It also implies that firms from developing and transition
economies may possess along with some countries at a similar level of development a more adapted management style than firms from Western countries, as
claimed by Balakrishnan (1975) and empirically documented by Pradhan in the
case of India (2002).

Can we agree with L. Wells's old statement that "the theories have done little
to answer why firms from LDCs (or TEs for that matter, comment by SM) invest
abroad" (Wells 1983: 13) or can we posit that the empirical data confirm the major
internationalization theories? Because the general theory of FDI has largely been
built on the experience of industrialized country investors, there are "inevitably
gaps in the possibility to apply this theory to emerging economies" (Buckley et al.
2007: 501). Recent studies tend to suggest that those theories do not explain the
"third wave of OFDI from emerging economies"[8] (Gammeltoft et al. 2010: 257).
Mathews (2002) found the "inadequacy of most leading theories of TNCs growth
and expansion" and offers "a process oriented account of dragon multinationals'
transnationalisation in which three key elements are emphasised: outward orientation, leverage through building linkages and achieving organizational efficiency
through integration" (Wai-chung Yeung 2002: 192).

Others (Lecraw 1977; Lall 1983) among the early authors assumed that the
existing theories could explain such internationalization. More recent articles on
this also claim that there is not much new in the internationalization of emerging markets' firms or those from TEs which would demand a modification of the
theory. Therefore, Dunning et al. (2008) believe that it is merely "old wine in new
bottles".

Outward FDI by five central European transition economies

There are very few studies on the OFDI by CEEs which go beyond evaluating
general flows and stocks. We therefore have to rely mostly on our own study
(Jaklič and Svetličič 2003), which also provides data on other aspects of internationalization. Concentrating on the same countries (without Estonia), Rugraff
(2010) came to similar conclusions, claiming that a small number of large, horizontal multinationals investing in the neighbouring countries account for the bulk
of the OFDI flows and stock.

Although investing abroad by state-owned enterprises started in socialist times
many decades ago, today it entails a totally new challenge. The early 1990s saw

slow progress in outward investment activities by large exporters with substantial international experience, whereas post-1997, and particularly 2000, has witnessed the speeding up of OFDI, also involving newcomers. The total stock of OFDI of the five CEEs (USD 4 billion in 2000) was and is still very modest internationally. It amounts to USD 130.3 billion, or an increase of more than thirty-two times. This is, however, only a small part of the overall OFDI by all TEs (not including EU members), which had accumulated to USD 487 billion by the end of 2014 or even more compared with the outward investment stock by developing economies of USD 4,833 billion by the end of 2014 (UNCTAD 2015: A 2).

The investors in our sample of CEEs are nearly twenty-eight years old on average, with some even dating back to before World War II, while many are spin-offs of old socialist, now disintegrated companies. They inherited management, brand names and business contacts and can hardly be regarded as totally new firms. Big firms are the most influential, quickest and most successful in their internationalization in terms of volumes, although the majority of sample companies have less than 250 employees.

> The gradually rising flows of OFDI following previous exports confirm that the sequential pattern of penetration does matter. Neighbouring countries, countries with strong trade relationships or cultural and/or historical ties/ vicinity have priority in investment location decisions made by all the surveyed countries.[9]

Market-seeking has been the most important motive of OFDI. Investing abroad has been an additional way to keep and increase market shares abroad. Lower labour costs have been, on average, the least important motive for investing abroad. Investors have been primarily looking for business opportunities and ways to exploit their FSAs, which often have a limited time duration.

What are the investors' competitive advantages?

> The reasons for the rapid rise of OFDI by selected CEEs can be classified into push and pull factors. The two push factors are the existing FSAs coupled with the limited opportunities to increase market shares in existing (small domestic) markets. Firms have realized that by exporting alone they can no longer keep their market shares abroad, that they also have to upgrade their foreign presence by establishing subsidiaries in order to be closer to customers (customization). On the other hand, the pull factors like globalization forcing firms to acquire economies of scale and scope have all been attracting investors to grasp the new opportunities emerging abroad. Some of them are also home-country-location based due to having once lived together in the same country.
>
> Among the relatively equally weighted different advantages, technological ones were the most important, followed by marketing knowledge.[10] There is, however, no systematic evidence as to whether such technological advantages are based on new products or new technologies or more on the adaptation of products and processes to local conditions.

The crucial source of FSAs of the surveyed investing companies is their management. This includes the capabilities of the managers, who undertook investments abroad before the theory would have predicted, and their strong vision at times when investing abroad was considered unpatriotic or at least unusual (in socialist times and the first years of the transition). Some managers had also developed a specific management style based on personal contacts and were highly assimilated to the culture of the host countries.

> Organizational know-how, as a specific type of FSA, was somewhat less 'important'. This type of advantage is temporary. Firms have to exploit it fast, before other competitors can catch up or outperform these advantages. It is therefore critical to achieve a *first-mover advantage* early and to upgrade other advantages before the advantage of how to do business in a specific environment expires.

The more risky environment found in other CEEs, less stability and predictability make firms choose FDI (internalization) as a safety-net solution in spite of the higher sunk costs. Companies have found it easier to protect their intellectual property and defend their original products against imitations when they have a direct presence (Jaklič and Svetličič 2003). Weak protection of property rights can be, contrary to traditional theoretical predictions, a motivation for and not a barrier to internationalization.

Third world multinational companies

The first internationalization of TW firms dates back to 1928, when the Argentine manufacturer SIAM (Sección Industrial Amasadoras Mecánicas) di Tella established a subsidiary in Brazil to produce gasoline pumps (Wells 1983: 1). Real internationalization started in the 1960s (Dunning 1981; Kumar and McLeod 1981; Lall 1983; Wells 1983; White 1983; Khan 1986; Tolentino 1992).

Dunning and Narula (1998) and Chudnovsky and Lopez (2000) distinguish three waves of such OFDI by TW firms. The first wave started from Latin America (LA) in the 1970s as part of the import substitution strategy of home countries. LA firms have spread abroad thanks to products meeting the needs of their growing domestic markets. The second stage is characterized by predominant Asian MNCs (from South Korea, Taiwan, Hong Kong and Singapore, and much later Malaysia, Thailand, China,[11] India and the Philippines) in the 1980s, while LA firms stepped back relatively. OFDI from newly industrializing countries accompanies the strategy of export promotion, growing markets in LDCs but also in order to benefit from the cheap labour there (the flying geese paradigm; Kojima 1960; Akamatsu 1961). The third stage, in the 1990s, exhibits the recovery of LA OFDI. The biggest Asian MNCs now compete with Western MNCs, as demonstrated by their investments in developed countries (Andreff 2003: 19). As in the case of CEMNCs, we also have wide heterogeneity among TWMNCs. They differ in terms of the timing, competitive advantages and motives. The development strategy also proved to be highly important for internationalization, as clearly demonstrated in the case of Asian and LA firms originating from totally different strategic backgrounds, like the system had been in the case of TEs. In both cases, we can see elements of the system- or institutions-escape type of investments, including tax escape (e.g. Cazura and Ramamurti 2014) due to underdeveloped institutions, their non-transparency and unpredictability (volatility of changes).

Comparing third world and central European transition economies' multinational companies

In spite of data and other limitations, it is possible to posit that there are more similarities than differences in internationalization development between the two groups of countries' firms. Authors researching both phenomena confirm the validity of the IDP paradigm (Chudnovsky and Lopez 2000; Andreff (2003), since both groups of countries' firms investing abroad do share many similarities in terms of the timing of internationalization, its evolution (by stages) and development level. LDCs' OFDI stock was at the level of today's TEs approximately twenty years ago (e.g. Gorynia et al. 2010).

Table 14.1 Key data and characteristics of TW and CEEs' MNCs

	TWMNCs	CEMNCs
Beginnings and developments	Three stages: a) 1960s to 1970s, mostly LA firms; b) 1980s (Asian firms); and c) 1990s onwards (Wells 1983; Chudnovsky and Lopez 2000). Exports preceded OFDI in 85% of cases (Wells 1983: 68)	Three stages: a) pre-transition infant stage; b) early beginning till 1996; and c) real upswing after 1997 Specific system-escape motivation in socialism (Svetličič et al. 1994) or institutionally based (Andreff 2003: 10). Exports almost always the first step before FDI.
Data on OFDIs and MNCs	USD 5–10 billion by the 1980s (Wells 1983: 2). USD 29–34 billion estimated stock of FDI by selected LDCs in 1982 (Dunning 1986). 1,964 subsidiaries abroad; the estimate goes up to 6,000–8,000 (Wells 1982 and 1983).	USD 1,483 million of OFDI by economies in transition or 0.1% of world OFDI flows in 1990 (Andreff 2003: 4).

	TWMNCs	*CEMNCs*
	1% of total OFDI stock in 1960, 3.2% in 1978 and 11.9% in 2000 (Andreff 2003: 18). USD 23–26 billion of inter-Arab and Arab investments in other LDCs (Svetličič 1987: 22). Stock for all developing countries in 2002 USD 849 billion[12] (UNCTAD 2003: 264).	USD 2.5 billion in the OFDI stock of the five CEEs in 1997 increased to USD 6 billion in 2001 (Svetličič and Jaklič 2003[13]) 863 affiliates in developed countries in 1992 (Andreff 2003: 4, 10).
Ownership of subsidiaries	Joint ventures and 100% owned (57% in manufacturing; Wells 1983: 3, 108). In other LDCs mostly joint ventures (90%; Svetličič 1986: 80). 65% of subsidiaries in other LDCs private, 20% state, 15% mixed (Svetličič 1986: 81).	Mostly 100% owned and greenfield
Ownership and type of investors	Mostly private, large and old firms. Only six qualify as a large MNC having more than six manufacturing affiliations abroad (Wells 1983: 9). 43% of investments in other LDCs are small, 20% medium and 16% large (Svetličič 1986: 77).	Originally state-owned trading companies. After the transition, private or mixed. Mostly manufacturing firms but expanding in trade as well. Major investors by capital invested are large old firms. SMEs prevail by numbers.
Type of activity	Trade units (Wells 1982). In other LDCs, mostly manufacturing (Wells 1983). Resource, market and assets augmenting (recently).	Sales units prevail before and during the transition. Production units more of a client-follower type. Mostly market, partly efficiency-seeking.
Geographical orientation	High regional concentration (Wells 1983: 4; Dunning et al. 2008: 167). Mostly other neighbouring LDCs, but also increasing in industrial countries.	In socialist times, advanced countries and resource-seeking/production in LDCs (political motives). Now a high regional concentration in less developed neighbouring TEs. OFDIs in emerging economies are very modest.

In both groups of countries, large firms are the dominant investors abroad. Flows are highly concentrated within the region. This provides strong support for the positive role of small cultural distance and/or institutional factors stimulating cooperation (see, for example, Kang and Jiang 2012). This role is relatively more important than in the case of advanced economies. It can be partly explained by the early stages of such internationalization in both groups of countries, where trust is relatively more important than in the later stages. This also applies to inter-Arab investment (e.g. Svetličič 1987). In the two groups of countries, systemic characteristics play an important role in the internationalization of their firms, albeit for different reasons. Socialism was to a certain extent a push factor for internationalization, while in the capitalist economies of LDCs' firms there were more

Table 14.2 The motivation of TW and CEEs' MNCs

	TWMNCs	*CEMNCs*
Motivation	Originally systemic based, avoiding quotas . . . (Wells 1982).	Dominantly market-seeking, also strategic-asset-seeking.
	Market-seeking less important, acquiring strategic assets, improving responses to customers.	Utilization of temporary FSAs (knowing how to do business).
	Lower labour costs as a defensive instrument (Wells 1983: 78).	Cultural proximity, minorities in neighbouring countries.
	Diversification of risks (Wells 1983: 68).	
	Cultural proximity.	
	Resource- and market-seeking (Dunning et al. 2008: 167).	
	Assets augmenting, recently (Dunning et al. 2008: 167).	
	Escape investments (Dunning et al. 2008: 167).	
Domestic push factors	Uncertain institutional environment, unfavourable foreign exchange and tax regimes.	Small domestic markets.
		System-escape OFDIs.
	Later, own innovations (Tolentino 1993).	Bad domestic investment climate, prohibitive taxation, political instability and high inflation and circumvention of export quotas (Andreff 2003: 18).
		Exploitation of specific knowledge and brand names' reputation in neighbouring countries/regions/former parts of the same country.
External pull factors	Less important than internal factors.	More important than in the case of TWMNCs.
	Recently, globalization.	EU integration accession.
	Regional integrations.	

limitations on the full functioning of market economies and import substitution strategies. In most countries, the exporting of capital was initially discouraged, if not prohibited. Many countries restricted imports, which stimulated firms to circumvent such barriers with tariff factories. Market-seeking has been the major driving force behind the internationalization of manufacturing firms together with other home-country push factors like an uncertain institutional environment, high inflation rates, underdeveloped markets, as well as unfavourable foreign exchange and tax regimes. "One can only operate successfully in a high inflation country by being on the spot and adapting price lists by the hour. It cannot be done by exporting or from a distance", said one Slovenian manager.

There are more differences in the strategies than in the motives. The Balakrishnan hypothesis (1975) has proved quite relevant to both groups of countries (relatively more in the case of early TWMNCs), meaning that it may be of (temporary) relevance in the infant stages of internationalization to adapt technologies while simultaneously upgrading their own specific advantages. Initially, they are more in organization and design than of totally new, quality products.[14]

The eclectic paradigm clearly states that investors must have some FSAs in order to qualify to invest abroad.

The process of such upgrading was faster in Asian countries because the outward-oriented development strategies and targeted industrial policies forced firms to meet targets in order to qualify for specific assistance for technological upgrading and achieving competitiveness. Import substitution strategies of LA and CE countries de-stimulated such efforts. Therefore, LA firms started to lag behind internationalization after their initial pioneering role. A small number of CE firms with ambitious and visionary managers started to strengthen their capabilities and invest abroad even in the 1960s (Yugoslav firms, for instance) in spite of such protection. Now the process of the catching up of 'dragon investors' is very rapid due in part to the better starting position of such firms in terms of technically well-educated manpower. Membership in the EU will also stimulate this process. It seems that a certain convergence is also occurring in the strategies.

Differences

The huge country differences within both groups of countries make comparisons very difficult, preventing reliable generalizations. First, there is an enormous difference in the number and size of the countries, their economies' stage of membership in integration groupings and previous development strategies. Firms from small countries are more driven into going international than those from large ones. TWMNCs, particularly Chinese, are mostly resource- or assets-seeking, while those from CEEs are not.

The stronger involvement of SMEs in the case of CEMNCs can be traced to macro-location-based factors, previously established networks in the common market of now disintegrated countries (so-called inherited investments; Jaklič and Svetličič 2001) or what Andreff (2003: 10) called "institutionally founded MNCs" established overnight as a consequence of the disintegration of countries in which

Table 14.3 The advantages and strategies of TW and CEEs' MNCs

	TWMNCs	CEMNCs
Competitive advantages	Location-specific, some brands, adapted technology, cheaper overheads, greater use of local inputs products/ services (Wells 1983: 48).	Macro-location institutionally based (the same systemic background).
	Specific skills in marketing, productive or technological knowledge (Lall 1983).	Knowing how to do business in a similar environment.
	Labour-intensive technologies and small-scale production (Lecraw 1977; Wells 1983; Agarwal 1986).	Cultural, historical, systemic and language vicinity.
	Tapping into external advantages and networks (Mathews 2002: 192).	Highly educated human capital, but lacking market/managerial experience.
	FSAs changing from the adaptation and assimilation of technology towards more own innovative FSAs (Cantwell and Tolentino 1990).	
Strategy	Cost- and following-the-customers based (Wells 1983: 54, 63).	No specific international strategies until the late 1990s.
	Niches abandoned by conventional TNCs (Chudnovsky and Lopez 2000: 37).	Defending previous export markets.
	Inclusion in global production chains.	Following the (industrial) clients.
	Recently, assets augmenting.	
	Hierarchical mode of organization (Brennan 2011).	Efficiency-seeking strategy rare (Andreff 2003: 17).
		Regional trading and production multinationals.
		Leapfrogging internationalization, born globals.

those firms operated before. In this way, such firms evolved from large domestic firms to small international ones in the new political reality.

The new information technology infrastructure also makes it easier for SMEs to internationalize today, particularly as suppliers to large MNCs (client-driven internationalization). It is now much easier to cut into so well developed global value chains at different stages of the smiling curve.

The timing of the starting period of internationalization was also different. TWMNCs commenced earlier, even before the 1960s, while only very few firms from socialist countries started to invest abroad then. The time lag of the internationalization of CEEs' firms is therefore about twenty-five years.[15] After 1997, the internationalization of CEMNCs seems to be faster, firms are leapfrogging over stages and some can even be considered born globals. This can be explained by: (i) globalization pull factors which are now much stronger than in the period of the first wave of TWMNCs' expansion; and (ii) better human capital capabilities. Ethnic ties are much stronger in the case of Asian TWMNCs than CEMNCs. While there are minorities outside homelands in CEEs, they are not as strongly or traditionally interconnected. They more facilitate than induce outward internationalization in infant stages. In the case of LA internationalization, Spanish or Portuguese languages have also played an important role.

Trade names have not proven to be a major driving force for OFDI by either TWMNCs or CEMNCs. Their relevance is of a somewhat different nature when it comes to investments in other LDCs or in industrial countries. TWMNCs initially designed some brand names to serve the specific tastes of developing countries' populations while, in the case of CEMNCs, we see more the exploitation of investors' general brand names originally established by exporting (customization). This is more the defence of existing brand names when threats of import limitations emerge, while in the case of TWMNCs we can talk more of the offensive penetration of brand names suited to local tastes. We can see more brand-seeking OFDI than brand-exploiting OFDI.

CEMNCs are also less inclined to regard their FDI as an instrument of the differentiation of risks, although this argument is stronger in the case of TWMNCs. The ownership structure of subsidiaries abroad also differs: TWMNCs are much keener to enter into joint ventures with local partners (Wells 1983: 115) than CEMNCs whose firms have wanted to control their operations abroad. The explanation is partly the system-specific increasing risks in the case of shared ownership and partly the type of FSAs. They are similar to those of local partners and therefore there is no need to acquire them.

Conclusions

The lack of reliable data and the heterogeneity of the two groups of countries prevent us from making any robust generalizations. While the eclectic paradigm has put much emphasis on location-specific advantages, those of home countries are relatively much more important in the case of TWMNCs, particularly when it comes to China, where major investors are large state-controlled firms with access to huge capital. Country-/location-specific factors make outward internationalization by firms from different countries specific. However, we believe that the general tenets of FDI theories still apply even when we talk of the system and similar escape types of outward investments or even in the case of a "reverse internationalization" pattern[16] or other specific investing country institutional characteristics (state ownership, available capital, policies, cultural characteristics, etc.). The relative weight and role of the different factors of internationalization vary, although similar factors play a role. "There are three potential arguments: capital market imperfections, the special ownership advantages and institutional factors" which make at least Chinese investments abroad specific, claim Buckley et al. (2007: 501). The uncertainties and political risks are not a barrier but an incentive to invest abroad due to the familiarity with such an institutional climate at home. Cuervo-Cazurra and Ramamurti (2015) added to the escape type of investments *institutional escape investments*, motivated by the desire to escape the home country's weak institutions and economic underdevelopment. Another category of escape investments is rooted in managers' motives aiming to reduce the negative country image of emerging markets, compared with advanced economies, which may negatively affect the international competitiveness of their firms (*discrimination escape*).

Policy is also taking on greater importance (like China's "Go Global" policy). There are also some ownership-specific advantages which are different than in the case of Western MNCs. Another modified factor that could be much more important is the role of cultural factors, of cultural proximity as a location-specific incentive to go abroad.

In spite of some 'early birds', investing abroad is a relatively new phenomenon for TEs' firms. Therefore, it is also too early to draw generalizations, although a robust test of the IDP model on the two groups of firms has confirmed that there are no significant differences among them in terms of the sequencing of internationalization (e.g. Andreff 2002: 377). Gorynia et al. (2010) confirmed the validity of the IDP for central and eastern European countries. Goldstein and Pusterla also established that China and Brazil are moving towards the third stage of the IDP (Gammeltoft 2010: 261).

Not only countries, but also firms' characteristics and strategies matter. Comparing CEMNCs with TWMNCs some forty years ago we can find several common features. This may indicate that outward internationalization is specific to the macro development level, location (transition) and FSAs and is more contingent on external environment conditions. Timing of the start of internationalization was quite similar in terms of the development level of the countries concerned. The modest beginnings in terms of volumes and mostly regional orientation were also similar, as was initially the kind of incremental internationalization. Only later did we see leapfrogging internationalization.

In the early 1980s, TWMNCs were comparatively small, their small-sized foreign affiliates were less numerous than those of Western MNCs and less scattered over a great number of host countries. MNCs from CEEs are also not (yet) global today. In LA the small size of the home country and domestic market in terms of purchasing power was a factor pushing local firms to invest abroad. The internationalization of CEMNCs was pushed more by internal factors (system escape, round tripping). The external environment and globalization trends later started to pull going-abroad strategies. FSAs were largely location based and system based and originated in a common history or in similarities of systems, cultures/languages and related factors. Many of their competitive advantages could gradually 'evaporate'. Therefore, firms are stimulated to start exploiting them very fast (first-mover advantages). Also similar are the institutional advantages of, say, Chinese MNCs abroad today.

For some authors, internationalization by firms from less advanced countries only confirms the mainstream FDI and internationalization theories. There are, however, also differences which may call for new theoretical approaches. These differences are more systemic and transition based. It seems that a certain productive combination between the Reading school and evolutionary approaches to internationalization (the Scandinavian school) is needed which could result in a 'leapfrogging eclectic investment path paradigm'. Van Tulder is developing a renewed approach to the stages theories.

However, Mathews (2002), Buckley et al. (2007), Li (2007) and Luo and Tung (2007) are right in claiming that their ownership advantages are fundamentally different from those of developed country MNEs. Yet such differences are gradually eroding, which can only mean that general resource-based theories can also be applied in the case of these firms' internationalization.

In order to establish whether both of these groups of investors can fit within the general theories of internationalization, we have to see what the similarities or differences with Western MNCs. The general difference is certainly that MNCs from advanced economies are driven more by cost considerations, while those from TW/emerging economies are driven more by gaining access to technology, know-how, R&D facilities and brand names in industrial countries (acquisition and augmentation of assets rather than exploitation). Therefore, host countries fear assets stripping, particularly when it refers to those coming from such a big and influential country as China. Such fears are, according to Charminade and Rebellotti (2015: 12), largely unfounded. They have not found any generalized predatory behaviour. The differences we identified or those by other authors (Dunning et al. 2008: 177) comparing developed country MNEs of the 1960s with emerging market MNEs in the 2000s seem not to jeopardize the general theoretical conclusions. However, some new elements have to be brought in by the third wave of emerging economies' internationalization,[17] since it has led to some "qualitative differences from emerging economies MNCs of earlier periods" (Gammeltoft et al. 2010a: 257). They enhance the role of contextual factors, including institutional ones which are more country-specific (see, for example, Mathews 2002; Luo and Tung 2007; Li 2007). Buckley et al. (2007: 1), for instance, found "Chinese OFDI to be associated with high levels of political risk in, and cultural proximity to host countries throughout, and with host market size and geographic proximity (1984–1991) and host natural resources endowments (1992–2001) and strong support for the argument that aspects of the special theory help to explain the behaviour of Chinese multinational enterprises".

Obviously, culture plays a much more important role in the internationalization of firms from both groups of countries. Contrary to the prevailing beliefs in the international business literature (Stahl and Tung 2015) assuming that culture is a barrier to international business, we see here that it can in fact stimulate internationalization.

Perhaps the biggest difference of those firms compared with the initial processes of Western MNCs' internationalization is the pace of internationalization and the context (enhanced globalization) in contrast to the case when the 'early birds' of such internationalization started the process. The modern wave of internationalization of emerging economies' MNCs and those from CEEs demonstrate leapfrogging types of internationalization (consider the acquisition of Volvo by the Chinese Geelly). Luostarinen's holistic internationalization model seems to be more relevant today (1979). Many firms have not started by expanding in neighbouring countries but in distant countries in terms of physical proximity and culture.

The OLI paradigm generally holds in spite of the enhanced role of country-of-origin-specific factors, for instance. The Uppsala or similar models partly hold, although leapfrogging has sped up the process, which has also happened in advanced economies with born global firms. Departures from the stage approach were already observed much earlier by Cantwell regarding the "diachronic involvement of American firms internationalized" (Cantwell 1997).

It is still impossible to say whether CEMNCs are a totally new animal substituting the previous "red multinationals" (Hamilton 1987). Much of such OFDI is still associated with capital flights or round tripping, related to transition instability, and cannot be explained by deeply rooted economic rationale alone.

Western multinationals needed several decades to grow into real global companies. Those from the TW needed a much shorter time to become world competitors, albeit they are still lagging behind the Western ones. The question is whether firms from TEs will also need less time to become true large multinationals, if at all. Our research seems to confirm this prediction. In this transitory period there will be many *small* departures from the general internationalization theories. In such a way, we will probably see a rejuvenation of 'old' theories, complementing theories from other areas of international business. New players are bringing new issues to the table that go beyond economics and business. We will perhaps see the development of more holistic inter- and multidisciplinary, multifaceted approaches. Yet it is almost impossible not to agree with Weick (1979), who asserted that a good theory is one which has general applicability, simplicity and accuracy. In such a spirit, it is not too fruitful to 'invent new theories' simply because there are some minor aspects not covered by old theories.

Notes

1 This is a modified and updated paper which was to be presented at the conference on *Global Business and Economic Development, January 7–10, 2004, Guadalajara, Mexico* (e.g. Chakraborty 2004).
2 It resulted in two books: Jaklič and Svetličič (2003) and Svetličič and Rojec (2003).
3 We are using third world, since it was the term mostly applied when some of such companies started. It has become less preferred in recent years.
4 The term third world MNCs was selected because originally this was the focus of authors publishing in the field. Recently, the same phenomenon is analysed under the term emerging economies' MNCs, mostly from BRICS.
5 For simplicity reasons, we will further omit transition economies.
6 The level of internationalization is still modest. The share of OFDI stock in GDP in 2011 was 11.6 percent for BRICS and 14.2 percent for the five CEEs (OECD 2013).
7 The survey contains data on 168 investing firms in 2000 with 477 subsidiaries abroad.
8 The first was until the mid-1980s, the second from the mid-1980s to the mid-1990s and the third from the mid-1990s until today.
9 Slovenian OFDI is concentrated in the successor states of former Yugoslavia, Czech OFDI in Slovakia, Hungarian OFDI in the Czech Republic, Slovakia and Romania (a strong national minority), while Estonian OFDI gravitates towards the Baltic countries.

10 Only in the case of Hungary do technological advantages have more weight, probably due to the many indirect investments from this country.
11 Such investments by Chinese firms started with the "Open Door" strategy encouraging investment abroad to integrate China into the global economy, although the only entities allowed to invest abroad were state-owned enterprises. The total investment of these first years was not significant and concentrated in the neighbouring countries, mainly Hong Kong. The regulations were liberalized after 1985 and a wider range of enterprises – including private firms – was permitted to invest abroad (Szunomáar 2014: 10).
12 LA and Caribbean 173, and Asia USD 632 billion.
13 If not otherwise stated, all data on the five CEEs are based on Svetličič and Jaklič (2003).
14 At first, it is mostly process and organizational.
15 The stock of OFDI by TWMNCs was then similar to that of CEMNCs at the end of the twentieth century.
16 Svetličič (2008) postulated that in the case of Slovenia, OFDI started before inward FDI. But this was because inward FDI was not allowed in the early socialist era of Yugoslavia.
17 In the first wave (1970s) OFDIs were directed more to other LDCs, in the second (1980s) more to developed countries, while the third wave (1990s) saw a return to LDCs again. The contemporary, fourth wave has seen the return of such investments again to developed countries, even via M&As (Dunning et al. 2008: 168).

References

Agarwal, J. P. (1986). Third world multinationals and balance of payments' effect on home countries: A case study of India. In K. M. Khan [ed.], *Multinationals of the South*. London: Frances Pinter Publishers Ltd., pp 184–195

Agtmael, A. (2008). *The Emerging Markets Century: How a New Breed of World-Class Companies Is Overtaking the World*. London, New York, Sydney, Toronto: Simon & Schuster.

Akamatsu, K. (1961). A theory of unbalanced growth in the world economy. *Weltwirtschaftliches Archiv, 86,* 196–217.

Andreff, W. (2002). The new multinational corporations from transition countries. *Economic Systems, 26*(4), 371–379.

Andreff, W. (2003). The new multinationals; Outward foreign direct investment from post-communist economies in transition. Mimeo.

Aykut, D. and Ratha, D. (2004). South-south FDI flows: How big are they? *Transnational Corporations, 13*(1), 149–176.

Balakrishnan, K. (1975). *Indian Joint Ventures Abroad: A Case Study of Foreign Investment from the Developing Countries*. A Research Proposal, Doctoral Candidate, Harvard Business School, Harvard University, Cambridge, MA, February.

Brennan, L. [ed.] (2011). *The Emergence of Southern Multinationals: Their Impact on Europe*. Basingstoke: Palgrave Macmillan.

Buckley, P. J., Clegg, L. J., Cross, A. R., Liu, X., Voss, H. and Zheng, P. (2007). The determinants of Chinese outward foreign direct investment. *Journal of International Business Studies, 38*(4), 499–518.

Buckley, P. J., Clegg, L. J., Cross, A. R., Liu, X., Voss, H. and Zheng, P. (2010). What can emerging markets learn from the outward direct investment policies of advanced countries? In Karl P. Sauvant and Geraldine McAllister with Wolfgang A. Maschek [eds.], *Foreign Direct Investment from Emerging Markets: The Challenges Ahead*. New York: Palgrave Macmillan, pp. 243–276.

Cantwell, J. (1997). The globalisation of technology: What remains of the product cycle model? In D. Archibugi and J. Michie [eds.], *Technology Globalization and Economic Performance.* Cambridge: Cambridge University Press, pp. 215–240.

Cantwell, J. and Tolentino, P. E. (1990). *Technological Accumulation and Third World Multinationals.* Discussion Papers in International Investment and Managements, No. 139, Reading: University of Reading. Mimeo.

Carlson, S. (1966). *International Business Research.* Uppsala: Acta Universitatis Upsaliensis.

Chudnovsky, D. and López, A. (2000). A third wave of FDI from developing countries: Latin American TNCs in the 1990s. *Transnational Corporations, 9*(2), 31–73.

Cuervo-Cazurra, A. and Ramamurti, R. (2015). *The Escape Motivation of Emerging Market Multinational Enterprises.* Columbia FDI Perspectives, Perspectives on Topical Foreign Direct Investment Issues No. 143, 16 March 2015.

Dunning, J. H. (1981). Explaining outward direct investment of developing countries – in support of the eclectic theory of international production. In K. Kumar and M. G. McLeod [eds.], *Multinationals from Developing Countries.* Lexington: Lexington Books, pp. 1–22.

Dunning, J. H. (1986). The investment development cycle and third world multinationals. In K. M. Khan [ed.], *Multinationals of the South.* London: Frances Pinter Publishers Ltd., pp. 15–47.

Dunning, J. H. (1988). The eclectic paradigm of international production: A restatement and some possible extensions. *Journal of International Business Studies, 19*(1), 1–31.

Dunning, J. H. (1993). *Multinational Enterprises and the Global Economy.* Workingham: Addison Wesley Publishing Company.

Dunning, J. H., Kim, C. and Park, D. (2008). Old wine in new bottles: A comparison of emerging market TNCs today and developed country TNCs thirty years ago. In K. P. Sauvant [ed.], *The Rise of Transnational Corporations from Emerging Markets: Threat or Opportunity?*, Cheltenham, UK; Northampton: Edward Elgar Publishing, pp. 158–172.

Dunning, J. H. and Narula, R. (1998). The investment development path revisited: Some emerging issues. In J. H. Dunning and R. Narula [eds.], *Foreign Direct Investment and Governments: Catalyst for Economic Restructuring.* London: Routledge, pp. 1–41.

Eriksson, K., Johanson, J., Majkgård, A. and Sharma, D. D. (1997). Experimental knowledge and cost in the internationalisation process. *Journal of International Business Studies, 28*, 337–360.

Gammeltoft, P., Barnard, H. and Madhok, A. (2010b). Emerging multinationals, emerging theory: Macro- and micro-level perspectives. *Journal of International Management, 16*, 95–101.

Gammeltoft, P., Pradhan, J. P. and Goldstein, A. (2010a). Emerging multinationals: Home and host country determinants and outcomes. *International Journal of Emerging Markets, 5*(3/4), 254–265.

Gorynia, M., Nowak, J. and Wolniak, R. (2010). *Foreign Direct Investment of Central and Eastern European Countries, and the Investment Development Path Revisited.* https://ideas.repec.org/a/jes/journl/y2010v1p21-36.html, accessed 19 June 2015.

Hamilton, J. (1986). *Red Multinationals or Red Herrings? The Activities of Enterprises from Socialist Countries in the West.* London: Frances Pinter Publishers.

Jaklič, A. and Svetličič, M. (2001). Slovenia's outward direct investment in the states of former Yugoslavia: A strategic or a defensive response? *Economic and Business Review, 3*, 299–323.

Jaklič, A., and Svetličič, M. (2003). *Enhanced Transition through Outward Internationalisation; Outward FDI by Slovenian Firms.* Aldershot, Burlington, Singapore, Sydney: Ashgate Publishing Ltd.

Johanson, J. and Mattsson, L. G. (1986). International marketing and internationalisation processes – a network approach. In S. Paliwoda and P. N. Turnbull [eds.], *Research in International Marketing*. London: Croom Helm, pp. 121–142.

Johanson, J. and Mattsson, L. (1993). Internationalisation in industrial systems – a network approach. In P. Buckley and P. Ghauri [eds.], *The Internationalisation of the Firm*. London: The Dryden Press, pp. 201–223.

Johanson, J. and Vahlne, J. E. (1977). The internationalisation process of the firm – a model of knowledge development and increasing market commitments. *Journal of International Business Studies*, *8*, 23–32.

Johanson, J. and Wiedersheim-Paul, F. (1975). The internationalisation of the firm – four Swedish cases. *Journal of Management Studies*, *12*(3, October), 305–322.

Kalotay, K. (2003). Outward foreign direct investment from economies in transition in a global context. *Journal for East European Management Studies*, *8*(1), 6–24.

Kang, Y. and Jiang, F. (2012). FDI location choice of Chinese multinationals in East and Southeast Asia: Traditional economic factors and institutional perspective. *Journal of World Business*, January, *47*(1), 45–53.

Khan, K. M. [ed.] (1986). *Multinationals of the South*. London: Frances Pinter Publishers Ltd.

Kojima, K. (1960). Capital accumulation and the course of industrialisation, with special reference to Japan. *The Economic Journal, LXX,* 757–768.

Kumar, K. and McLeod, M. G. (1981). *Multinationals from Developing Countries*. Lexington: Lexington Books.

Lall, S. (1983). *The New Multinationals*. Chichester and New York: John Wiley.

Lecraw, D. (1977). Direct investment by firms from less developed countries. *Oxford Economic Papers*, November, 442–457.

Li, P. (2007). Towards an integrated theory of multinational evolution: The evidence of Chinese multinational enterprises as latecomers. Journal of International Management *13*, 296–318.

Liuhto, K. and Jumpponen, J. (2003). *The Russian Eagle Has Landed Abroad,* Lappeenranta: Lappeenranta University of Technology.

Luo, Y and Tung, R. (2007). International expansion of emerging market enterprises: A springboard perspective. *Journal of International Business Studies 38*, 481–498.

Luostarinen, R. (1979). *Internationalization of the Firm*. Helsinki: Helsinki School of Economics.

Mathews, A. J. (2002). *Dragon Multinationals: A New Model for Global Growth*. Oxford and New York: Oxford University Press.

Mattsson, L. G. (1985). An application of a network approach to marketing: Defending and changing market positions. In N. Dholakia and J. Arndt [eds.], *Alternative Paradigms for Widening Marketing Theory*. Greenwich, CT: JAI Press, pp. 263-288.

McMillan, H. C. (1987). *Multinationals from the Second World*. London: Macmillan Press.

OECD (2013). *FDI in Figures*, Paris, January.

Penrose, E. T. (1959). *The Theory of the Growth of the Firm*. New York: Wiley.

Pradhan, J. P. (2002). *Determinants of Outward Foreign Direct Investment from a Developing Country: The Case of Indian Manufacturing Firms*. Mimeo.

Prahalad, C. K. and Hamel, G. (1990). The core competence of the corporation. *Harvard Business Review*, May–June, 79–91.

Razin, A. (2002). FDI flows: A critical look. *NBER Reporter*, 16–18.

Rugraff, E. (2010). Strengths and weaknesses of the outward FDI paths of the central European countries. *Post-Communist Economies, 22*(1), 1–17.

Stahl, G. and Tung, R. (2015). Towards a more balanced treatment of culture in international business studies: The need for positive cross-cultural scholarship. *Journal of International Business Studies, 46*(4, May), 391–414.

Svetličič, M. (1986). Multinational production joint ventures of developing countries, their economic development and specific features. In K. M. Khan [ed.], *Multinationals of the South*. London: Frances Pinter Publishers Ltd., pp. 67–87.

Svetličič, M. (1987). South-South public enterprise investments and the role of the Arab investors. In M. Svetličič [ed.], *Joint Ventures among Developing Countries: The Arab Experience*. Ljubljana: ICPE, pp. 17–32.

Svetličič, M. (2004). Central European transition economies' multinationals – are they different from third world multinationals? In C. Chakraborty [ed.], *Proceedings of the 8th International Conference on Global Business and Economic Development, January 7–10, 2004, Guadalajara, Mexico*. Montclair: Montclair State University, 2004.

Svetličič, M. (2008). Reversed internationalization path: The case of Slovenia. *AIB Insights, 8*(1), 3–9.

Svetličič, M. and Jaklič, A. (2003). Outward FDI by transition economies: Basic features, trends and development implications. In M. Svetličič and M. Rojec [eds.], *Facilitating Transition by Internationalisation*. Aldershot, Burlington, Singapore, Sydney: Ashgate Publishing Ltd., pp. 49–76.

Svetličič, M. and Rojec, M. [eds.] (2003). *Facilitating Transition by Internationalisation; Outward Direct Investment from Central European Economies in Transition*. Aldershot, Burlington, Singapore, Sydney: Ashgate Publishing Ltd.

Svetličič, M. in cooperation with Rojec, M. (1987). *Investment among Developing Countries and Transnational Corporations*. Harare: Research Centre for Cooperation with Developing Countries, Ljubljana and Zimbabwe Institute of Development Studies.

Svetličič, M., Rojec, M. and Lebar, S. (1994). Internationalisation strategies of Slovenian firms: The German market case. In K. Obloj [ed.], *High Speed Competition in a New Europe, Proceedings of the 20th Conference of EIBA*, Warsaw, December 11–13.

Szunomáar, Á. [ed.] (2014). *Chinese Investments and Financial Engagement in Visegrad Countries: Myth or Reality?* Budapest: Institute of World Economics, Centre for Economic and Regional Studies of the Hungarian Academy of Sciences.

Thomsen, S. (2010). Emerging market multinationals: Legal challenge ahead. In Karl P. Sauvant and Geraldine McAllister with Wolfgang A. Maschek [eds.], *Foreign Direct Investment from Emerging Markets: The Challenges Ahead*. New York: Palgrave Macmillan, pp. 447–462.

Tolentino, P. E. (1992). *Technology Innovation and Third World Multinationals*. London, New York: Routledge.

Turnbull, P. W. (1987). Challenge to the stages theory of the internationalisation process. In P. J. Rosson and S. D. Reed [eds.], *Managing Export Entry and Expansion*. New York: Praeger, pp. 21–40.

UNCTAD. (2003). *World Investment Report 2002*. Geneva.

UNCTAD. (2015). *World Investment Report 2015*. Geneva.

Van Tulder, R. (2010). Toward a renewed stages theory for BRIC multinational enterprises? A home country bargaining approach. In Karl Sauvant, Geraldine McAllister and Wolfgang Maschek [eds.], Foreign Investments from Emerging Markets. New York: Palgrave Macmillan, pp. 61–75.

Wai-chung, Y. (2002). Review of the book: *Dragon Multinational: A New Model for Global Growth* by John A. Mathews (Oxford and New York: Oxford University Press 2002). *Transnational Corporations, 11*(3), 191–194.

Weick, K. E. (1979). *The Social Psychology of Organizing* (Topics in Social Psychology Series), 2nd edition. New York: McGraw-Hill.

Wells, L. Jr. (1982). The third world grows its own multinationals. *International Management*, January, 39–40.

Wells, L. Jr. (1983). *Third World Multinationals; The Rise of Foreign Investment from Developing Countries*. Cambridge, MA: MIT Press.

Wernerfelt, B. (1984). A resource-based view of the firm. *Strategic Management Journal*, 5, 171–180.

White, E. (1983). The international projection of firms from Latin American countries. In K. Kumar [ed.], *Multinationals from Developing Countries*. Lexington: Lexington Books, pp. 155–186.

Yiu, D. W., Lau, C. and Bruton, G. (2007). International venturing by emerging economy firms: The effects of firm capabilities, home country networks, and corporate entrepreneurship. Journal of International Business Studies, 38(4), 519–540.

15 Looking at central European and BRIC FDI through the lens of investment development path theory

Michał Zdziarski

Introduction

The internationalisation of companies from emerging markets is becoming an area of primary interest in IB research (Buckley, Clegg, Cross and Liu 2007; Luo and Tung 2007; Yiu, Lau and Bruton 2007; Brennan 2010). We can observe increasing levels of investment flows in a direction opposite to the well-explored internationalisation of established firms from developed to emerging economies. The share of developing countries in global FDI flows is increasing, and investments from one developing country to another are also becoming more common. Yet there is relatively little published research presenting the strategies, models and patterns of internationalisation of firms based in emerging economies (Mathews 2006; Bonaglia, Goldstein and Mathews 2007; Yiu, Lau and Bruton 2007; Brutton, Ahlstrom and Obloj 2008). Studies on investment flows and stocks among emerging, recently industrialised and developing countries are also rare, and often indicate that the IDP paradigm has limitations in explaining the changing net outward investment (NOI) positions of countries that are subject to changing GNI and are catching up with industrialised economies (Narula and Dunning 2000; Jaklič and Svetličič 2002; Boudier-Bensebaa 2008; Sathye 2008; Gorynia, Nowak and Wolniak 2009; Gorynia, Nowak and Wolniak 2010a; Narula and Guimon 2010).

This paper responds to calls to further explore FDI that proceeds "the other way round" (Yamakawa, Peng and Deeds 2008). The focus of this chapter is on investment from the BRIC countries – Brazil, Russia, India and China – to the Visegrad group consisting of Poland, the Czech Republic, Slovakia and Hungary. The four Visegrad countries of central Europe have only recently come to be classified as developed and joined the club of OECD members. The FDI stocks from and into these four countries have historically deviated from the predictions of investment development path (IDP) theory (Boudier-Bensebaa 2008; Gorynia, Nowak and Wolniak 2010a; Narula and Guimon 2010). The major goal of the research presented in this chapter is to establish whether FDI net positions among the BRIC and Visegrad countries fit the IDP stages model.

The chapter is organised as follows: in the first section I briefly present the IDP theory, and in the second I review IDP research on FDI in the context of central European countries. In the third section I present the results of an empirical study of FDI flows between the Visegrad and BRIC countries. In the final section, conclusions are presented concerning the explanatory value of IDP in the specific context of investment flows among recently developed and rapidly developing countries.

Investment development path

Outward FDI involves the establishment of a new entity in a foreign country, and is considered to be the most advanced stage in the process theory of internationalisation (Johanson and Vahlne 1977), in which firms make greater commitments than simply increasing their foreign sales (McDougall and Oviatt 2000). The eclectic paradigm of internationalisation suggests that countries' FDI stocks depend on three major factors: ownership, location and internalisation advantages. It is therefore often referred to in IB research as the OLI paradigm. Ownership advantages result from the competitive advantage of domestic firms versus their global rivals; location advantages relate to the host country's attractiveness resulting from labour arbitrage, natural resources, infrastructure, institutional setting and local demand; while internalisation advantages are derived from the ability to benefit from low transaction costs (Dunning 1971). The IDP concept was introduced by John Dunning (1981) as part of efforts to develop a model linking the OLI paradigm of internationalisation to the relative position of a country's development (Buckley and Castro 1998). The IDP model predicted initially four, and later five, phases, in which the balance between inward and outward FDI changes is dependent on the level of economic development, usually measured by levels of GNI or GDP per capita (Dunning 1981; Dunning and Narula 1996; Narula and Dunning 2000). The model of NOI changes depending on economic development measured by GNI per capita as presented in Figure 15.1.

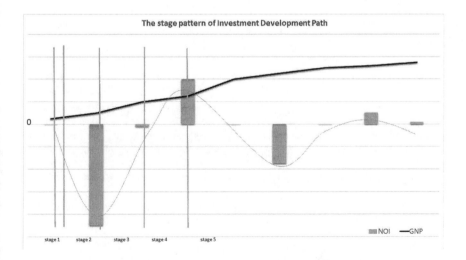

Figure 15.1 The stage pattern of IDP

In the initial phase of early growth in GNI per capita, NOI is negative and a small amount of early inward investment occurs. In stage 2, the net investment position becomes even more negative, as incoming investments increase and outward FDI is only beginning to emerge. The situation changes in stage 3, as more local firms improve their competitive positions through interactions and spillovers from global companies. In stage 4, NOI becomes positive and stabilises. This is the characteristic situation for developed, industrialised economies, in which FDI flow levels generally increase. A summary of the motivations and dynamics predicted by the IDP stage model is presented in Table 15.1.

Table 15.1 Evolving dynamics and motivations of inward and outward FDI across the IDP stage model

IDP Stage	FDI Dynamics	Key Investment Motivations
Stage 1	No or very little IFDI. Very little OFDI. NOI negative.	OFDI mainly motivated by drive to take advantage of the country's natural resources. As L advantages improve, resource-based motives arise, followed by market-seeking motives. Mainly "system escape" motives for initial OFDI.
Stage 2	Growing IFDI, weak OFDI activity. Negative NOI values, although the slope of the NOI curve decreases later in this phase before it reaches its minimum value.	Mainly market-seeking motives, and labour arbitrage in labour-intensive industries for IFDI. Resource-seeking motives in OFDI, often to other emerging markets, and system escape motives to locations with institutional advantages. Domestic firms lack O advantages.
Stage 3	Rising IFDI, growing OFDI activity. The slope of the NOI curve reverses and reaches 0 towards the end of this stage.	Market-seeking motives, L advantage exploration and efficiency-seeking investments as manufacturing base emerges. Based on spillover effects, domestic firms build O advantages – the range of motives expands to include market seeking, technology seeking and risk/asset augmentation.
Stage 4	OFDI stocks continue to rise faster than IFDI. NOI becomes positive and increases to reach its maximum.	Exploitation of the country's specific advantages becomes the primary driver of OFDI. L advantages become based on created assets, and O advantages increase in importance.
Stage 5	This stage is characteristic of leading developed countries in which NOI often fluctuates around zero with high levels of both OFDI and IFDI.	NOI position will depend on short-term evolution of exchange rates and economic cycles.

Source: Author's own work based on Dunning (1986), Narula and Dunning (2000), Gorynia, Nowak and Wolniak (2010a).

The IDP model has been empirically tested in a variety of national and regional settings, including some smaller, recently industrialised or developing markets such as India (Sathye 2008), Ireland (Barry, Gorg and McDowell 2001), Portugal (Buckley and Castro 1998), Poland (Gorynia, Nowak and Wolniak 2009), central Europe (Boudier-Bensebaa 2008; Narula and Guimon 2010; Gorynia, Nowak and Wolniak 2010a) and Austria (Bellak 2001). The results of all of these studies are inconclusive, and indicate that empirical data may be quite distant from what would be expected based on GNI per capita levels in a given country or region. Therefore, specific institutional, economic and historical settings need to be considered as an important context for IDP theory.

IDP-grounded research in central and eastern Europe

As Narula and Guimon (2010: 9) point out, any attempt to analyse investment development paths for central and eastern European countries needs to consider carefully the very specific historical and political context. Indeed, the internationalisation of firms from central and eastern Europe is very specific given their historical contexts. These countries, politically dependent on the Soviet Union after World War II, were governed for over fifty years under institutional settings known as communist regimes and centrally planned economies. Economically they were organised based on central planning, with market transactions and firm-level hierarchies playing limited roles as mechanisms of resource allocation. The allocation of resources was almost entirely organised by a country's communist party and its agencies, including central and local government institutions. Communist parties were granted country-level political monopolies by the Soviet Union, which directly controlled and influenced their conduct in all spheres of social and political life, including economic relations and internationalisation. Market institutions such as stock exchanges, property laws and monetary systems were either nonexistent or weakly functioning. State-owned companies had little autonomy to make strategic decisions on such matters as FDI. Exports were centralised and monopolised within specialised state-owned agencies, and it was not up to the discretion of managers of state-owned firms to decide the levels and directions of foreign sales. With some variation among countries of the communist bloc, private firms did not exist, except for some small enterprises providing basic services or being active in agriculture. Inward investments from foreign companies were hardly possible.

Under these conditions, the initial FDI structure deviated from the IDP paradigm (Boudier-Bensebaa 2008). In central and eastern Europe the wave of outward FDI occurred earlier than any inward FDI, in contrast to the proposition of Dunning and Narula (1996: 35) that in initial internationalisation phases the stream of inward FDI will flow before outward FDI emerges. This fact can be interpreted as an effect of the Soviet policy which aimed to access technologies and resources from competing blocs of democratic countries. An alternative, or perhaps parallel, explanation is that FDI served as a defensive instrument of "system escape" (Jaklič and Svetličič 2002) to mitigate the inefficiencies of central planning.

The transition from centrally planned, Soviet-dependent economies into market-oriented, sovereign democracies began with negotiated revolution and the Solidarity movement in Poland. The Warsaw Roundtable agreement between Solidarity and communist party leaders was followed by a complete transition in institutional settings in Poland. In a chain reaction, the transformation of all countries in central and eastern Europe quickly followed. While central European countries shared much historically, especially their dependence on the Soviet Union, their cultural background is rooted in a much longer history, resulting in important differences that include, but are not limited to, countries' FDI profiles (Boudier-Bensebaa 2008; Gorynia, Nowak and Wolniak 2010a; Narula and Guimon 2010).

Countries also differed in their approach to the transformation and institutional change from centrally planned to market-oriented economies. Many state-owned companies were sold through privatisation to foreign investors in the initial years of transformation, which resulted in high levels of FDI inflows through brownfield investments. Brownfield investments are considered to bring higher risks of crowding-out effects than greenfield investments (Narula and Guimon 2010). For example, in the list of the 500 largest companies in Poland, foreign-owned companies outrank both private Polish companies and state-owned companies in terms of both absolute number and cumulative revenues, which indicates that a crowding-out effect is indeed observable. It is also noteworthy that over 80 percent of the banking sector, measured in terms of assets, is owned and controlled by foreign banks. Banks play an important role in internationalisation as providers of the financial resources needed for foreign expansion.

Investment development path studies presenting aggregate data for Poland prove that inward FDI is much higher than outward FDI, a pattern that can be observed with different magnitudes for all countries in the region (Gorynia, Nowak and Wolniak 2007; Boudier-Bensebaa 2008; Gorynia, Nowak and Wolniak 2010a). This pattern is characteristic for countries in the second stage of the IDP paradigm. The level of outward investment in central and eastern Europe is substantially lower than what one would expect looking at indicators such as GNI per capita or the technological and educational capabilities of those countries (Narula and Guimon 2010). Gorynia, Nowak and Wolniak (2010a) decomposed inward and outward FDI dynamics at country level to show that Poland is simultaneously in stage 2 of the IDP framework when total FDI is considered, and at stage 4 if the analysis is performed versus other central and eastern European countries.

IDP predictions for Visegrad and BRIC countries

I decided to follow the approach of Gorynia, Nowak and Wolniak (2010a) and to decompose IDP into country-level and regional-level analyses, in order to present investment stock positions for four central European countries – Poland, the Czech Republic, Hungary and Slovakia – versus the four BRIC countries: Brazil, Russia, China, and India. This is followed by an aggregated, regional level of analysis in which I investigate the explanatory power of IDP by looking at FDI stocks in the Visegrad region versus the BRIC countries. Since historically the Visegrad countries

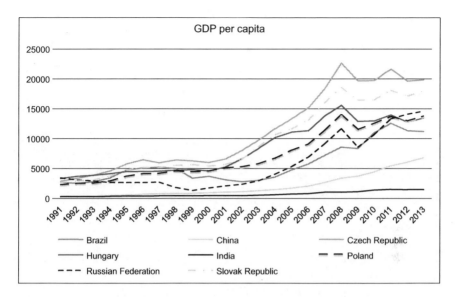

Figure 15.2 GDP per capita for Visegrad and BRIC countries in current US dollars
Source: Author's own work based on World Bank data on GDP per capita.

were under the dominant influence of the Soviet Union, which transformed in part into what is now the Russian Federation, I will also look separately at regional-level relations among the three BRIC countries that are very distant institutionally, culturally and politically from the central European countries: Brazil, India and China. This choice is also motivated by relative levels of GDP per capita, which differ between Russia and the other countries in the BRIC group, as shown in Figure 15.2.

All of the countries analysed here increased their levels of GDP per capita in the period from 1991 to 2013. Russia stands out among the BRIC countries when this indicator of economic development is considered. Its GDP per capita levels are marginally higher than those of Poland and Hungary in the early and late periods of the analysed time frame. For India, China and Brazil, GDP per capita levels are lower than the corresponding indicators in the Visegrad countries. Thus, in addition to institutional factors, we should expect different IDP patterns for Russia and the other BRIC countries, driven by relative economic development. The Czech Republic and Slovakia, which have higher levels of GDP per capita than Poland and Hungary, can also be expected to differ in terms of observed patterns and pace of change between stages in their NOI position versus the BRIC countries.

The net outward investment position of the Visegrad countries versus the BRIC countries, plotted in double lines in Figure 15.3, is driven mostly by the mutual NOI position with Russia, plotted in a solid black line. We can observe that these two curves indeed fit very closely to each other, while the amplitude of NOI values versus the remaining three countries – China, India and Brazil – is several times lower than that against Russia. There are two possible locations of the observed

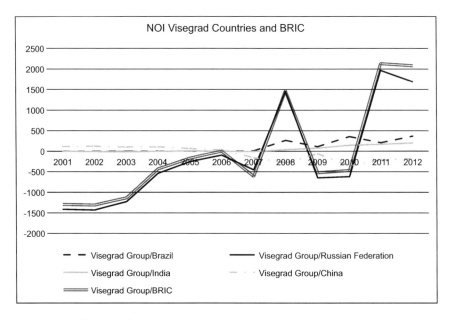

Figure 15.3 NOI position of aggregated Visegrad countries versus BRIC countries in millions of US dollars for 2001–2012

Source: Author's own work and calculations based on FDI stock data from UNCTAD.

levels of NOI among the Visegrad countries vs. BRIC in the twelve-year period of observation on the curve predicted by IDP theory. It is either at the boundary between stages 3 and 4 or on a part of the curve in stage 5, in which NOI fluctuates around zero. Another possible interpretation, given the relatively stable and parallel growth of GDP per capita in the observed time frame, is that NOI also remains around zero if there is no re-balancing occurring among the specific economies under investigation.

If one compares the NOI levels of the Visegrad region vs. the countries of the BRIC group excluding Russia, as shown in Figure 15.4, it can be observed that with the exception of one year (2007), NOI is positive in the analysed period of 2001–2012. Starting from 2008 it increases, to reach approximately $380m in 2012. This phase of increasing NOI from 2008 onwards is similar to what happens in the case of NOI vs. Russia, as shown in Figure 15.3. These dynamics, with positive and steadily increasing NOI, seem to fit stage 4 in the original IDP model.

The NOI position of the Czech Republic – the country with the highest GDP per capita in the analysed group – is predominantly driven by its investment position with respect to Russia. This was positive until 2008 but took negative values from then on. The double line curve for NOI against all BRIC countries behaves very similarly (Figure 15.5). The plots showing the bilateral net investment position against Brazil (dashed line), India (grey solid line) and China (grey dotted line) moved in a reverse direction to that for Russia (black solid line) in the last four

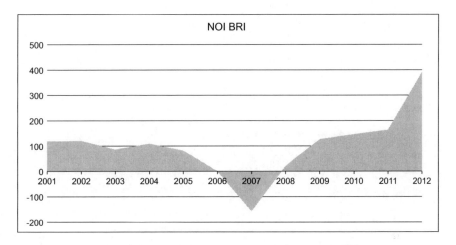

Figure 15.4 NOI position of aggregated Visegrad countries versus BIC (Brazil, India and China) countries in millions of US dollars for 2001–2012

Source: Author's own work and calculations based on FDI stock data from UNCTAD.

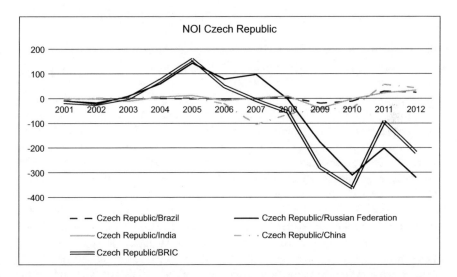

Figure 15.5 NOI position of Czech Republic versus BRIC countries in millions of US dollars for 2001–2012

Source: Author's own work and calculations based on FDI stock data from UNCTAD.

years of observation. Since 2009 the Czech Republic has improved its NOI position against the BIC countries and moved into a positive balance with all three of them. A positive balance in NOI is only achieved in stage 4 of the general IDP model when a country's overall stock of investment is considered. The NOI balance against individual countries may, however, vary quite significantly during

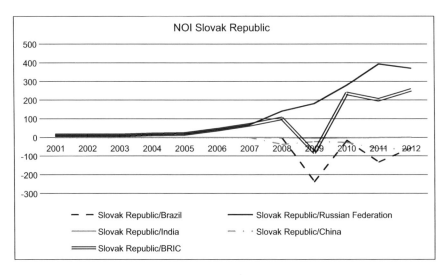

Figure 15.6 NOI position of Slovak Republic versus BRIC countries in millions of US
dollars for 2001–2012

Source: Author's own work and calculations based on FDI stock data from UNCTAD.

the IDP phases based on aggregated country-level data. In the case of the Czech
Republic, we can observe differing trends in NOI position when Russia is considered separately from China, India and Brazil.

Slovakia become independent from the Czech Republic only in 1992, and relative levels of GDP per capita remain similar for the two countries. Their curves
of GDP per capita run in parallel (see Figure 15.6), and they remain the most
developed countries among the eight observed economies based on GDP per capita
measures. In terms of their NOI position curves, however, we can observe different patterns between the Czech Republic and Slovakia in the period 2001–2012.
Overall, Slovakia has improved its NOI position versus the BRIC countries, and
recorded positive values for all observed years with the exception of 2009, while
the Czech Republic was initially positive but moved into negative values of NOI
after 2008. The NOI position of Slovakia versus Russia has improved greatly since
2008, which is exactly opposite to the case of the Czech Republic. However, Slovakia has a negative NOI position against the BIC countries. We can note that the
NOI position is least balanced in Slovakia's relationship with Brazil.

It is not surprising that Hungary's NOI position against the BRIC countries
is dominated by its relationship with Russia, for which the amplitude is much
higher in both directions depending on the observed time frame (Figure 15.7).
It should be noted that Hungary has the highest range of absolute values of NOI
among the Visegrad countries. Since 2008 its NOI position against Russia was
quite strongly negative, but unlike in the case of the Czech Republic this trend
was reversed, and since 2010 the Hungarian economy has improved its NOI
position against Russia to achieve significantly positive values. The amplitude

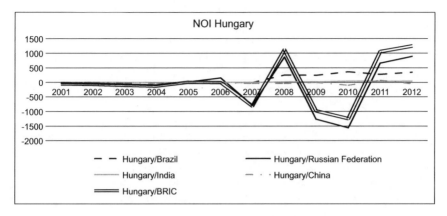

Figure 15.7 NOI position of Hungary versus BRIC countries in millions of US dollars for 2001–2012

Source: Author's own work and calculations based on FDI stock data from UNCTAD.

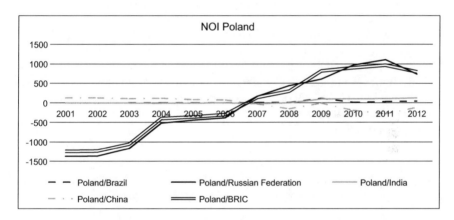

Figure 15.8 NOI position of Poland versus BRIC countries in millions of US dollars for 2001–2012

Source: Author's own work and calculations based on FDI stock data from UNCTAD.

of imbalances is much lower for the remaining three countries from the BRIC group. Hungary, in contrast to Slovakia, enjoys a positive NOI position against Brazil over the whole period of analysis, and a position close to zero with respect to India and China.

The curve of Poland's NOI versus the BRIC group is distinct from that obtained for the other countries – it moved from negative to positive values in 2007 and has remained significantly positive since then (Figure 15.8). Similarly to the other countries in the region, its NOI relationship with Russia dominates the overall aggregated data – the regional curve (double line) fits quite well with the curve showing NOI position against Russia (black solid line). In the second part of the period under analysis, the NOI position against Russia follows a similar pattern to that seen in Figure 15.6 for Slovakia. The plot of Poland's NOI position against China moves in the opposite direction to that for Russia. The position against China was positive until 2007 but took negative values from 2008 to 2012. The NOI balance with India and Brazil remains around zero.

While there is no common pattern in the trends in NOI position for bilateral relationships among the eight observed countries, the general NOI position for the Visegrad group of countries against other developed countries is clear – they increased their negative stock of FDI in the analysed period of 2001–2012, in which GDP per capita levels generally improved in the region (Figure 15.9). The overall negative value of the NOI position more than doubled in the observed period, from –88,191.9 to –176,993 million US dollars. This rapid decline is characteristic of stage 2 of the IDP model, which confirms earlier findings about the region (Boudier-Bensebaa 2008; Gorynia, Nowak and Wolniak 2010a).

Table 15.2 presents a summary of the findings for pairs of countries.

The table summarising trends in NOI between pairs of countries indicates that there is little commonality in the observed patterns. On the contrary, we may observe trends going in different directions, if we compare for example the NOI balance of the Czech Republic against Brazil, India and China with that against Russia. While the NOI balance with the first three economies moves to positive values, it moves in the opposite direction in the relationship with Russia. Russia has distinct patterns of NOI balance with all Visegrad countries – there is no other country in the BRIC group to which it has a similar pattern with respect to any single Visegrad country.

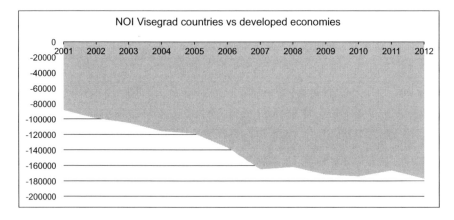

Figure 15.9 NOI position of Visegrad countries versus developed countries in millions of US dollars for 2001–2012

Source: Author's own work and calculations based on FDI stock data from UNCTAD.

Table 15.2 Summary of NOI patterns for pairs of countries

Country	Brazil	Russia	India	China
Czech Republic	Fluctuating around zero, then negative changing to positive	Positive changing to negative	Fluctuating around zero, then negative changing to positive	Fluctuating around zero, then negative changing to positive
Hungary	Fluctuating around zero, then positive	Fluctuating around zero, then negative changing to positive, followed by change to negative and again positive values	Fluctuating around zero	Fluctuating around zero
Poland	Fluctuating around zero	Negative changing to positive	Fluctuating around zero	Positive changing to negative
Slovakia	Fluctuating around zero, changing to negative	Positive	Fluctuating around zero	Fluctuating around zero, changing to negative

Source: Author's own work.

Conclusions

Overall, in the analysed period from 2001 to 2012, the NOI position of the Visegrad countries against the BRIC group of countries moved from negative to positive values. This effect was driven mostly by FDI imbalances with Russia, which seem to fluctuate more often and with greater amplitude than those with the remaining BIC countries. Fitting the trends to the IDP model, we find that the relative situation of this group of countries is similar to what is expected to happen between stages 3 and 4, when the balance of FDI stocks moves from negative to positive values. If we break down the group further, the NOI position of the Visegrad countries against Brazil, India and China is positive over the entire time frame of the analysis with the exception of 2007. This positive balance positions the trend more towards stage 4. The observed differences among bilateral relationships, as well as major differences in the NOI position of the Visegrad countries against the BRIC countries compared with that against other developed countries, supports the idea of more detailed, regional inquiry into the composition of country IDP patterns. The case of Russia clearly shows that common history and institutional links matter and make the relationship quite distinct from those with other regions that may look similar if only GDP per capita values are considered. The paradoxical performance of Visegrad countries against the expected IDP stage model during the last twenty-five years, in which their GDP per capita has improved quite substantially while they remain in stage 2 of the model, suggests a need to rethink the IDP paradigm so as to acknowledge the different types of capitalism that are emerging in the contemporary world. The IDP model is based on an idea of the convergence expected to emerge as countries, and the companies located in them, become more like the known ones in the developed world. The widening NOI gap among recently developed Visegrad countries and the different pattern observed for this group versus BRIC countries indicate that convergence is not the only pattern that we should expect.

Bibliography

Barney, J. B. (1991) 'Firm resources and sustained competitive advantage', *Journal of Management, 17*: 99–120.
Barry, F., Gorg, H. and McDowell, A. (2001, 04 approached 06–06–2015) 'Outward FDI and the Investment Development Path of a Late-Industrializing Economy: Evidence from Ireland'.
Bellak, C. (2001) 'The Austrian investment development path', *Transnational Corporations, 10(2):* 107–134.
Bonaglia, F., Goldstein, A. and Mathews, J. (2007) 'Accelerated internationalisation by emerging markets' multinationals: The case of the white goods sector', *Journal of World Business, 42(4):* 369–383.
Boudier-Bensebaa, F. (2008) 'FDI-assisted development in the light of the investment development path-paradigm: Evidence from central and eastern European countries', *Transnational Corporations, 17(1):* 37–68.
Brutton, G., Ahlstrom, D. and Obloj, K. (2008) 'Entrepreneurship in emerging economies: Where are we today and where should the research go in the future?', *Entrepreneurship Theory and Practice, 32(1):* 1–14.
Buckley, P. and Castro, F. (1998) 'The investment development path: The case of Portugal', *Transnational Corporations, 7(1):* 1–15.
Buckley, P. J., Clegg, L. J., Cross, A. R. and Liu, X. (2007) 'The determinants of Chinese outward foreign direct investment', *Journal of International Business Studies, 38:* 499–518.
Dunning, J. H. (1971) *The Multinational Enterprise.* London: George Allen and Irwin.
Dunning, J. H. (1981) 'Explaining the international direct investment position of countries: Towards a dynamic or development approach', *Review of World Economics, 117(1): 30–64.*
Dunning, J. H. (1986) 'The investment development cycle and third world multinationals', in *Multinationals of the South* edited by Khushi M. Khan, 15–47. London: Frances Pinter.
Dunning, J. H. and Lundan, S. M. (2008) *Multinational Enterprises and the Global Economy.* Cheltenham: Edward Elgar.
Dunning, J. H. and Narula, R. (1996) 'The investment development path revisited: Some emerging issues', in *Foreign Direct Investment and Governments: Catalysts for Economic Restructuring* edited by J. H. Dunning and R. Narula. London: Routledge, pp. 1–41.
Duran, J. and Ubeda, F. (2001) 'The investment development path: A new empirical approach and some theoretical issues', *Transnational Corporations, 10(2):* 1–34.
Gorynia, M., Nowak, J. and Wolniak, R. (2009) 'Poland investment development path: In search of a synthesis', *Economic Policy in Emerging Economies, 2(2):* 153–174.
Gorynia, M., Nowak, J. and Wolniak, R. (2010a) 'Foreign direct investment of central and eastern Europeam countries, and the investment development path revisited', *Eastern Journal of European Studies, 1(2):* 21–37.

Gorynia, M., Nowak, J. and Wolniak, R., (2010b) 'Investment development paths of central European countries: A comparative analysis', *Argumenta Oeconomica, 1(24):* 65–88.

Jaklič, A. and Svetličič, M. (2001) 'Does transition matter? FDI from Czech Republic, Hungary and Slovenia', *Transnational Corporations, 10(2):* 67–104.

Jaklič, A. and Svetličič, M. (2002) 'Outward FDI by Selected Transition Economies; Comparative Evaluation'. Paper presented at the Annual Meeting of EIBA – European International Business Association.

Johanson, J. and Mattsson, L. G. (1987) 'Internationalisation in industry system: A network approach', in *Strategies in global competition* edited by Neil Hood and Jan-Erik Vahlne. London: Routledge, pp. 287–314.

Johanson, J. and Vahlne, J. (1977) 'The internationalisation process of the firm – a model of knowledge development and increasing foreign market commitments', *Journal of International Business Studies, 8(1):* 23–32.

Luo, Y. and Tung, R. (2007) 'International expansion of emerging market enterprises: A springboard perspective', *Journal of International Business Studies, 38*: 481–498.

Mathews, J. (2006) 'Dragon multinationals: New players in 21st century globalisation', *Asia Pacific Journal of Management, 23(1):* 5–27.

Meyer, K. E. and Peng, M. W., (2005) 'Probing theoretically into central and eastern Europe: Transactions, resources, and institutions', *Journal of International Business Studies, 35:* 600–621.

Narula, R. and Dunning, J. H. (2000) 'Industrial development, globalisation and multinational enterprises: New realities for developing countries', *Oxford Development Studies, 28(2):* 141–167.

Narula, R. and Guimon, J. (2010) 'The investment development path in a globalised world: Implications for eastern Europe', *Eastern Journal of European Studies, 1(2):* 5–19.

Sathye, S. (2008) 'Investment development path theory and the case of India', *International Review of Business Research Papers, 4(1)*: 299–309.

Rugman, A. M. and Verbeke, A. (2004) 'A perspective on regional and global strategies of multinational enterprises', *Journal of International Business Studies, 35(1):* 3–18.

Verma, R., and Brennan, L. (2011) 'The investment development path theory: Evidence from India', *International Journal of Emerging Market 6(1)*: 74–89.

Yamakawa, Y., Peng, M. W. and Deeds, D. L. (2008) 'What drives new ventures to internationalize from emerging to developed economies?', *Entrepreneurship Theory and Practice, 32(1):* 59–82.

Yiu, D. W., Lau, C. and Bruton, G. D. (2007) 'International venturing by emerging economy firms: The effects of firm capabilities, home country networks, and corporate entrepreneurship', *Journal of International Business Studies, 38(4):* 519–540.

Part VI
Conclusion

16 Emerging multinationals in Europe

What have we learnt?

Caner Bakir and Louis Brennan

Introduction

Emerging multinational corporations (EMNCs) are a new and powerful force in global competition and are challenging the incumbency of much older global companies from the developed world. In 2014 MNCs from developing economies alone accounted for a record share of 35 percent of global FDI. The aim of this book has been to improve our understanding of EMNCs' behaviour in Europe. The preceding chapters of the book have provided a range of perspectives on this behaviour. In this concluding chapter, the main findings are summarised under four main headings:

- Characterising and quantifying EMNCs in Europe;
- Drivers, motivations, and strategies of EMNCs in Europe;
- Country-specific EMNCs in Europe; and
- Country and industry studies.

Characterising and quantifying EMNCs in Europe

De Beule and Jaklič offered a comparative overview of EMNCs in Europe. They showed that while the presence and the impact of Southern multinationals in Europe has increased in recent years, the trend varies across European countries and regions. Southern multinationals are aware of the diversity of Europe and pursue a range of different strategies. They compared the extent (number), sectors, business activities, and corporate parents of European subsidiaries from various Southern multinationals by analysing in detail the firm-level investments made in Europe. In order to facilitate their analysis, some countries were grouped together given their common characteristics, location, or economic background. In terms of the extent of investment, the number of investments clearly demonstrates that Western Europe is a more attractive investment location than Central and Eastern Europe. While the predominance of Western Europe as an investment region is clear for most home countries and regions of origin, there are a few notable exceptions (e.g., Russia and Central Asia invest equally in CEE as in western Europe). In terms of sectoral comparison, the industrial sector and the service sector have attracted an equal number of investments, or about 45 percent each.

Western Europe has attracted slightly fewer industry investments than service investments while the reverse is true of CEE. More than half of the investments in CEE are industrial, compared with one in three for services. CEE has also attracted somewhat more primary investments (10.3 percent) than Western Europe (6.5 percent). There is also a clear link between home country comparative and competitive strengths in particular sectors and the outward investments from these countries. In terms of business activities, the analysis indicates huge differences between Western Europe on the one hand and Central and Eastern Europe on the other.

As far as differences with regard to the home country or region are concerned, a number of significant differences can be observed. All in all, Southern investors are clearly more attracted to Western Europe than to Central and Eastern Europe. With the exception of intraregional CEE investment, one of the few noteworthy types of Southern investments in the region relate to manufacturing investments. In CEE, the most important business activity is clearly manufacturing. This is followed by retailing and marketing and sales. Business services are limited, while there are almost no headquarters or R&D projects in CEE, especially if we exclude CEE projects into their home region. In general, companies from CEE are the most prolific investors in their own region, which should come as no surprise. The prevalence of Central and Eastern European investors is most notable in retail marketing and sales, and business services.

The question of FDI data availability and quality is of central importance for analysts and policymakers in the face of the growing activities of emerging multinationals from emerging economies and their international investments across many regions and sectors. Europe has experienced increased FDI inflows from Southern multinationals, especially since the global economic crisis, and several initiatives for improved data compilation have been launched since then.

Jaklič and De Beule have demonstrated that tracing the pattern of FDI and MNC behaviour has become a growing challenge, particularly given that FDI and MNEs have a growing impact on the development of economies. They presented recent developments on data coverage and changes in data monitoring after the latest EU enlargement. The authors reveal how most data compilers have tried to improve data gathering and coverage, enhanced cross-country and cross-institutional cooperation and validation, and implemented new methodologies and approaches. Having compared the coverage among different sources, the quality of data was assessed by the authors. They conclude that there has been an increasing gap between business intelligence, in terms of volume, quality of data, and speed of updating, which is used in corporate strategies, and the quality of data supporting economic policies either at the country level or at the EU level. They have highlighted how the existing data coverage, deficiencies and changes influence data analysis and derived related policy implications.

Since the recent literature on emerging markets outward FDI (Sauvant 2008; Ramamurti and Singh 2009; Brennan 2011; De Beule and Duanmu 2012; De Beule and Van Den Bulcke 2012) has found Southern multinationals to be quite heterogeneous, they emphasize that analysis based on macro-level aggregate data may often not reveal this heterogeneity and development. Whereas changes that have been introduced recently have raised standards and improved data availability, the authors conclude that challenges remain as far as data compilation and data usage are concerned.

Drivers, motivations, and strategies of emerging country multinationals

In Chapter 4, Srai explored the drivers and motivations of EMNEs' that have sought to establish a key element of their value chain within the European market, and the potential policy implications thereof. He examined EMNEs integration into global value chains through EU acquisitions and alliances and the need to differentiate between those long-term investments that enrich the EU's supply base, from the more predatory moves that seek to transfer out activities.

Then the chapter considered different patterns in the innovation and technology development of EMNEs, including more incremental product innovations, an appetite to invest in production processes, and business models that exploit home-country low cost labour advantages. Accordingly, Srai asserts that policymakers should recognise that the competitive innovation environment will challenge established firms whilst enriching competition.

In addition, he showed that EMNEs' responses to current reshoring activities of developed-country MNCs may provide entry points for EMNEs into Europe. However, for Srai, this may result in the decline of EMNEs in their home countries as MNCs reshore in favour of EU located suppliers. Fieldwork studies suggested that policies that support reshoring will have greatest impact where proximity to markets and technology encourage localisation strategies.

Srai argues that 'product' and 'sectoral' considerations suggest that EMNEs' competitive advantages are most favourable where their home-country advantages of low cost labour and scale enable economic international supply. However, policymakers should consider where national strategic assets, such as infrastructure, defence, and supply security considerations, require European safeguards. EMNEs that are considered national flagships by their home country, particularly state owned enterprises, may by their very scale and nature possess competitive capabilities that will support global reach. However, their favourable home market conditions may provide these EMNEs with advantages that might fall outside traditional EU competition norms.

In Chapter 5, Weusthoff and Meckl considered the motivations of EMNC M&As in developed countries. They argued that while the competitive position of EMNCs has been characterised by a focus on country-specific cost advantages, recent theory and anecdotal evidence indicate that intellectual capital in the form of technology, management, brands, and networks is still the most significant competitive disadvantage for EMNCs. Thus mergers and acquisitions might enable EMNCs to change their international role. Based on the LLL model, they identified intellectual capital as a central strategic motivation for EMNCs' M&A transactions in developed countries. Based on a data sample of M&A transactions with acquirers from BRIC countries and target companies located in the EU-25, they found that EMNCs are selecting targets with significantly high values of intellectual capital. Their findings are consistent with the theoretical background of traditional and EMNC-specific learning theories explaining M&A as an instrument for acquiring missing skills.

Thus they advocate that Western firms, considered as potential acquisition targets by EMNCS, should emphasize the company-bound intellectual capital during the transaction process. At the same time, they advise that appropriate incentive systems should be developed to encourage EMNCs to make a long term European commitment.

In Chapter 6, Dura and Drigă focused on outward foreign direct investments from Russia, analysing their spectacular development and their impact upon developed and emerging European countries. They concluded that the outstanding growth of Russian multinationals demonstrate that they are becoming redoubtable competitors within the global business environment. They further concluded that the drivers of outbound investment by these firms match the conventional group of motivations of multinationals from developed economies, viz., market-seeking, resource-seeking, technology-seeking and efficiency-seeking. They assert that the unprecedented expansion of Russian multinationals in the last fifteen years can be explained with the assistance of the LLL and Uppsala models. Dura and Drigă consider that the position of being "latecomers" was turned by Russian multinationals from a disadvantage to a significant advantage which allowed them to penetrate market niches that multinationals from developed countries had overlooked. Through the rapid assimilation of knowledge and new technologies from their business partners, Russian corporations managed to skip over several decades of multinational evolution as compared with their counterparts from developed economies.

Nükhet Vardar addressed Turkish EMNCs and analysed the impact of their motivations on their degree of internationalisation and their performance. She found that marketing and branding reasons were the most critical motives that led Turkish EMNCS to engage in FDI in the EU. Her results indicate that Turkish MNCs investing in the EU mainly employ an asset-seeking approach.

Country-specific EMNCs in Europe

In this section of the book, EMNCs from China, India and Turkey were considered. In Chapter 8, Hay aimed to better understand the strategy and the idiosyncrasies of Chinese investors in Europe in her thorough analysis of Chinese MNCs' identity, modes and forms of investments, destinations, activities, and motives, while taking into consideration concrete examples. She argued that their strategies have largely evolved over the last decade, in line with the rise of the Chinese economy and firms; they are becoming increasingly closer to those of incumbent multinational companies. Thus she concludes that the motives and strategies of Chinese investors in Europe – and in the world – are becoming closer to those of established multinationals, insofar as they are now seasoned, hold standard technologies, and, very importantly, are currently able to make real innovations, especially "cost innovations". At the same time, they seek to increase their market positions at the international level and to operate in high added-value activities.

In Chapter 9, Bakir and Acur investigate recent geographical and sectoral spread, motivations, and competitive advantages of TMNCs in Europe and whether these investments represent theoretical and empirical challenges to existing knowledge or can be explained within the existing theoretical frameworks that have been used to explain developed-country MNEs. They argued that the largest TMNCs employ multiple strategies in developed- and developing-country markets in Europe. Most of their greenfield investments are in developing or in transition economies. They relied mainly on FSAs (dynamic capabilities) obtained at home, such as managerial knowledge, expertise, technology, local/regional brands and distribution channels, and expertise in operating in weak institutional environments abroad in these markets. In contrast, most of their acquisitions have been in developed countries where TMNCs not only exploited their current FSAs obtained from home CSAs but also aimed to explore FSAs obtained from host CSAs through their subsidiaries. In greenfield investments, TMNCs mostly exploited their FSAs obtained in home markets. They also exploit traditional locational advantages or CSAs such as economies of scale and leadership in home market, geographical, cultural, and institutional proximity. Further, this chapter shows that structural complementarities such as financial and economic crises and currency appreciations reinforce internationalisation of TMNC. It also highlights that a parent in the home market and a subsidiary in a developed host market can develop effective organizational mechanisms that transfer their unique resources and capabilities into FSAs of one another in an effort towards a global consolidator strategy.

In Chapter 10, Milelli focused on Indian MNCs in Europe. He showed that these were essentially private companies, more often family owned or/and managed, and very represented in services such as IT. Their strategies focused mainly on expanding or cornering new market shares. Given those features, they tended to be dissimilar to Chinese firms in Europe. He concluded that Indian firms have generally followed a cautious investment behaviour: when they look for target companies and when they take control, they have the patience not to push for immediate changes by imposing their way of doing business.

Elia, Piscitello, and Scalera have offered new empirical evidence on the strategies employed by Chinese MNCs to upgrade their technical competencies, namely by putting in place external knowledge sourcing through international collaborative innovation, in Chapter 11. They demonstrated that institutional and cultural distance tend to boost (rather than to hamper) the contribution of the network of subunits to the innovative activity of the parent companies. Thus, they have concluded that Chinese MNCs engaged in collaborative innovation are likely to benefit from an increase in the effectiveness of the knowledge sourcing and transfer process and an accelerated catching-up. They advise that managers of multinational firms should try to exploit their network of subunits to trigger this phenomenon, by taking advantage of the institutional and cultural distance rather than fearing it. From a policy perspective, they advise that policymakers of the host countries should better understand to what extent the collaborative innovation undertaken by emerging countries also benefit their host economies or whether potential risks of knowledge leakages hold.

Country and industry studies

This section of the book contained four chapters that focused on country studies, viz., Norway, the Visegrad countries of Eastern Europe, Central European transition economies and the white goods industry. In Chapter 12, Heum and Pires shed some light on the extent to which multinationals from some of the major emerging economies, the so-called BRIC countries, are directly involved in the Norwegian economy. Contrary to what is observed in other countries, they found that investments of BRIC country multinationals in Norway represented a small share of total foreign investment in Norway. With the exception of two large investments by Chinese multinationals, they have not gained importance in the last decade. They assert that the reasons for this are due to the specificities of the Norwegian economy: Norway is not a member of the EU, it is a high wage country, it was not affected by the financial crisis, and it is a high tax country.

In Chapter 13, Zdziarski concluded that the patterns of FDI among Central European countries fit the theoretical IDP model, suggesting that the theory works well for countries with similar institutional settings. He analysed the BRIC countries, which are increasingly active in global FDI flows in terms of the degree to which FDI involving those countries and the Visegrad countries of Eastern Europe fit the IDP model. He found that the overall NOI position of the Visegrad countries against the BRIC group of countries has moved in the period 2001 to 2012 from negative into positive values. He argued that the paradoxical performance of Visegrad countries against the expected IDP stage model during the last twenty-five years in which they improved GDP per capita quite substantially but remained in stage 2 of the model highlights the need to rethink the IDP paradigm in order to acknowledge different types of capitalism that emerges in the contemporary world.

Zdziarski, Srai, and Rezk explored the embeddedness of supply chains of emerging vs. developed-market multinational companies in a global value chain in Chapter 14. They applied methods of social network analysis to a comparative study of global supply chains in the white goods sector. This sector is uniquely composed of established MNCs like Electrolux and Whirlpool and new, Southern multinationals like Haier and Arcelik. Their exploratory analysis offered insights into the structure of buyer and supplier relationships in the white goods global value chain that constrains companies forming the industry. Thus they concluded that networks not only create opportunities for accelerated internationalisation, but can powerfully constrain its scope and force alternative strategies to globalisation.

In Chapter 15, Svetličič evaluated the recent expansion of selected Central European firms' outward FDI and compared this expansion with that of early third world multinationals and those coming from emerging countries recently. In both cases, the most advanced countries proved to be the biggest investors abroad. Both groups of investors followed certain stages in which the macroeconomic strategy of the home countries proved to be important. For Svetličič, however, the recent pace is much faster. Firms leapfrog stages. There are also many differences between groups and within them. One is the more important role of pull factors (globalisation) in the case of latecoming investors abroad from transition and emerging economies. He argues that the modern wave of internationalisation of emerging economies' MNCs and those from CEEs demonstrate leapfrogging types of internationalisation.

Conclusion

This final chapter of the book has presented a summary of the contributions in the preceding chapters. This summary has followed the structure of the book focusing on the themes addressed in each section of the book. These themes have encompassed the characterisation and quantification of EMNCs in Europe, the drivers, motivations, and strategies of EMNCs in Europe as well as incorporating consideration of country-specific EMNCs in Europe and country and industry studies.

References

Brennan, L. (2011) 'Southern Multinationals and Their Impact on Europe: What Have We Learnt?' In Brennan, L. (Ed.) *The Emergence of Southern Multinationals: Their Impact on Europe*, Basingstoke: Palgrave Macmillan.

De Beule, F., and Duanmu, J. (2012) 'Locational determinants of internationalization: A firm-level analysis of Chinese and Indian acquisitions' *European Management Journal*, 30, 3: 264–277.

De Beule, F., and Van Den Bulcke, D. (2012) 'Locational determinants of outward foreign direct investment: An analysis of Chinese and Indian greenfield investments' *Transnational Corporations,* 21, 1: 1–34.

Ramamurti, R., and Singh, J. V. (Eds.) (2009) *Emerging Multinationals in Emerging Markets.* Cambridge, UK: Cambridge University Press.

Sauvant, K. (2008). *The Rise of Transnational Corporations from Emerging Markets.* Cheltenham: Edward Elgar.

UNCTAD (2015) *World Investment Report 2015*, Geneva.

Index

Printed in Great Britain
by Amazon

17368780R00160